TWO SIDES TO EVERY GLORY

AC/DC

AC/DC - TWO SIDES TO EVERY GLORY
The Complete Biography

by Paul Stenning

A CHROME DREAMS PUBLICATION

First Edition 2005

Published by Chrome Dreams
PO BOX 230, New Malden , Surrey
KT3 6YY, UK

WWW.CHROMEDREAMS.CO.UK

ISBN 1 84240 308 7

Editorial Director Rob Johnstone
Editor Tim Footman
Cover design Sylwia Grzeszczuk
Interior design Marek Krzysztof Niedziewicz

TWO SIDES TO EVERY GLORY

AC/DC

THE COMPLETE BIOGRAPHY

PAUL STENNING

In the research and preparation of this book the following sources have been used, I remain indebted to all the relevant authors.

Websites

www.crabsodyinblue.com
www.daveevans.au.com
www.acdccentral.com
www.kolumbus.fi/nononsense/
www.ac-dc.net/
http://www.bluemud.org/article/16683
http://www.superseventies.com/faq_acdc.html
www.acdc-faq.fsnet.co.uk/
www.rockdetector.com
www.buoy.com/~bonfire/bonrel.html
www.hem.passagen.se/honga/database/v/valentines.html

Books

Highway To Hell: The Life And Times Of Ac/dc Legend Bon Scott, Clinton Walker, Verse Chorus Press, U.s. 2001
Ac/dc The World's Heaviest Rock, Martin Huxley, Saint Martin's Press 1996
Get Your Jumbo Jet Out Of My Airport (Random Notes For Ac/dc Obsessives), Howard Johnson, Helter Skelter Publishing 1999
Ac/dc: The Definitive History, The Kerrang! Files (Various), Virgin Books 2001
Maximum Ac/dc, The Unauthorised Biography Of Ac/dc (Audio Book), Chrome Dreams 2000
Magazines
Kerrang!, Classic Rock, Metal Hammer, People, Record Collector, RIP, Circus, Spin.

All AC/DC lyrics quoted in this book are courtesy of
E.B. Marks Corp.
J. Albert & Son Pty Ltd.

Photographs courtesy of

Redferns
LFI
Starfile
Barry Plummer
Rex
Paul Stenning
Big Eddie Richmond

Many thanks to the following for their encouragement and co-operation in the composition of this work: Clinton Walker, Chris Barnes of Six Feet Under, Joel McIver, Steve Armstrong, Jeff Cureton, Dave Evans, Paul Di'Anno, Mike Browning, Tom O' Dell, Rob & all at Chrome Dreams, Mark Evans, Vincent Lovegrove, Susan Marino, Colin Burgess, Ian Cant, Russell Clark, Richard Selby.

Special Thank you to Mac, Mum, Claire and my devoted partner Isla.

This book is dedicated to Tommy Vance (11th July 1943 – 6th March 2005, R.I.P.) for his inspiration and devotion to rock music.

Music author and journalist **Paul Stenning** specialises in listening to and writing about rock and heavy metal. He is currently a regular contributor to the hallowed pages of Metal Hammer, Terrorizer and Record Collector magazines, and has previously written for countless other publications and websites. He has also produced several works on the art and majesty of hard rock and heavy metal. He has interviewed numerous bands and artists from those genres including Iron Maiden, Alice Cooper, Meatloaf (who also serenaded Paul into agreeing copy approval!) Judas Priest, members of AC DC and Guns N' Roses, among a host of other top names.

His previous book *The Band That Time Forgot - The Unauthorised Biography Of Guns N' Roses* has sold in excess of 25,000 copies worldwide and has recently been published as a revised edition.

Paul lives in Manchester, England, with his fiancée and the meanest of furry kittens.

Introduction

'Ridin' down the highway, Goin' to a show, Stop in all the by–ways, Playin' rock n' roll. Gettin' robbed, Gettin' stoned, Gettin' beat up, Broken boned. Gettin' had, Gettin' took, I tell you folks, It's harder than it looks… It's a long way to the top
If you wanna rock 'n' roll' 'It's A Long Way To The Top (If You Wanna Rock 'N' Roll)'

So began AC/DC's arduous introduction to playing rock n' roll. The beauty of the band in general – and of Bon Scott's lyrics in particular – was their ability to translate the harshness of life onto the page, onto 'wax' and into bars, clubs, concert halls, arenas and ultimately, the muddy environs of the festival circuits. Their music has always been simple, the words to the songs even simpler. Yet, where others have tried, and indeed many have, to copy or imitate this effective simplicity, most have failed to come anywhere close to the power of AC/DC.

Bon Scott was a rock n' roll genius. The 'DC front man for five years moulded the band into an act which quickly filled a cleverly observed niche. They kept it remarkably straightforward at times, but there was clearly something different about them. In fact the nuances of their stage show, and indeed their studio work, were many. For one they had Angus Young who dressed as a schoolboy and dispersed enough energy during a gig to fuel a small country. He duck walked across the stage and played like his life depended on it. In many cases it really did. Without rock music the members of AC/DC had little else, and certainly nothing they really wanted. Travelling from show to show meeting women and getting high was all part of the deal, but the real kick was the one hour show the group was afforded on a nightly basis. Soon that hour would progress to two, as AC/DC built a fan base which grew with every sweat drenched performance. They came from a strange base that combined Scotland with Australia and this, in part, lent them an edge few other outfits could match.

It was an essential element of their collective personality and it came out in their music. Their outlook was deeply British and straightforward yet they also carried an Aussie air of arrogance and unmatchable flair. The music was to the point, direct – and so were the interviews. The photo shoots displayed the vital ingredients for a perfect rock band; Bon's maniacal grin; Angus's youthful looks and tiny frame; brother Malcolm holding things together and the other members – who gradually came and went – all playing their part. They epitomised the genre.

The original core of AC/DC held firm through a number of legendary recordings. Their titles now fall off the tongue as rightfully heralded rock classics. No group before or since has been able to match the power, majesty and pure verve of *High Voltage, Dirty Deeds Done Dirt Cheap, Let There Be Rock, Powerage* and *Highway To Hell*.

Each of these records are now more than twenty years old yet you wouldn't know it to hear them. Sure, the early production was slightly raw and undoubtedly plain but this was a charming aspect of AC/DC. It is a compliment that, in the 21st century, bands all over the world try regularly to capture that 'garage' sound. In recent times it has worked to such an extent that groups influenced by the Anglo–Aussies, from The Hives to The Strokes, have achieved great success building a modern take upon the 'DC blueprint.

Angus and co. would not begrudge them their chance. After all, part of AC/DC's easily identifiable sound is their basic approach to early rock n' roll and blues. They simply beefed it up and found a street urchin to utter poetic yet hard and edgy words over the clear–cut backdrop.

Part of the group's allure was their inability to pen a bad song. Although their critics would suggest that every track sounded alike, this was really to AC/DC's advantage. The songs were somewhat recognisable with the first hit of a familiar chord – and when Bon screeched over the musical backing the recognition was complete. There *were* similarities within every track – as indeed there are with all the finest groups – yet, equally, enough variation to mark out each one as an original, unique and endearing composition .

The beauty of AC/DC however was not to last in its most distinctive form. Bon was not their first singer yet he was their most identifiable. He brought the band respect and appreciation from across the world, and along with Angus stood as a focal point in the most successful rock group of the late seventies.

In retrospect, perhaps it was not meant to exist for longer than a few years. Bon was to die during 1980 in questionable circumstances. It could easily have spelled the end for the group. Many, including the remaining members themselves, thought it would, and some would suggest it should have. For the band to still be around twenty–five years later, having not once split up is an achievement in itself. That they came back after Bon's tragic demise with an acknowledged benchmark in heavy rock, and one of the best selling albums of all time, is testament to their determination and creativity. Bon was the soul of AC/DC, yet so too is their current vocalist, the man who took his place – with no shortage of trepidation.

It shouldn't have been so easy, yet it seemed like destiny when the new line up went on to achieve such extraordinary success. An Englishman, Brian Johnson stepped into the most difficult empty shoes in all of rock n' roll. Nobody thought Bon could be replaced, and indeed he could not. But to Brian's eternal credit, he didn't try. What he did do was become a different type of front man with his own agenda, personality and vocal style – albeit with a respectful nod to the band's past. This humble yet powerful approach turned AC/DC's comeback album, *Back In Black,* into a masterpiece. And the fan's loved him for it.

Some would argue that the group has failed to attain the same creative heights since, but still the records are made and the records sell. Virtually every two years since 1980 there has been new band product. There have been highs and lows, but during the loftier moments there is still no act in the world who can touch the mighty AC/DC. Every year they play live and almost every time the venues – still arena sized – are sold out. Their longevity is staggering and their appeal enduring. Acknowledged by musicians of every denomination, and by the media alike, AC/DC continue to surprise and delight their fans old and new. 30 years in the business and still going strong, AC/DC are an institution.

Two Sides To Every Glory is a fitting mark of respect to all that AC/DC have achieved and created. This is the entire story of the band. It begins where no other work has dared to tread, in the slums of Glasgow and the depths of the Youngs' childhood and continues through Bon's troubled adolescence, moving onto the fateful union that was to create the subject of this book. Complemented by interviews with those who knew the band members best, as well as with the line up past and present, this is the ultimate 'DC bible and an ideal accompaniment to the stacks of albums on your shelves baring the lightning logo. So sit back, relax and crank the stereo with the recording of your choice and enter their world. This is rock; this is the sonic power surge of AC/DC.

'You wanna see me do my thing
All you gotta do is plug me into high
High voltage rock n' roll' 'High Voltage'

Chapter 1 – Career Moves

"As a kid, I was never one for the Cliff Richard thing with the tennis racket. I was more interested in getting my fingers around the guitar neck." Angus Young

In 1960, Glasgow, the largest city in Scotland, was a dirty, dark, smoggy, industrial town. Today the same essence survives, but back then there was a more insular grimness, which gripped the area like fetid black tar. Glasgow was also dangerous. Street crime was an issue, but overcrowding and poor housing were a greater risk for those on low incomes. The city was increasingly overpopulated, and people were crammed into dank tenements.

So crowded were the living quarters that a new town called Livingston was built to the east of the city, to accommodate the Glasgow overspill. The local economy was in limbo and many native Glaswegians faced the stark choice of remaining in their city and suffering poverty, or moving elsewhere to find better living conditions.

On the other side of the world however, Australia was still savouring the effects of its post–war economic resurgence. The country was hungry for foreign migration and the government was increasingly targeting the Brits. The princely sum of £10 per head was offered to those bold enough to sail south.

In 1963 the Young family took the bait. Margaret and William Young took eight of their nine children to Sydney, in the New South Wales territory of this enormous country. These included Angus, born on the 31st of March, 1955, and brother Malcolm, two years older.

It was, to put it mildly, a culture shock. If Glasgow was dank and gloomy, Australia was (literally and metaphorically) the land of sunshine, a situation exemplified by the locals' adoration for the Beach Boys. The influence that the California quintet had on Australian culture at that time seemed to give Angus Young particular cause for concern. He later said, "When my family immigrated to

Australia you'd see these kids that had nothing to do with the real thing, but they all looked like they came out of *Hawaii Five–O*. Standing there with these great lumps of wooden board. I'd never seen a surfboard in my life. But they had all got these bits of wood, and they were all going, 'Suurrfun Yew Ess Ayyy.' I went home to my mother and said, 'Mum, I think we're on another planet.'"

Jeff Cureton was a school friend of the Young brothers. "My brother and I grew up in our early years in the Burwood area of Sydney," he recalls. "We both attended Burwood Public School and that's where we met Angus, Malcolm and their cousin Sammy Young. Wee Sammy, as their family would call him, was in my class. Angus was in my brother's class. We used to go around to their house a lot, until we moved to Haberfield. They lived on Burleigh Street in Burwood. I remember we loaned the boys our slot car track for a while, and we were over there one night and Harry Vanda and George Young (older brother to Angus and Malcolm) were there playing with the slot car track at the rear of their house. Angus was given a beautiful red Jaguar and the tyres had knobs, from a radio. That was very cool, 38 or so years ago."

Cureton was a constant companion of the two young Scots. "On the weekends around June we would ride to Strathfield to an old fruit shop that sold fireworks, penny bangers, thunder bangers, roman candles. You know all the good stuff. Anyway, we would go to Homebush Bay, set up on a bridge there and set the bangers off. We would light them and wait till the wick would burn just inside the banger then we would drop it in the water like a depth charge. We loved it and had great fun doing it, a lot of things got blown up back then, all in fun."

According to another schoolmate, Bill Clark, Angus started smoking at about 8 years old. "He thought he might become a jockey because of his size. Both he and Malcolm were convinced early that anyone could be pop stars. They were caught smoking out of school but in school uniform on a train. The school uniform must have been the impetus for Angus to wear a school uniform on stage during his earlier shows – including the cap!"

*"The Headmaster used to call me up every second day or so
and say, 'well, Young, what have you been up to this time?'"*
Angus Young

Bill and Malcolm were in the same class and often travelled
together on the same train to school. "Our public transport at that
time did not have automatic doors", explains Clark "and they would
hang outside the carriages and walk from one door to the next. Aca-
demically not strong and very disrespectful to their teachers. This
seemed to add to their aura. They lived in a small semi–detached
house which I think still stands just behind the police station. Their
mother was nice, and a bit plump–ish." Steve Armstrong was a good
friend of both Angus and Malcolm. "I met them jointly as they pretty well did everything and went everywhere together in those days,"
he says. "Ashfield Boys' High was an all–boys school that used to
be a Technical College. From memory, about 800 students attended
from years 7 to 12. Wasn't a bad school, some strict teachers. This
was back in the days when corporal punishment was allowed".

This didn't seem to deter the Young brothers, especially Angus. As Steve recalls, "My earliest memories of the boys are that
Angus was a smartarse! He had an attitude where he thought he
could say and do anything and get away with it, which he did. He
was a larrikin[1]. On the other hand Malcolm was the quieter of the
two and held the interest of the girls, he was a bit of a pretty boy.
I got the impression Angus was always in the shadow of Malcolm,
especially where the girls were concerned. But Angus had that real
attitude and was not frightened to display it to anyone. Through the
week they would have to do their guitar lessons after school so we
didn't see them when school finished, they would go straight home.
But at the weekends they would get the bus and come down and
hang out with us, it was a pretty large group and they were just two
of the boys, it was great." In 2005, Armstrong remembers his time
with the Young brothers as if it were yesterday and he remarks, "I
still get a kick out of telling people that I knew them and that my
wife Coralie used to go out with Angus before we met. He was 14
and they used to meet at Ashfield Swimming Pool on weekends
sometimes and have a little kiss, so she tells me."

Big brother George, who had also been on the boat from Scotland, had befriended Harry Vanda (real name Johannes Jacob Hendrickus Vandenberg) upon arriving Down Under, and soon the guitar–playing pair had formed a beat combo they called The Easybeats. The line–up also consisted of singer Little Stevie Wright, drummer Gordon 'Snowy' Fleet and Dick Diamond on bass guitar.

The name was chosen to roll off the tongue as naturally as 'The Who' or 'The Beatles'. Indeed, the band would quickly become the Sydney equivalent of The Beatles, expanding further afield and becoming known as Australia's biggest pop group during the mid '60s. The link with the Fab Four was accentuated by the fact that drummer Snowy was a Liverpool native, and before decamping for Oz, had been a member of The Mojos, who had played on the same circuit as The Beatles, The Searchers, Gerry and The Pacemakers and other Merseybeat acts. The band's manager Ted Vaughan soon met up with Ted Albert of the music publishing house J. Albert and Son, and a subsidiary called Albert Productions was formed in order to accommodate The Easybeats. The group then secured a deal with EMI's Parlophone imprint, the same label The Beatles were signed to in the UK

"I got to know George had become famous with the Easybeats," remembers Steve Amstrong, "but I never actually met him. I loved the band though, loved their music. I didn't view Angus and Malcolm any differently just because George was their older brother, nobody did you know. But I think both George and the boys' parents were major influences on their career because they used to say that guitar practice was a *must*. They would have to do homework first and then it would be guitar practice, every night in the week."

By the summer of 1965 The Easybeats were starting to peak in Australia. They were now attaining a level of stardom previously reserved for The Beatles, indeed the level of adoration for the band was similar to 'Beatlemania', and was quickly dubbed, 'Easyfever'. During 1965 and early 1966 they released a string of hit singles, all written by Young and Wright, including 'For My Woman' (which reached No. 5 in the Australian charts), 'She's So Fine' (the bands first No. 1), 'Wedding Ring' (No. 6), 'Women (Make You Feel Alright)' (No. 1), 'In My Book', 'Come And See Her' (No. 1), 'I'll Make You Happy' (No. 1), and 'Sorry' (No. 4). Additionally, the Wright–Young song writing team penned 'Step Back' which became a chart–topping hit for Johnny Young (no relation) in 1966.

That same year, before returning to Britain, The Easybeats recorded a farewell television show, *The Coca Cola Special*. This became one of the most famous manifestations of Australian music television from the sixties. Tragically, after recording the show Harry Vanda returned home to find his wife, Pamela had committed suicide by overdosing on sleeping tablets. Vanda was undeterred by the tragedy and followed his plans through to travel to England with The Easybeats. The trip was to be fruitful. With Shel Talmy, producer for The Who and The Kinks, at the controls, the band recorded 'Friday On My Mind' which hit No. 6 on the UK charts, followed by an American release where it charted at No. 16. By this stage, Harry Vanda had supplanted Stevie Wright as George Young's songwriting partner. The band was soon making an impact throughout Europe, when they were offered a tour with The Rolling Stones. The shows were a success and The Stones invited The Easybeats to America where they went down equally well. However after a few line–up changes, the band remained in England. Though they would score minor hits in the US charts with 'Good Times' and 'Falling Off The Edge Of The World', lack of promotion and management attention meant that The Easybeats felt they were not able to capitalise on their initial promise. To make matters worse, they were boycotted by some US radio stations for the mild sexual nature of a few of their songs. The band subsequently lost momentum and despite several more minor hits, they disbanded in 1970.

Vocalist Stevie Wright remained in the music business and recorded two solo albums, *Hard Road* and *Black–eyed Bruiser*. He even had a No. 1 single in Australia with the song 'Evie'. *Hard Road* featured Malcolm Young on guitars and there were rumours that Angus also made an unaccredited appearance. Despite this success, Wright later slipped into substance addiction and spent much of the '70s out of the limelight. However, he did manage to join a 1986 reunion tour with the Easybeats. He re–entered the spotlight in 2004 when The Wrights, a supergroup headed by Nic Cester of

Jet, released a cover version of The Easybeats' hit 'Evie', produced by Harry Vanda.

After The Easybeats split up in 1970, Vanda and George Young (who were later referred to as the 'Dutch Damager' and 'The Gorgeous Glaswegian') returned to Sydney to work for Ted Albert in his newly formed Albert Productions organisation. They continued to work on music together and were to work on several successful projects, most notably Flash and the Pan and The Marcus Hook Roll Band. It was this latter project in 1973 that featured the first credited appearances for both Angus and Malcolm Young, after they had appeared at the recording sessions of the album *Tales of Old Granddaddy*. It was at this time that Harry Vanda and George Young began to take a more serious interest in production and studio work.

The Easybeats' success had intrigued both Malcolm and Angus, who looked up to George and thus wanted to emulate his achievements. It was indeed his influence that had encouraged the two younger brothers into beginning their guitar practice. The musical achievements of the Young brothers, including those of another sibling, who played saxophone in a local group, had not gone down well with Mr Young Senior however. He thought his sons should be working regular jobs and not fumbling around with music, regardless of George's success at playing to hundreds and thousands around the country and beyond, he did not consider it real work. At school the boys were supposed to keep quiet about George being in a band, but when one headmaster found out, he taunted the youngsters and they also had to endure teasing from classmates.

Not to be deterred however, the brothers had decided they wanted to play music for a living. George provided Malcolm with ad hoc advice on guitar techniques, and his protégé was to make swift progress. Angus was often found emulating his older brothers, and he too began to play the guitars around the house, until finally his mother bought him his very own.

A friend of George had given Malcolm a Gretsch guitar, and he has stuck with this brand ever since. Once Happy with his Gretsch, Malcolm gave the older Hofner instrument he had previously used to Angus.

The two boys were heavily into the sound of Chicago blues as they were growing up. As Angus would later say, "I like a lot of the Chicago thing, and a lot of different players. Elmore James, I very much like that style of playing. When you hear it you think it's very simple, but it's not. It's actually very clever, and he executed it so well. And you never hear it even if you see someone and go, 'Oh, they're going to imitate it,' they never pull it off. And B.B. King is another one. Buddy Guy is a great player. And I like Johnny Winter. He's got a lot of power in his blues. He runs a great variety. And he's always played like that. I regard him as a Hendrix or something. For rock and roll I like Chuck Berry's playing. His things are a bit of an art."

"Malcolm would always tell me 'don't tickle the guitar, hit the bugger!'" Angus Young

At school Angus stood out from the pack. Other kids would be sucked in by the top 40, or whatever was popular at the time, whereas Angus was going backwards through time, seeking out as much heartfelt blues as he could find. In Australia the records would often be on import only, but Angus would make sure he could pick up Little Richard or Muddy Waters. He later said, "When I was young, one of the earliest records I heard was Little Richard's 'You Keep a Knockin'" I think I nearly invented rap with that record. I'd take the needle and keep putting it back on to the same spot, to the blues bit, over and over again, because that was the best part of the song. My mother said, 'You touch that needle one more time and you're going to have a very sore fist.' But I couldn't help it. I just loved that one bit. And I was never a lover of the harmony type stuff. For some reason that seemed too... '*eeuuuewww...*' it brought in that sweetness. When I heard the Beach Boys I thought it was an older version of the Chipmunks."

At that time, the minimum school leaving age in Australia was fourteen years and nine months old. Neither Angus nor Malcolm was about to hang around any longer than was required. Initially, in keeping with their father's wishes, the two found jobs, though not exactly standard employment. Angus worked as a janitor, and as a printer for a soft porn magazine called *Ribald*. Malcolm worked as a sewing machine maintenance mechanic in the Berlei brassiere factory. In their spare time, they followed their true vocations. Angus had formed his own outfit, which he dubbed Tantrum, while in 1971 Malcolm joined a group called Velvet Underground (no relation to the Lou Reed version). The original singer in this band had, coincidentally, been a man called Brian Johnson.

Notes

1. Larrikin: an Australian term meaning rascal or scallywag.

MEMORIES

Jeff Cureton on the good old days with Malcolm and Angus:
"We lost contact with Angus and Malcolm when we moved
to Haberfield. When I was 18 some friends and I drove up to
Kempsay, surfing. We met four girls up there; we stayed in
their house for a few weeks before we went to Rock Hamp-
ton. One of the girls– her name was Jenny – had a baseball
hat with a big A on the front, she kept talking to the other
girls about Angus this and Angus that. After a few days I
said, 'who is Angus?' She replied in a cheeky voice, 'Angus
Young from AC/DC'. I said, 'I know him; I grew up with
him'. You can imagine what the girls said: 'Yeah, bullshit.'
So I said, 'OK, when I get back to Sydney I will go to his
house and say hello for you. Angus and Malcolm were over-
seas on tour. His Auntie let me in so I could talk to Angus's
Mum, so as I walked in she said, 'I remember you, you're
the one that knocked off all the Easter eggs.' I won't go into
that any further!"

Chapter 2 – Gorillas Of Glam

"AC/DC is just a tough, driving rock and roll band...five dwarfs that make a big racket." Angus Young

Velvet Underground was never going to be a full–time or serious band for Malcolm Young; the peak of the band's success was a few support slots for a singer called Ted Mulry. Frustrated, Malcolm left for pastures new. Shortly afterwards, Mulry approached the group to act as his backing band. They accepted, ditching singer Dave Evans.

Evans originally arrived in Australia from Carmarthen in South Wales, aged five, and settled in North Queensland with his family. "I remember arriving in Townsville and thinking how beautiful everything looked from magnificent Castle Hill which overlooks the city to the ocean and Magnetic Island which looks like a stone's throw from the esplanade," he recalls. "It reminded me of Carmarthen Bay, where my family and I used to visit before we emigrated, with the castle overlooking the ocean, but of course the weather was a bit colder. My family moved west to Charters Towers soon after and it was like going to another planet really. It was hot, dry and brown. I was mortified. I was used to the greenness of Wales and earlier, Townsville. It was a shock. I did however receive a very good education there, as Charters Towers is known as the education centre of the north due to the many schools and colleges there."

After forming his first band In Session, in Charters Towers when he was seventeen, Evans moved to Sydney. "I started listening to The Beatles, Rolling Stones, The Kinks and The Who when I was in high school but there was no rock band in Charters Towers, only a band called The Trisonics. They played at our school dances. I joined together with three other young guys – a couple of them who I went to school with – and we formed a pop/rock band called In Session and then the locals finally had the choice of two bands; which worked fine for both of us."

Evans explains why he moved to Sydney: "I guess that with the locals telling me how good I was, I suppose I believed them, and knew that if I wanted to make a record that I had to move to where the action was, I asked the other boys in my band to come with me but they did not have the same confidence and ambition as I did, so I had to head to Sydney alone."

Sitting in his Bondi flat one day, after his stint with Velvet Underground had ended, Evans heard a knock at the door. It was Angus Young. Evans obviously knew of Malcolm Young, and every Australian and his granny knew about George. But Angus was an unknown quantity.

"He arrived with almost waist–length hair and green teeth and he was so tiny," Evans remembers. "The first thing I thought was 'Jeez, another Young brother? Christ, how many are there?'" Angus asked Dave if he wanted to join his band Kentuckee. "He was pleasant enough but when he played me the music he was into at the time I found it too guitar–orientated without enough vocals so I declined his offer to join his band."

But Angus didn't have far to look for a willing musical accomplice. Malcolm was putting together a new band, and was experimenting with different instrumental line–ups. After toying with the introduction of a keyboard player, he realised he could get a thicker sound by employing another guitarist; and who would be better than his proficient little brother Angus? The choice was easy for Angus; it was either stay rooted in depressing dead end jobs or go for his ultimate ambition, to play in a full time rock n' roll outfit. Kentuckee was going nowhere fast and the chance to play alongside his older brother was something he grasped instantaneously, although according to Malcolm he did harbour some doubts. "He was like, 'oh, I don't know mate'", Malcolm recalled in 2003. "He said, 'I know you're all right, but those other guys…' Luckily it made sense when he came down to rehearse with us."

Whether Angus had quite imagined the group in the same way as Malcolm was another matter. In keeping with the prevailing visual images of the current popular rock acts, he foresaw long hair and huge boots, similar to glam–rock bands such as Slade and Sweet. However, the brothers were unanimous in what they wanted the new outfit to sound like. They discovered like–minded musicians in drummer Colin Burgess (ex–Masters' Apprentices), Larry Van Kriedt and, turning up like a bad penny, Dave Evans who had answered an advertisement for a "ballsy rock singer" placed in the *Sydney Morning Herald*. Evans arrived to meet the band for a jamming session at an abandoned office complex in Newtown, Australia and met Malcolm for the first time. (He had joined Velvet Underground after Malcolm had left the band). According to Evans, "We all met and had a jam. It was good. We played a few Bad Company covers, Free, some Rolling Stones and it felt good. We all shook hands and said 'Yes. We have a band.' We didn't have a name but we had a band."

Colin Burgess remembers, "I first got involved around 1973 before Christmas. This guy rang me up and said 'Malcolm Young wants to form a band.' At the time I didn't even know who Malcolm was but I knew all about George and Harry and that he was George's brother so we set up a rehearsal and it sounded great. At the time it was only a three–piece but Malcolm's guitar playing was just fantastic."

Larry Van Kriedt remembers meeting the Young brothers for the first time, "I first met Angus and Mal in August 1969. I lived in a migrant hostel and Angus used to go there. The first time I saw him he was wearing a school uniform, carrying an electric guitar and smoking a cigarette. He was 14 or 15. I had a real Gibson guitar and I could play it so we became friends and he introduced me to his family. I used to go to their house every weekend for about a year. I always brought my guitar. Angus, Mal and I would sit around exchanging riffs on our guitars. We were all very good! I stopped seeing them for a year or two. One night I got a knock on my door and a friend of mine called Robbie Lord asked if I wanted to go and jam with the boys as they heard I had bought a bass. So we jumped in his car and went to a rehearsal studio in Newtown. I was 19 then and had a baby boy. I used to bring him to rehearsals sometimes and I was worried that he would get his ears damaged. Today he plays with me in my band called Afram. I was probably only in AC/DC for about four months. But it seemed like longer. Everyone could see that it was going somewhere."

There is confliction in how the AC/DC name came about. According to some it was Malcolm and Angus's sister–in–law Sandra who came up with the name AC/DC – to signify power and energy. More likely, it seems the name came from the back of a vacuum cleaner or sewing machine. (In electrical jargon the abbreviation stands for Alternating Current/Direct Current.)

Of course, 'AC/DC' is also a slang term for bisexuality, but the defiantly hetero rockers appear to have been completely unaware of these connotations. In their minds, AC/DC referred to the electricity they squeezed out of their guitars and amps. Nevertheless, several gay clubs would offer to book the group assuming their name indicated some degree of sexual flexibility, a scenario that wasn't as distressing as it might have been for the band members. "Upfront, bisexual women would come in and hold up vibrators. They had t–shirts with holes cut out in the front, and their boobs were poking out. It was great!" Malcolm later described.

Luckily for AC/DC there weren't many rock acts in Sydney and even fewer consisting of musicians that had developed as quickly as Angus and Malcolm. So it was easy to book a gig and after a few of rehearsals the confident musicians strode onstage on New Year's Eve, 1973, in a small Sydney nightclub called Chequers, situated at 79 Goulburn Street. Dave Evans recalls: "I was very excited as it was the premier rock venue in Sydney. It was more packed than usual, as it was New Year's Eve and we went on and really rocked the place. It was magic."

Their set was, like that of many new bands, a collection of cover versions of their favourite musicians. In keeping with their influences, AC/DC played a rollicking set of Rolling Stones, Chuck Berry and Beatles numbers[1]. They had even managed to perform some original material such as the unrecorded 'The Old Bay Road' and 'Midnight Rock'. Despite Malcom's dreams of glitter–rock flamboyance, they all wore jeans and t–shirts.

Members of the audience knew they were witnessing something with bags of potential. There was something in the way the boys attacked their instruments, with the fervour of youth but the ability of veterans. The band returned to Chequers less than a month later, and played other gigs throughout Sydney. For these dates Larry Van Kriedt played saxophone while Malcolm took over on bass.

The line–up was tweaked several times over the next six months as slowly Malcolm and Angus became the mainstays of the group and experimented with an influx of new musicians. Though it caused frequent grumbles over their inability to hold down a true line up, it was valuable for the two guitarists as it honed their twin playing abilities and they equally improved by playing alongside so many talented players. These included Rob Bailey (ex–Flake), who replaced Larry Van Kriedt on bass, and a succession of drummers after Colin Burgess had been sacked following a collapse at a gig in Chequers. Burgess remembers the night he fell out of the band. "One night I came along to do the gig and I'd had a couple of drinks beforehand but I wasn't drunk. I've never fallen off my drum set in my life, not before or since. What happened was I bought a drink and left it on one side so I could go and check the set–up of my drums and I came back about half an hour later, grabbed my drink and downed it because we were about to go onstage. Then we were onstage and my head is going all over the place, I felt like jelly and I did this really long drum–roll around the kit and ended up rolling on the floor."

Dave Evans adds, "we carried Colin offstage and I didn't really know what had happened. Ten minutes later Malcolm walked up to me and told me they had sacked him. When it happened I was in shock, I liked Colin, I still do."

"Malcolm said 'You're so drunk you can't play, so you've got the sack,'" sighs Burgess. "I had to sit down for a while anyway when I came offstage because I was still like jelly. Someone must have spiked my drink or something..."

The replacements for Burgess were Ron Carpenter and Russell Coleman and finally Peter Clack (like Bailey, ex–Flake). It was Clack who held firm long enough to be the drummer for the AC/DC incarnation which would record its first single in June 1974. The band cut the tracks in Albert Studios, Sydney. The two songs recorded were 'Can I Sit Next To You Girl' and 'Rockin' In The Parlour', both produced by Harry Vanda and George Young. Come July the single had been pressed and released throughout Oceania, in

Australia on Albert Records and in New Zealand on Polydor. "I was on cloud nine as I got onto the bus from Bondi to travel into the city to the recording studio" remembers Dave Evans. "It was a dream come true to be produced by Harry and George. I just did everything I was told and didn't really open my mouth except to sing."

Though he was out of the band, Colin Burgess still had this to say of the single he helped construct, "I thought the track, 'Can I Sit Next To You Girl', had great potential. I'd played in bands that had had lots of hits, and I thought, 'Here we go again, on another roll'. I knew they were going to be big, and they were."

As their fame spread, the band members began to ditch their denim–and–t–shirt garb, and donned costumes. Again, they unwittingly encouraged rumours about their sexual proclivities by camping it up. The drummer was a harlequin clown, Angus alternated between a schoolboy and Zorro, the bassist was a motorcycle cop, Malcolm was a pilot while Evans was a stereotypical glam pop star. In fact, their penchant for costumes seems to prefigure the band that put gay macho subculture on the map a few years later.

"That was a long time before the Village People," Evans says. "We were a heavy rock band and we just came out of left field – we certainly turned heads. But not long after we put our first single out, The Skyhooks came along and they pretty much had the costume thing down pat. We decided to get rid of the gear. The only one that was retained was Angus's schoolboy." Angus's year of birth was publicised as 1959 to play into the schoolboy image. This would have made him 14 years old when the band formed in 1973. It was Angus's sister Margaret who had suggested he wear the schoolboy attire permanently as he had once tried the costume in a previous group. But before he settled on the image that would identify him for over 30 years, he could be seen in an assortment of outfits, including a gorilla suit (dressed in which he would burst out of a cage), Spiderman (with a spider's web made of rope as a backdrop), and Superman, or rather Super–Ang (with a phone booth on stage where he could change).

Angus: "In the beginning I'd wear whatever I thought was appropriate, but the schoolboy suit was the one that stuck. Being in the gorilla suit, I thought I was going to perspire to death. And I couldn't see where I was going – I wandered straight into the audience. The first thing they saw was me. It was like a cold slap in the face. And they thought, 'Is it a joke?' First reaction was people would sort of giggle. And Malcolm would say to me 'Shut 'em up! You can play.' It was a good thing because they were going to remember us for the little guy in the short pants who looks like he's having an epileptic fit. But the thing is you had to play."

Angus did not always keep his clothes on however. Quite often he would take off his jacket when the temperature inside a club was stifling. He would habitually then pull his shorts down to moon at the audience. All this form of theatre was indeed entertainment, and Angus refers to it as "cheap cabaret". There was a catalyst for his newfound distraction tactic.

"One time we were playing this big festival in England and there was this woman photographer with a real Dolly Parton physique. She gets up and walks across the front stage, and of course more than half the audience were hot–blooded males; so they're all following her with their eyes and my brother says, 'You better do something quick to get their attention back.' So I mooned 'em. That certainly jolted them back quick. Very popular with the law too. Oh yes."

The antics of AC/DC and particularly Angus led to acceptance from the always–entertained audience but there was always someone who didn't appreciate them. "I remember at a theatre at Long Island, a guy kept throwing drinks at me. I warned him a couple of times, and then he hit me on the side of the head with his metal container. So I jumped in the crowd and let him have it. As soon as I jumped off stage and saw the height of this guy, I thought to myself, 'You fool.' Luckily, one of our crew guys got me out of it, because this guy was big. But I figured if all else failed I could bite him in the kneecap."

Playing in clubs was a learning curve in itself, but dressing as a camp schoolboy was not entirely conducive to acceptance in the rougher establishments that AC/DC would play in their early days. Angus: "We started in clubs and clubs could be a little rough and tumble. Many a guy dived on stage. Once, in Perth, some clown's getting at me all night, he gets onstage and puts me in a headlock.

So I defend myself. Well, he got in for the shock of his life. I know I look teeny up there, but that's the worst time to give me grief. When I put that school suit on, I go into another thing. It takes over. Malcolm says, 'It's like he's possessed!' It is two different people. And this clown decides he's going to come into your planet. You know, I decided to evict him."

Despite heckling or the odd scrap, Angus would religiously keep his outfit on, claiming he would feel naked without it. As for being possessed as Malcolm described, this was simply down to being so concentrated on playing guitar. The intense and sweaty act was as much about playing the notes correctly as it was about keeping the audience amused.

The importance of image, and the dominance of the Young brothers, began to cause bad blood within the band. Dave Evans had long hair and planned to keep it that way. As he remembers, "Malcolm told me I had to cut my hair and wear sunglasses on stage. It wasn't the image that I wanted. I wouldn't cut my hair for anyone. My old man told me when I was 16 'Get a haircut or piss off'. So I left home."

'Can I Sit Next To You Girl' was to feature heavily on Australian television. A clip filmed at the Last Picture Show Theatre in Cronulla was shown on the only national rock television show, *GTK*. Dave Evans' look was perfect for TV, though it might not have necessarily suited AC/DC, even at that time.

Another problem was bad management from those becoming involved with AC/DC, according to Evans. As he remembers, "We were playing big gigs, had a single in the top ten but we didn't have any money. We were struggling to get money together to buy a bloody hamburger. I was enjoying the life. I expected the money to take care of itself but the cash wasn't forthcoming. I started questioning the guys about the management and thinking the manager, Dennis Laughlin, must be ripping us off. It got pretty heavy between me and him, I mean he had a perm and was flying around the country to get to gigs. We were struggling around in clapped out trucks."

Sometimes laughter would accompany those early trials and tribulations and the band felt like a unit, even under difficult circumstances. Evans tells the story of the most bizarre gig AC/DC ever played. The group had agreed to play at a Greek wedding. The bride's brother was a close friend of the band, and had lent them a PA whenever they needed one in the past. AC/DC were to be paid for the gig but were confused when told they would be playing in a suburban backyard. There was to be no stage, just a lawn to stand on.

Evans continues, "We did a set – a bit of Chuck Berry, a bit of Rolling Stones – the stuff we were doing then. Then we had a break. The people were very generous and gave us plenty to eat and drink. The father of the bride came up to me and asked us if we could play 'Zorba The Greek' – an instrumental piece. I said 'Mate, we're a rock n' roll band. There's no way.' Then Malcolm said, 'Give me a minute'. He went away and practised for a while, all from ear. That's how good the guy was. Then Malcolm said 'Tell him, yeah. We'll do it'. The band went back and played following Malcolm's lead. It was an instrumental piece so I was in the clear. It sounded good. We killed 'em. The people at the wedding danced and cheered when it was over. I hope they all remember that day. The one and only time AC/DC ever played 'Zorba The Greek'."

It was a light moment in an otherwise frustrating time for the up and coming AC/DC, who had been garnering a huge reputation from Perth to Adelaide, where their single had already been a big hit. "We were travelling from Adelaide to Perth along the Nullabor Plain. The road wasn't sealed at the time, just a rough track," remembers Evans. "About three quarters of the way across we got a flat tyre. The truck didn't have a jack. So we all get out of the truck and it starts to rain. If not for the kindness of a passing traveller, AC/DC might still be out on the Nullabor Plains. The Good Samaritan came along and dug the hole under the wheel single–handed. Without waiting for the expressions of gratitude, the guy jumped back in his car and took off. The band was saved."

"The biggest problem I had with AC/DC in those early days, being a touring unit, and not having much money, was keeping everything together, keeping everyone happy. There's a few dope smokers in the band, right? Instead of giving everyone fifty bucks a week, it's

*like, alright, whatever you need, we'll get it. Thirty bucks a week
plus a bag of dope, a bottle of Scotch. Well, Angus was a pain in the
arse, because he says, 'Fuck ya, I don't drink booze, or fuckin' take
drugs'. I'd give him a bag of fish and chips, a Kit–Kat, a packet of
Benson and Hedges and a bottle of Coke." Dennis Laughlin.*

Evans was still unhappy at the relatively disorganised state
of affairs surrounding AC/DC. Instead of listening to Evans' concerns and attempting to improve the situation Malcolm decided it
was time to start touting for a new vocalist. According to Evans the
band had been jamming with another singer whilst he was still in
AC/DC. By this time Michael Browning was managing the band
and it was he who had hired Ronald Belford Scott, better known as
Bon, to be the band's driver. It was not in Scott's nature to be a mere
hanger on to a touring band; he had designs on being in the group
itself. He nagged at Malcolm to allow him a chance at drumming
for the band, before he more cheekily attempted to become singer.
Bon told Malcolm, "Get rid of that fucking poof you got up there,
I'd fucking love to have a crack at that with you guys." As the guitarist remembered, "he went back to the hotel, smoked a few joints,
goofed around on the guitar and instantly we just knew this ruffian
was right."

Dave Evans: "Bon joined the band and stepped right into my
shoes. There was already an established group with a hit record out
and a natural stage act. He was good. He became a caricature just
like Angus. Now I know I'm not seen as the essential AC/DC singer.
To me, the core of the band is with Bon. The classic songs are the
ones Bon did. Bon Scott was the voice of AC/DC but it didn't do
him any good." There were to be no sour grapes from the group's
first successful singer however. "By the time I left AC/DC, the band
was already established and had a hit record. So I get some personal
satisfaction knowing that. Any band that's successful over 25 years
is just a great act. To me the Rolling Stones are an institution and
AC/DC, well, you'd put them right up there with them. To be part of
the group at that founding stage well, I'm pretty proud of that."

Says Evans: "I will never forget a conversation I had with
Doug Parkinson when I was just starting out as a singer in Syd-

ney when I was in my early teens. Doug was a very well–known Australian star singer and still is. He asked me: 'Do you know the reason why most bands split up?' I didn't really know. He said to me – 'women!' And left me to ponder. I found out the hard way. When AC/DC first started Malcolm used to encourage me to talk to the female fans before and after the gigs to make fans out of them. Well it certainly worked a treat. We gained a strong following very quickly and as lead singer I certainly had my pick of the best–looking girls, and there were plenty of them of course." Evans' words regarding others in the band are at odds with those of school friends of Angus and Malcolm who have previously described how the brothers were quite popular with females. And it seems unlikely this appeal would have faded once the boys were in a group taking to a stage every night. Nevertheless Evans' description of the climax to his falling out with the band is as follows: "At first me getting girls was a great thing for the band, but increasingly jealousy turned into hateful resentment as even though Malcolm and Angus were huge talents and great performers they weren't popular with the opposite sex and both did not even have girlfriends the whole time I was in the band with them. I also felt that there was also a resentment from Angus because of the fact that I did not join Kentuckee."

By the time of Evans' departure AC/DC had progressed to playing such notable venues as the Sydney Opera House. Evans recalls, "This was the first time that rock was to be played on the main stage there. It was just over the top with seven or eight thousand people outside still trying to get in. It was just unreal to be there on the main stage of the world famous Opera House! What a rock venue. Stevie Wright (ex–Easybeats) came on after us as the main act, as he had the hit record 'Evie' out at the time."

But the high times weren't to last, for Evans at least. A fracas with AC/DC's manager seemed to be the catalyst to end his time in the group. "There was a lot of tension already built up on this my last tour with the band," Evans recollects. "We were touring with a hit record but we hadn't been paid for ages. We were eating fish and chips when we could get them while performing at the top venues in the country. We just wanted to know why. Back then we didn't have any idea of the running costs of gigs plus accommodation plus hire cars and trucks plus roadies' wages. There was probably a good reason for the lack of funds for the actual stars themselves, though I couldn't figure that one out. I guess things were never explained to the band and things came to a head after a night of drinking. It became a little heated between the manager and me and a few fists were thrown but I don't think anything connected. Anyway it was broken up quickly but that was the incident that sealed my fate as far as my position with AC/DC was concerned. I had just made an important enemy."

Evans's contribution to rock mayhem was not over, however: he went on to front Thunder Down Under, Hot Cockerel and, most memorably, glam–rock purists Rabbit.

Notes

*1. The full list of cover versions the band played was: 'Shake, **Rattle & Roll**' (Big Joe Turner), '**Heartbreak Hotel**' (Elvis Presley), '**Baby, Please Don't Go**' (Big Joe Williams, made famous by Them), '**No Particular Place To Go**' (Chuck Berry), '**Jailhouse Rock**' (Elvis Presley), '**That's Alright Mama**' (Elvis Presley), '**Jumping Jack Flash**' (Rolling Stones).*

TAKEN FROM THE OFFICIAL RABBIT BIOGRAPHY FROM CBS – CIRCA 1976

'Dave Evans makes no apologies for the unveiled aggression of his voice, movement and song lyrics. "Rock and violence are closely connected," he says, "I used to try to strangle my aggression on stage – but since I've been in Rabbit I've found it impossible. When you play music like ours, you've got to be honest enough to realise that violence is a part of everyone's personality – and they want to turn it loose. Kids in today's world – especially girls – are told not to. That's why we use shock tactics."

Dave commits his whole mind, body and energy to each per-formance and the result is saturation level rock. "Our music is nothing if it isn't taken to the limit," he says. "If we can't let go, how can we expect our audience?" For Dave "letting go" is pushing his body to the point of agony and his voice to the extreme of forcefulness.'

Chapter 3 – The Chameleon

"I have always wished them the best as, being a founding member, I will always be a part of the band too." Dave Evans, 2005

Bon Scott first saw AC/DC in Adelaide, South Australia, when the band was supporting Lou Reed on his Australian tour. Vincent Lovegrove (ex–singer of The Valentines with Bon) introduced him to AC/DC. "Bon used to hang with the band when we played in Adelaide," remembers Dave Evans. "He knew George Young and Harry Vanda; in the 60s, Bon's old band recorded one of The Easybeats' songs, 'My Old Man's A Groovy Old Man', with Vince. Vince now had a booking agency and did the bookings for AC/DC in South Australia. He told Bon about the two younger Young brothers."

By the time he met up with AC/DC, Bon had already led a colourful life. Born on the 7th of September, 1946, in Kirriemuir, Scotland, he was christened Ronald but soon acquired the nickname Bon, short for 'Bonnie Scotland'. Like the Young family, the Scotts emigrated to Australia; in their case they followed Bon's sister who had moved to Melbourne a year earlier. It was in Melbourne that he started his education, at the Sunshine Primary School. His family would later relocate to Western Australia where Bon joined North Fremantle Primary. In 1959, aged 12 Bon started at John Curtin High. During this period he had become a proficient bagpipe player and was an under–17s pipe band drum champion for five consecutive years. His mother Isa, who would always call him Ron, remembers: "There was a pipe band nearly every week, every Saturday night, marching through the square. Ron was mad on drums before the pipes. He would hit biscuit tins or the breadboard."

"My new schoolmates threatened to kick the shit out of me when they heard my Scottish accent. I had one week to learn to speak like them if I wanted to remain intact. 'Course, I didn't take any notice. No one railroads me, and it made me all the more determined to

speak my own way. That's how I got my name, you know. The bonny Scot, see?" Bon Scott.

Ian Cant was a school friend of Bon's and says of the time: "North Fremantle in those days was a great place to grow up. I'm glad I was born there; it was a great place for Bon too. He was, to me, a little bit of a larrikin; he had an aura that showed up from a very early age. He had something that attracted people to him, his easygoing air. We both attended John Curtin High School where we had good teachers and a good environment and all the students at that time had fun." Russell Clark, another friend of Bon's, says of Fremantle: "It's an environment that really encourages people to enjoy themselves."

In part due to his love of music, Bon was not cut out for academic work and he would thus often find himself in trouble in school. "He was into everything," recalls Isa, "a mind of his own. He went walking by himself; I never had to do anything. He never used to come home from school. He'd just go off with some of his little mates and never think of coming up the hill. I used to have to chase him, so it started young! He was mischievous, I'd say, more than anything. Not naughty; he just had a mind of his own and if he wanted to do something, that was it."

The courts did not see Bon in quite the same way. An article in the *West Australian* on March 13th 1963, reported the crime which saw Bon sent to the Riverbank Juvenile institution for his increasing misdemeanours:

'A 16 year–old youth pleaded guilty in the Fremantle Children's Court yesterday to charges of having given a false name and address to the police, having escaped legal custody, having unlawful carnal knowledge and having stolen 12 gallons of petrol.'

Being sentenced to time at a boys' home was preferable to facing his parents, whom Bon felt he had disappointed. Until the age of 18, he was placed in the care of the Child Welfare Department. The mistake he had made left Bon feeling low, and he missed out on seeing his grandparents who had travelled from Scotland to visit the family. In many ways he spent the rest of his younger years trying to atone for his early behaviour and close friends of his would say that later in life Bon was more determined to be successful in an attempt to make up to his parents for what had happened.

When Bon emerged from custody he had made the decision to make a full time career of music. He had long wanted to be a professional drummer and the appeal had increased when Bon began to dream of travelling the world and meeting as many women as he possibly could. He felt it was a more suitable career for a person of his character and intrigue and it certainly beat the alternatives. Since leaving school, Bon had held a series of odd jobs: driving a tractor, labouring on fishing boats and working as an apprentice weighing machine mechanic. He even attempted to join the Australian army but they pronounced him 'socially maladjusted'.

In 1965 Scott joined his first real band in Perth, known as The Spektors. He drummed, and although he also sang when the need arose, he was initially convinced that his musical future would be behind the kit. Little is known about his time with The Spektors, but despite Bon not being in the band for very long, it appears that it was nevertheless a good education in group politics and writing and recording music.

Richard Selby, an Australian musician who would go on to form The Troubadours, recollects his first meeting with Bon. "It was at St. Patrick's church where they had a Sunday rock n' roll dance. There would be bands coming, wonderful rock n' roll bands and we would be there, watching the band. That was a good part of our growing up because there was always something happening with music in North Fremantle. Before we actually got into bands we were watching other bands and that encouraged us to practice more and try and form our own group. In 1964 I joined the Troubadours and it was about the same time The Spektors were happening. I think we played a couple of gigs together at a place called the Big Beat Centre along with other bands like Russ Kennedy and Johnny Young and The Strangers."

Vincent Lovegrove also remembers seeing Bon play with The Spektors. "Bon used to get up and sing maybe three or four songs a night", he says. "We often as not found we were playing the same venues. I was a singer in The Dimensions, later called The Winztons, and he and I struck up a friendship. Bon and the singer would swap places halfway through their set, and Bon would sing whilst the singer would drum. The singer's name was John Collins, a good solid singer, but a bit straight. He was also a good drummer.

"Bon was a postman in the daytime, and I was a menswear clothing salesman. He'd drop the mail in to the menswear shop in Fremantle. Bon lived in North Fremantle with his mum, dad and brother. There were a lot of cabarets in Perth at the time and there was also a lot of mining going on around the area at that time and the miners used to work on and off – they would work for six months and take three months off and they would accumulate a lot of cash and spend it in these clubs. The only problem was the bands they wanted to have there were what we called top 40 cabaret bands. There was no originality so therefore there were a lot of places that opened up in the surf clubs along the west coast, places like the Swanbourne Stomps."

In 1966 Bon and Vince formed The Valentines. Bon was 20 years old. They shared vocals and were backed by Ted Ward on rhythm guitar, Bruce Abbott on bass guitar, Wyn Milson on lead guitar, and drummer Warrick Findlay. "We cooked up this idea of combining the best of each other's bands, and forming our own", says Lovegrove. "We were influenced by Sam And Dave and other soul music, along with the Small Faces, so we decided to form a band with two singers. We would take turns to sing the main vocal line, while the other would harmonise."

Though Bon was not brimming with confidence in his own vocal style he nevertheless was secure enough to put his voice to tape. Unlike his eventual singing with AC/DC, in the '60s Scott's voice was soft but in keeping with the pop and often psychedelic approach of The Valentines and of the music scene at the time. Within weeks of their live debut The Valentines had made an impression on the local concert going public, and played shows at venues such as Canterbury Court and the Swanbourne Surf Livesaving Club (more commonly known as the Swanbourne Stomp). "We worked off each other a lot," Lovegrove says of their duel vocal duties, "because we weren't really confident enough to do it on our own. We had a pretty wild stage act for the time, we used to jump on and off amps and have fire bombs going off onstage and all sorts of weird stuff. And we fired off each other, we definitely gelled and we would work stuff out beforehand, what we would and wouldn't do."

The Troubadours' Richard Selby recalls: "They were both pretty smooth but Vince was more laid back than Bon. Vince had this star aura, Bon had an aura of mischief, this twinkle in his eye, the look on his face that would bounce off Vince, the cool one. It was interesting to see."

"I met Bon in 1967", Russell Clark recalls. "We were post-men together. He laughed all the time and really enjoyed himself but with Bon it was like two lives. He would come to work but virtually have the clothes on he had been working in at night, you know, and not have his uniform on. He'd just say where he'd been playing and where he was *going* to play he said to us 'why don't you come and see us one night when we are playing?' We went to the Swanbourne beach when he played at the Swanbourne Stomp down there. My mates and I used to go to different stomps around the area and he happened to be in one of them. He was a likeable chap; easy to get on with. His personality, I would say, was better than his singing! In the end he was more known for his singing than his personality but I think he had both and that was one of his plus points."

Another band that resided in Adelaide at the time was The Twilights, who were the only other group in the area to utilise two vocalists. In both cases this led to respect for the seamless integra-tion of the two singers' styles, as well as adoration from the female audience members. According to Bon, he had switched to vocals as "the singer would get more chicks". In the 1960's, Perth only had one record label and its owner, Martin Clarke, took pride in know-ing about all bands that operated throughout Australia. His Clarion label knew The Valentines could be on the verge of success and so Clarke approached them, claiming their signatures in March 1967. Less than a year after they had formed, the group had found a label and released their first single. For this they chose a cover version, Arthur Alexander's 'Everyday I Have To Cry', whilst on the B–side they recorded 'I Can't Dance With You', a Small Faces number. Inevitably, the record did very well in The Valentines' locality, reaching the Top 5 in Perth alone.

The band then recorded six tracks for Ron Tudor's June Productions, which were leased to the Philips label. These included a version of Harry Vanda & George Young's 'My Old Man's A Groovy Old Man' and the self–penned 'Juliette'. These two became hits for The Valentines when released on an EP. The second single was less successful, however; a Stevie Wright/George Young composition entitled 'She Said', released in August 1967, only just managed to scrape into the Perth charts. There was a slight improvement in February of the following year, when the double A–Side 'I Can Hear The Raindrops'/'Why Me?', both Lovegrove/Ward compositions, reached number 30 on the Perth charts, but still failed to score elsewhere.

Later The Valentines were rumoured to be moving label and joining the ranks of the Sunshine company. However, the group remained with Clarion to release their fourth and last single in July 1968. 'Peculiar Hole In The Sky' was another gem from the Easybeats' vaults, written by Harry Vanda and George Young and produced by Paul Aulton. The B–side 'Love Makes Sweet Music' was a cover version of a song by progressive jazz rock British band The Soft Machine. The Valentines now moved base to Melbourne where they joined New Dream and The Zoot as forerunners in the 1960s boom of Australian psychedelic pop.

The relocation to Melbourne was inspired by a 'battle of the bands' competition where the winner could receive a free trip to London. "It was a nationwide competition where each state had a winner," Lovegrove recollects, "and we won Perth, and our prize was to go to Melbourne to compete in the nationals, and that was a big trip for us. So we decided to use that as our gauge as to whether we should leave Perth for good. We went over and of course we played in a big hall, there were five thousand screaming fans and there were another 12 or so bands on. You only got to do two songs but you could work out a really good stage act for two songs. We didn't win but for the four days we were there, we went to every single club in Melbourne, and saw that it was a completely different world to where we came from. We decided there and then, 'this is it, let's go'. Six months later we left to go to Melbourne permanently."

Lovegrove remembers one incident, which stirred up problems in the Valentines camp. "When we hit Melbourne we made a band decision that we were not going to smoke pot or take any drugs," he explains. "I can remember me and Bon went up to Sydney one time and it was the first time I had ever had a joint, we went and saw this band that we knew and the keyboard player invited us back to his place to smoke some dope. We were both nervous as shit and we went back there and smoked and were shit scared. We just sat in the corner of the room giggling and wondering whether we should be there and eventually we just slid our way out of the room, you know completely paranoid before bursting out laughing. Then we ran back to the hotel we were staying in which only had one room for the whole band. And of course the rest of the guys knew immediately that we had smoked and we were ostracized and told we were going to be kicked out of the band. We laughed at that, considering we had started the band. So we went out to a club and got shit–faced drunk because we couldn't believe the gall of the guys in the band thinking they could throw us out. We saw them again the next morning. We always used to have breakfast around the corner; we used to go there and have fresh orange juice because after a hard night drinking it's good to have a bit of orange juice. We were on one table and the band was on another table and they wouldn't speak to us because we were still stoned. Anyway eventually a member of the band came over and said 'It's ok – we'll let it go this time – you can still be in the band.'"

There was to be a high profile drugs bust involving The Valentines, although it was not clear exactly which members were involved, or exactly what the forbidden substances were. This gave the band publicity, but it was something they didn't want hanging around their necks. As Lovegrove explained, "Bon and I agreed we were going nowhere. We were only being kept alive by publicity about pot, not by what we were doing, which was good but we weren't playing at the right places and we got lost basically. So Bon and I decided we had the right to do it because we had formed the band in the first place – we would leave the band and would get on with other things. We announced our decision to the band and it didn't go down all that well with them or our management at that stage but we felt it was for the best."

The Valentines had provided a useful initiation into the music world for Bon Scott. He had experienced life in a popular touring group and though the songs were rarely their own and fell on the lighter side of rock, his introduction to rock n' roll was complete.

In his liner notes for Bon's next project, Glenn A. Baker (an Australian based music writer and broadcaster) remarked that he "encountered Bon Scott a number of times during the 70s and each meeting served to increase my incredulity that a performer's public image could be so at odds with his real personality. Bon really was a sweet man. He was warm, friendly and uncommonly funny. He did not breathe fire, pluck wings off flies or eat children whole. And while his daunting stage persona of lascivious leers and blood curdling howls was by no means fraudulent, it was most certainly a professional cloak that could be worn at convenient moments."

Bon went to Sydney to put together a new band, which he did with the remnants of Levi Smith's Clefs. Fraternity was another leap forward for Bon and his adaptable persona and voice. He grew a beard, eventually looking something like Arthur Brown (a British singer famed for his notorious pyromaniac stage routine) crossed with Scottish comic Billy Connolly. This was not unusual for the time, yet for Bon, wearing leather sandals and outlandish clothing was slightly at odds with his core instincts, especially when compared with his later, no–bullshit image. Fraternity were clearly a more exciting visual prospect than The Valentines were ever going to be, but musically they fell somewhat short, despite favourable reviews at the time. Their whole purpose was to attempt to be an Australian version of Bob Dylan's former backing group The Band.

Fraternity then moved to South Australia after being offered management and financial support by businessman Hamish Henry. *Go–Set* magazine featured an interview with Vince Lovegrove and Bon at this time where it was noted: "Bon Scott, vocalist, recorder and timbale player, is constantly in a dream world of his own but he's having a ball. He says: 'the point is, the dollar sign is not the ultimate. We want to try and help each other develop and live. So that the thing inside of us, whether it be creative or not, is satisfied. Something makes us tick and it's up to people to satisfy that something. We are satisfying ourselves and others by creating an environment."

Lovegrove remembers that he and Bon both had "eclectic musical tastes, but we were also into creating a stage act, an exciting stage act, and that was probably just as important to us as two 20/21 year–olds as our music, rightly or wrongly. It was an experimental and pioneering time in rock music in those days. Particularly in Australia, because we were so isolated from the rest of the world."

According to Lovegrove, "Bon had found his niche with Fraternity. That was what he needed; when he left us he became a showman. He was what they needed as well; he was a front man with a good voice. They believed they were the best band in the world and were going to conquer the world. It was also a time of many magic mushrooms being dropped and lots of alcohol being drunk and that became part of Fraternity as well."

The group of aspiring hippies regularly returned to their spiritual home of Sydney. Their recordings were issued on the Adelaide independent label Sweet Peach but the reception was lukewarm. The music could not stand up to scrutiny beyond a live environment, where they had developed a reputation for exciting performances. Thus the album *Livestock,* released in 1971, made little impression. John Robinson wrote the wonderful 'Seasons of Change' for the band, but it was the version by his own group, Blackfeather, which cracked the charts. There was a further connection for Bon however, as he appeared on the Blackfeather album, *At The Mountains Of Madness,* which has since been rightly heralded as a cult classic. Oddly enough, it wasn't his singing that featured on the album, but his skills with the recorder.

Fraternity won the prestigious *Hoadley's National Battle Of The Sound*s in 1971, although this did not help with their attempts at releasing a hit record. But *Go–Set* gushed at the band's stage show: "Fraternity came on and nearly rocked themselves off stage and half the audience nearly rocked themselves onto the stage. Superb harmonica and superb vocals by that guy out of the old Valentines. What's his name again? Oh, you know him."

After becoming disillusioned with the Sweet Peach label in late 1971 Fraternity released a number of singles on the small Raven label before recording their second long–playing record. The resulting *Flaming Galah* album was more of a rock record than its predecessor, and left behind many of the band's fans. In an effort to find a more broad–minded fanbase, the band and their entourage decamped to England, where the glam rock scene was at its stack–heeled peak. The group, and the hangers on (16 people in all, plus Clutch the dog) would remain in England for 18 months, living in a huge four–storey house in Finchley, London. At one stage they played alongside Status Quo in the south coast town of Bournemouth, but the denim–clad boogie legends were so polished that they blew Fraternity away.

The group decided a name change was necessary, quickly altering their moniker to Fang. But success still evaded them and by 1973 the members were bickering on a daily basis. By August Fraternity/Fang would play its last ever gig at a festival in Windsor. Some of the members, including Bon, hung around in London as the group disintegrated, finding work in a nearby pub, behind the bar. But by Christmas both Bon and Irene decided to return to Adelaide. They'd had enough of each other by this point and were quarrelling constantly. Irene went to live with her parents, while Bon moved in with Bruce Howe of the Mount Lofty Rangers and his wife and son. The Rangers were something of a cult band in Australia, featuring many of the country's top musicians, including Robyn Archer, Jimmy Barnes (who went on to front Cold Chisel), Chris Bailey (later leader of The Saints), Mauri Berg and 'Uncle' John Ayers.

Howe was hopeful that Bon could patch up his differences with Irene, but any optimism seemed to disappear after one particularly heated argument between the couple. Bon stormed out of Irene's parents' house and immediately crashed his motorcycle. The accident left him with missing teeth (which would require him to wear a dental plate), a permanently damaged leg and a smashed jaw.

During the resulting lay–off, Bon worked with Adelaide musician Peter Head (aka Beagley) who wrote the songs 'Round And Round And Round' and 'Carey Gully' for him. Subsequently Scott performed with the Rangers, but by 1974 he was working as an occasional roadie for AC/DC.

"If you saw the way Bon drove, you'd know why he ended up singing! We knew all along that Bon would be perfect for us. We first got together one afternoon and straight away we worked out two songs. From that point, you could tell the guy had great talent."
Angus Young

It was Vince Lovegrove who initially introduced his old Valentines pal to AC/DC as he explains, "Contrary to what other stories you may hear. I was working as an agent and journalist at the time, and managing some acts, including Cold Chisel. I knew George Young and Harry Vanda from our Valentine days. They wrote a lot of our songs for us. Anyway, George's two brothers, Angus and Malcolm, had just started this band called AC/DC who wore funny clothes like The Valentines, but they had that riff rock thing underlying, with an early version of Malcolm's rhythm chop playing. It was actually started by other Australian acts such as Billy Thorpe and The Aztecs, and a band called Carson, and perhaps one of Australia's best ever bands, The Dingoes. But to Malcolm's credit, he really expanded the sound, and experimented with it, and forged a new sound, which was the basis of 'the Australian sound' that so many bands mimicked after that...like Rose Tattoo and The Angels and many others." Rose Tattoo would become friendly with AC/DC and Bon Scott in particular would become close to RT leader, Angry Anderson.

Lovegrove continues: "Bon was recovering from his accident, and he needed a place to stay and needed some money. We were both living in Adelaide and it was just a couple of years after The Valentines broke up and Bon had been in Fraternity. He stayed at my home to live, and I gave him some work painting the office and driving bands around. George had asked me to look after his two little brothers, Angus and Malcolm, as their manager was ripping them off at that time. I loved AC/DC then; I could see they were going to be world–beaters. They were unique, nothing like them then. So I booked them as much as I could, bringing them to Adelaide from

Sydney, mostly at a loss for me, but as a favour to George. I would pay them the cash directly instead of giving it to their manager.

"One day Malcolm told me they were going to sack their singer, and he asked me if I knew anyone. I told him about Bon, and that I'd introduce him that night as they were playing at my venue. They said to me that Bon was too old, that they wanted someone young. I told Malcolm that Bon could rock them 'til they dropped, that he could out rock them anytime."

Vince Lovegrove seemed to be the only person who truly knew Bon Scott would be perfect for AC/DC. As he remembers: "When I told Bon, he told me they were too young, that they couldn't rock if their lives depended on it. On outside appearances, to all and sundry at the time, it did not seem like a good match. But I knew both parties and I knew they would compliment each other. I knew it would work, even though nobody else thought so; AC/DC, Bon, anyone else. It seemed so obvious to me. Anyway, that night, backstage, I introduced Malcolm and Angus to Bon. It was strange because their lead singer was there at the time, and I knew, and they knew, but he didn't. After the show we all went back to Bruce Howe's place for a jam session (he was the bass player for Fraternity) and they rocked on until dawn, doing Chuck Berry songs."

According to Lovegrove, the band matchmaking session worked a treat. "Next day, Bon came around to the house, packed his bags and said he was going to Sydney to join AC/DC. He was in the back seat of their hire car. They were in the front. We waved goodbye, and that was that. A legend began."

The band's then manager Dennis Laughlin had been regularly filling in for Dave Evans who at this time was calling in sick a great deal. Nevertheless, they managed a six weeks residency at Perth's Beethoven Disco, as the unlikely support act for a well–known transvestite called Carlotta. By September Laughlin called Bon to ask if he would like to join the band as full–time singer. He didn't have to think too long, believing even early on that AC/DC were capable of going far and insisting that they would go further with him at the helm rather than Evans whom he called a "drongo".

Bon joined the group at the end of September and appeared with them on stage for the first time at the Pooraka Hotel for a jam session. Angus recalled: "The only rehearsal we had was just sitting around an hour before the gig pulling out every rock n' roll song we knew. When we finally got there, Bon downed about two bottles of bourbon with dope, coke, speed and says, 'right, I'm ready,' and he was too. He was fighting fit. There was this immediate transformation and he was running around with his wife's knickers on, yelling at the audience. It was a magic moment, he said it made him feel young again." According to Vince Lovegrove, Bon had told him he liked the guys in the band and thought they were going to be big, because he was going to sing for them."

"It keeps you fit – the alcohol, nasty women, sweat on stage, bad food – it's all very good for you" Bon Scott

After Dave Evans played with the band in Melbourne he was given his marching orders.

"After my split with the band I was surprised that Bon was the new lead singer as he was a lot older than us, and he was recovering from a bad motorbike accident, and was splitting with his wife", says Evans. "He was not really together. He did not go down well in Sydney at their first concert there without me, as the crowd was expecting me but they moved to Melbourne to regroup." The gig Evans refers to was the band's first official concert with Bon as frontman, at the Brighton Le Sands Masonic Hall in Sydney. Though the crowd was indeed expecting Evans, it was clear to all in attendance that AC/DC had made a good choice with a replacement vocalist. Scott did not have the looks of Evans but what he lacked in 'pretty boy' status he made up in pure charisma and brash confidence, a trait which dissuaded people from disagreeing with him to his face.

Angus commented on meeting Bon: "When Bon first came along and saw me and Malcolm he sat behind the drums and started bashing away. We said 'we know a good rock n' roll drummer, what we want is a great rock n' roll singer', hence the song we recorded. This is what we wanted. For us it was great. He was a striking person. He did have the stuff legends are based on. I was in awe too, being the youngest. I laughed my head off and he laughed when he saw me. He said to Malcolm 'Do you want me to sing like some-one?' Malcolm said: 'No we're asking for you not anybody else. We don't want a clone, we want you and what you are.' He loved that. He loved the fact that he could get on and be himself. He said to himself 'I never got what I wanted to be.' Being in a pop band the front guy would always have the image for the little girls. Bon used to call himself the background singer, the rhythm singer. He had the talent and nice guy looks. Some people wanted him to cover up his tattoos and all sorts of stupid things."

Upon joining AC/DC it seemed Bon was finally where he had truly wanted to be ever since joining his first band – front man, lead singer, lyric writer and all in whatever style he wanted. He could go on stage wearing jeans and a t–shirt, or even women's undergar-ments, and the other members couldn't care less. This would never have happened in The Valentines or Fraternity.

"I've never had a message for anyone in my entire life. Except may-be to give out my room number." Bon Scott

Chris Gilbey worked for the Albert production company and experienced AC/DC with both Bon Scott and Dave Evans. He re-members: "To be honest, the early tracks with Dave were not that impressive to me. However it was a George and Harry play and they were developing the band in the studio and they recorded a bunch of tracks with Dave. I don't have much recollection of what they recorded with Dave. Frankly it was when Bon joined the band and started writing lyrics that sounded like graffiti that I started thinking that this was a band that was going to go somewhere. Bon was a great guy who had a tremendous attitude and great stage pres-ence – a fantastic communicator."

During AC/DC's first gig with Bon there were already signs of the front man's excessive nature. "We got into the dressing room and there's a bottle of bourbon, a line of coke, some speed and a big fat joint laid out", recalled Angus. "Bon came in and guzzled the lot! I said to Malcolm, 'if he can walk to the stage, let alone sing, it's gonna be something.' But he got out there and this huge, hurricane yell came out. The whole place went, 'what the fuck is this?' Plus, there was the look of him. He had all these tattoos and a t–shirt with a big drawing of his cock on it!"

In November 1974 Michael Browning, manager of the Hard Rock Café (Melbourne), became AC/DC's full time manager. Together they all moved into a house in Melbourne where there was apparent nightly debauchery. Nevertheless, though the band clearly knew how to party, especially with Bon now on board, they could also work hard and fast. Within ten days the group had recorded their first album, which they named *High Voltage*. This was undoubtedly influenced by the AC/DC name itself and was perhaps a discreet assertion that the name represented power and energy as opposed to sexual preferences. It also covered the base of the music, which was somewhat lo–fi, straight to the point good time rock n' roll with an added kick; the verve of youth and the unmistakable howl of Bon Scott.

George Young and Harry Vanda manned the controls behind the production desk whilst George played bass himself on some songs. Session musician Tony Currenti was enlisted to finish the drum parts as Peter Clack and John Proud had only played on one track each. The band now had a real record to stand behind and after a tour of South Australia finished the year off in style with a New Year's Eve gig at Festival Hall in Melbourne. By their own admission they would pretty much play in front of anyone, and often did. Every type of fan could be seen at an AC/DC show, from gays who assumed they were named for a different reason, to typical girl groupies and the standard male rockers – this was an act that could transcend boundaries. The *High Voltage* record was to set them well on their way down the road to glory.

VINCENT LOVEGROVE PROFILE

Vince Lovegrove is something of a renaissance man who has tried his hand at many things during the course of his life. He came to the fore as a film maker in 1978, by producing the first ever international documentary on Australian music, 'Australian Music To The World'. In 1987 he completed a documentary called Suzi's Story, which was commissioned by Home Box Office in New York and 20th Century Fox in Hollywood. The subject of the film was Lovegrove's wife, who had recently died of A.I.D.S. In 1994 he made another film about the illness, which this time focused on his son Troy who had also passed away after contracting the disease. Both films were to win numerous awards internationally, and both achieved Emmy award nominations. They became the most successful portraits of the A.I.D.S. virus ever to be made into documentaries and are still shown around the world.

Lovegrove retained a musical slant to his work, managing the group Cold Chisel, which featured Bon Scott's Fraternity understudy Jimmy Barnes, at the start of their career and he also acted as The Divinyls' manager from 1982 to 1985. During this time the increasingly successful ex–Valentines vocalist resided in New York for four years. Briefly he would manage AC/DC before deciding he wanted to spend more time with his family and resigning. By 1994 he was still involved in management and rescued old friend Jimmy Barnes' career, achieving great success for him in the south of France. However after 18 months he stepped down as Barnes' manager in order to forge a writing career.

Since then he has been an international correspondent for many international magazines and newspapers, in the fields of music, entertainment and sociology. He became entertainment editor for the world travel magazine, 'TNT', based in London, and is now the magazine's regular features writer and columnist. He has also been writing 'Lovegrove Ear On London', a regular Internet column, for a number of years. He is based in London, a single father, a one time widower, and two times divorcee. As previously mentioned he lost his second wife and his son from that marriage to the tragic A.I.D.S. virus.

"I don't mean to sound blasé at all, but that's life and life is all relative", he says. "You have things that have crushed you that would mean nothing to me, and vice versa. A wife and a son are hard to lose, but you can either go under with them, or swim and survive. You have to do that really, because the only other choice is to give up and there's no fun in giving up. That is not to say I am not saddened by loss, or by those who have gone. Not at all, I am very saddened, and it hurts and it leaves scars, but one must learn from death, after all it is part and parcel of the process of life, and life is for living. I have become a better person for all the sadness and sorrow, and I appreciate each minute of life even though it sometimes is dark and desperate. It's dark and desperate right now, but there's always light, the sun always rises. And there's always what the departed leave behind for you, and that's their soul."

Chapter 4 – I'm Alright, Jack

'Here is the rock that rolls, not moving too fast or too slow. This is the rock that rolls, as soon as it hits you you'll know.' Stray, 'The Rock'

On the 25th January 1975 AC/DC played the fourth and last Sunbury Festival, a Woodstock – type affair in Melbourne. The big name band that day was Deep Purple, but the event did not exactly go according to plan. Purple were not originally scheduled to be the last band to go on but they did not expect AC/DC to follow them once they had played their set. A brawl broke out on stage with 20,000 audience members watching, intrigued to say the least. Virtually everyone became involved from roadies to George Young, and the band members themselves. The upshot was that AC/DC had to leave the festival without playing a single note.

Despite this embarrassment, they were still on a high, having recorded their first full–length album, *High Voltage*. Initially the record was only released in Australia, (not exactly the rock n' roll capital of the world) but it began seeing success in other territories as an import. Although, up to this point, AC/DC had not played live outside Australia, thousands of fans across the world were picking up on the AC/DC phenomenon. The Deep Purple incident helped to boost their notoriety.

Alberts Productions' Chris Gilbey helped the band come up with the concept behind their first album. "I came up with the album sleeve," he remembers. "The idea was a power substation with a dog peeing against it. As I recall, the title was mine. It just seemed like the logical title for an album by a band called AC/DC. It also positioned them as being a rock act rather than as an act that was involved in cross–dressing. But the really interesting thing was that the band loved the title and went and wrote a song called 'High Voltage'. Unfortunately (or fortunately) the song wasn't finished until the album was well into production and we couldn't add it to the record. The album had started selling extremely well as a result of the first one or two singles and we had this track in the can with the same title as the album. I decided to take the rather crazy step of releasing 'High Voltage' as a single when it wasn't on an LP of the same name. If you did that these days, they would shoot you!"

The seemingly irrational step paid off in the end, as Gilbey explains. "Anyway, what happened was pure magic. The single became a big hit. The album went on to become an even bigger hit without the song 'High Voltage' on it! And by the time we had sold a load of albums we were ready to release the next full–length, which did have the song on it, but of course had a different name and that second album was an instant hit. Amazing stuff!"

"His first words when he got out of the car were, 'I'm Bon.' Then he looked down and went, 'Ah, I've put on my wife's underwear.' And that was his introduction to the band." Angus Young

Anyone who read AC/DC's lyrics was also in for entertainment. With Bon as the chief wordsmith (he would tell journalists, "I am the poet with this band"), the songs were always simply constructed but memorable. Nowhere was this more evident than on the track Bon had written about his by now ex–wife Irene. The title 'She's Got Balls' pretty much said it all. But the song also illustrated Bon's ability to forgive and forget. Regardless of his problems with Irene, which had eventually led to the divorce, the song was something of a respectful paean. Indeed he respected a lady more when she had balls so to speak. Bon didn't want 'yes' men or women around him; as he said in 'She's Got Balls', he liked 'spunk'.

"She's got balls my lady / Likes to crawl my lady / Hands and knees all around the floor / No one has to tell her what a fella is for," grins Bon on the album version. It didn't do much good with the lady it was written for however.

"Irene had complained to Bon that he'd never written a song about her", Angus said later. "So he wrote 'She's Got Balls' and she left him! When he joined us she told him, 'Bon, it's either them or me.' He said, 'Well they're a good band…' Irene is probably the only person who knew him really well. Even though they parted, he always got along great with her."

The album *High Voltage* and its first single, 'Baby Please Don't Go', entered the Australian charts in March. In June 1975, the band released 'High Voltage', the single. With their lead single in the charts they played a show at Melbourne's Festival Hall. The gig was filmed at the suggestion of the band's management who wanted to tout AC/DC to record companies around the world. They would need some form of licensing abroad to spread the name further.

Another problem was the group's unstable rhythm section. Rob Bailey and Peter Clack were fired and in their place were the returning Larry Van Kriedt on bass and new drummer Phil Rudd. Van Kriedt lasted only a few days however, and Malcolm or George would play the bass parts until a more permanent solution could be found.

"We saw more of Bon than his family did, especially us three. It was always me, Bon & Malcolm. We hung out together. Go to clubs together, get thrown out of clubs together..." Angus Young

Phillip Hugh Norman Witschke Rudzevecuis, aka Phil Rudd was born May 19, 1954 in Melbourne and had made his name with the Colored Balls, a skinhead band formed by guitarist Lobby Lloyd and singer Angry Anderson (who went on to form Rose Tattoo). This band was perfect for bikers and other rabble–rousers during the early seventies. Their genre was known as 'yob rock', exemplified by the British legends Slade.

With Rudd in place the band felt they could truly push on as they now had more comradeship than ever before. In March AC/DC had an unexpected turn of fortune when the b–side to their second single 'Baby Please Don't Go', 'Love Song (Oh Jene)', gained airplay in Australia and became their biggest record to date, hitting number 10 on the national charts the following month. It was a Big Joe Williams cover song but seemed to suit AC/DC down to the ground. It was the first song on the *High Voltage* album and no doubt many listeners had assumed it was a Young brothers composition.

The timing was perfect to hire a permanent bass guitarist. Mark Evans (no relation to the departed singer) was born on March

2nd, 1956 in Melbourne, and he first met AC/DC when they played a date at the Station Hotel in his native city. The accepted story has been that Evans had been barred from the venue the night before, after being thrown out for fighting. Despite this, he and a few mates returned to the bar the following evening to watch AC/DC, but eagle–eyed bouncers spotted them and ejected them once more. Both Bon Scott and roadie Steve McGrath jumped in and persuaded the hotel management to let Evans and his friends stay. The introduction was made and after Evans learned of the bands need for a bass player he expressed his interest.

However, Evans remembers the connection with AC/DC rather differently. "That story is not quite true," he winks. "It was Station Hotel, in a suburb of Melbourne, where I lived. And I did meet the guys when they were playing in that hotel. But the thing about fighting, that was not quite right. That was our manager's idea. But I met the guys in the Station Hotel. The link between me and the band basically was a good friend of mine, who was roadie for them – a guy called Steve McGrath – and he mentioned that they needed a guitar player. As Malcolm was playing the bass at that stage and the band was just four–piece. But when I got in Malcolm said that he wanted to play guitar, so I became bassist overnight. We did one audition, which was on the Sunday afternoon. Then we played next Tuesday night at the same hotel again. We never used to rehearse that much. The audition that I did was the only rehearsal. That was about it, we started gigging around Melbourne."

Evans' opening appearance was on the bands' first television performance. The ABC network asked AC/DC to play for their *Countdown* show and it was inevitable which song they would play. 'Baby Please Don't Go' went down well with the audience, as did Angus's outfit. He decided to be dressed as a super hero; Super Angus had made his first television appearance. Though the backing music was pre–recorded, the vocals were live.

The producers liked the fun–loving image of the band – cheeky but clean – and AC/DC was asked to make another appearance in April on the same show. Yet the viewers could not have expected what they were about to see. As Clinton Walker puts it in his biography of Bon Scott, AC/DC had "stomped into the yawning gulf" of missing gritty rock n' roll, "too late, too ugly to be glam, too clever to be metal, too soon, too dumb to be punk."

As Mark Evans suggested, the fans could see the truth: "There wasn't any bullshit involved like high heels and make up." AC/DC were clearly a breath of fresh air in a stagnant period for serious rock n' roll. Covering tracks like the Big Joe Williams blues standard accentuated the band's influences, but proved how music created long ago could be brought screaming into the modern era with a flick of the volume control and an outpouring of energy.

"My life changed pretty rapidly because the band was doing between six and eight shows in a week," comments Evans. "In Melbourne at that time there were a lot of hotels that staged gigs. It wouldn't be unusual for us to do three gigs in one day. It was pretty hectic. I had left school and I worked for a telephone company. I was there about six months but I was going nowhere. I had to get away from that; fortunately the band came along at the right time. It changed my life pretty dramatically; first I was working for the government next thing I'm playing in a dirty rock n' roll band. It was the time of my life."

"I'm 33. Before AC/DC I'd played with lots of bands in Australia. You're never too old to rock & roll." Bon Scott, shortly before his death.

As Angus later remembered, "On one of the early tours of Britain we had the vice squad on tour with us the whole time. 'Cause Bon, he took to using French language you know? Well, he had colourful language anyway. I remember there was this one time in Australia, playing in these outback places where we'd have to put up money. And if we did anything wrong like me pulling my pants off or Bon swearing or anything, we'd lose the bail money. The mayor and the councilmen would come along to the show and monitor us. They thought it was a great thing. They invented it, not us. It was their way of trying to stamp us out. So I remember Bon getting up there and saying, 'I've been told we can't say "fuck". Okay, we won't say "fuck". I've been told we can't say "shit". Okay, we won't say "shit". They left out "suck", but we won't say that either...' You know? Our bank books didn't grow but our popularity did."

Despite not being the prettiest chap ever to play on a stage, Angus Young had grown to be a focal point for the female members of an audience. They thought he was cute and cheeky enough to be attractive, not to mention energetic. Angus was the star of the band's live performances, but this was equally an achievement that should be ascribed to Bon Scott. Angus stole the limelight, but Bon was sensible (and devoid of ego) enough to allow him the spotlight whenever he desired. Bon was the unselfish lead singer, who did his job and only needed to get his point across; he was able to leave aside claims for personal stardom or front man demands. This was a group of mates; no one cared who got the kudos because they all trusted each other's contributions to the band. Perhaps this is where Dave Evans was never going to be a permanent fixture in the line–up. According to some, even the band itself, he was more of a stereotypical rock star. This would not have worked for AC/DC for very long.

The group's appeal was that they looked pretty much like everyone who was in the crowd, the only real difference was that they were on stage and could play rock n' roll rather well. The audience could identify with its icons, which some would argue is not what people want from escapist type music. AC/DC begged to differ, without worrying too much. The showman aspect of its performance were the antics of Angus, which amounted to little more than duck walking across the stage and playing as if he were 'possessed'. It was a natural reaction to the music, and the audience could sense it.

In the section '12 Ways To Alter Your Consciousness Without Drugs' in his *Book Of Lists*, author Russ Kick writes: "Music – whether it's loud, crunching rock and roll that makes you feel like you've taken speed, or ethereal chanting that lifts you out of your body, music has a myriad of ways of changing your state of being. And that's just from listening to it. Playing it can take you into a zone where nothing exists but you and the music." This would describe Angus's state of being perfectly.

Come April, AC/DC was asked to return to *Countdown* to play 'Baby Please Don't Go' again. Bon didn't tell anyone his intentions, but he arrived in an outfit that would have made Heidi proud. He burst onto the stage in blond pigtails and a schoolgirl uniform, his cheeks streaked with rouge. The band was unaware that Bon was going to be so committed to his performance, but found it hilarious. Unfortunately, neither the producers of the show, nor the sedate television viewers, looked at his frolics so kindly. The incident sparked outrage and the station was inundated with complaints. AC/DC had truly staked their claim as rock troublemakers. They didn't seem put out by the publicity; the notion of 'any publicity is good publicity' seemed appropriate. Though they would not be invited back to *Countdown* for a while, it wouldn't really matter.

Anything associated with the band was fair game for the media. Where so often the newspapers have to create stories to sell numbers, the copy with Australia's finest was plain and truthful, often endorsed by a member of the group . The following appeared in the *Truth* newspaper in Melbourne: 'POP STAR, BRUNETTE AND A BED: THEN HER DAD TURNED UP!'

Dave Dawson spoke to Bon, who told him: "The girl's father had warned me once before not to sleep with her. But she is 17 and capable of making up her own mind. I had returned from Sydney the night before and she was there waiting there for me. We were making love when our roadie Ralph knocked on my bedroom door and said someone wanted to see me urgently. I told him to come back in two hours because I was busy. Eventually I went to the door and was sprung by the girl's father. I was wearing only shorts. He said 'I can see you've got your fighting shorts on.' He took out his false teeth and said, 'come outside'.

"I followed him outside where he had two of his mates, in their 30s. He said 'where's my daughter?' I said, 'She will have gone by now. You are always bashing her up.' Suddenly he started punching me in the head and body. He knocked me into a rose bush and dragged me through it. Then his two mates came over and dragged him away. They could see that because I was just 5' 5" I didn't have a chance. That was the worst beating I have ever had. My manager Mike Browning took me to a dentist who couldn't stop laughing when I explained how my dental plate was smashed and my teeth were knocked out. It wasn't so funny because the dental bill will be at least $500. The girl's father has never given her any love and he certainly showed me none. After he bashed me he said 'if she is not home by night I will send another ten blokes around to bash you.' I'm certainly not going out of my way to see her again."

Though this story will inevitably bring a smile to the face of any reader, it highlights a few aspects of Bon's personality most unlike the rough dirty rocker of legend. Firstly the line where Bon says he was 'making love' to a girl. Thousands of leery, greasy rockers would have used more explicitly physiological terminology. This was not merely a groupie fumble, and the account highlights a tender, loving side to Bon's persona.

Secondly, in the response to the girl's father Bon expressed concern that her Dad was beating her. The fact he confronted the father with the fact was courageous in itself. It was probably the thing, which caused him a heavier beating. And in the midst of all this, most unlike any other rocker you could care to name Bon has no qualms about admitting he was clearly going to lose a fight because he's outnumbered and outsized, nor did he assert his manliness by talking up the fact he had been in a fight and that it didn't matter to him to have received a thumping. On the contrary, Bon stated he would not see her again – it was clearly too much trouble for the both of them with a father like that.

It seems certain people were jealous of Bon and those who had the opportunity, got their revenge. Here was a charismatic guy with no cares in the world, the singer in an emerging rock band, doing as he pleased. Fine upstanding folk would not stand for it: it simply wasn't done to appear on television dressed as a schoolgirl, or to fool around with *their* ladies. AC/DC was by now a collection of superstars in Melbourne, and indeed throughout the country. By the end of June, *High Voltage* had been certified gold in Australia.

In late August, the band would attempt to play a series of free concerts at the Myer store in Melbourne. Somewhat naïvely, they did not realise the furore this would evoke, and in the end their set was truncated when 10,000 fans stormed the store on the first day. The place was virtually ripped to shreds and the plug was pulled after just two songs. Drummer Phil Rudd had to be replaced by Colin Burgess for several gigs after he broke his thumb during a fight at the Matthew Findlers Hotel in Melbourne.

Fortunately, singer and drummer had overcome their injuries when the time came to record the next album. There was a set pattern for songwriting. Malcolm would generally come up with the basic guitar parts and Angus would mimic them before cultivating his own style around the groove. The tunes formed a framework around which Bon could then craft his own lyrical magic. There is little doubt that the songs on the album, called *T.N.T.*, could have been handled by Dave Evans, but what everyone was beginning to realise was that Bon Scott had a special kind of charisma that few could attain. Best of all, his was a natural talent; he didn't have to try, other than perhaps to top up his confidence with the aid of a few drinks. But this was all the more remarkable; like all the best frontmen and most memorable performers Bon would play just as well drunk as he did when sober. The glint in his eye was not the product of alcohol; it was real.

For Bon, joining AC/DC was the pinnacle of his achievement. His earlier days in Australian groups were all about practise. The Valentines and Fraternity were passable bands in musical terms, but somewhat low on character, and this would eventually lead to their downfall. Most of their songs were cover versions. With AC/DC, Bon had free rein to wield his pen in any way he wished. The words would come to him as quickly as riffs would occur to the Young brothers. The song titles were good enough to sell an album alone; when coupled with the energetic buzz of the music and Bon's fiery vocal delivery, *T.N.T.* was destined to become a classic album.

It was released at the end of 1975, and would soon sell more than 100,000 copies. By this stage, AC/DC were by far the biggest rock 'n' roll band in Australia. It was no surprise, given the songs they had at their disposal. The lyrics were often about real life–situations or dreams and aspirations. Though Bon was by now singer in a famous rock n' roll band, he sang about *wanting* to be which was appealed to listeners who might not be in such an exalted position.

'It's A Long Way To The Top (If You Wanna Rock n' Roll)', 'Rock n' Roll Singer', 'Live Wire' and 'Rocker' were rebellious anthems that had little variety in terms of themes but an abundance of brute force. But the most notorious track, and a song that would be included in their live set for years to come, was 'The Jack'. The song was originally called 'The Clap' and its eventual title is another slang term, this time specifically Australian, for a sexually transmitted disease. The song itself refers to the many women who visited the group when they shared a house together.

The title track also had particular resonance for AC/DC, and for Bon Scott in particular. His words were always inextricably linked to his personality and the listener would always assume – usually correctly – that Bon was referring to himself. With 'T.N.T.' this was especially evident. "Women to the left of me / And women to the right / Ain't got no gun / Ain't got no knife / But don't you start no fight," warns Bon, and you believe him.

The term 'likeable rogue' certainly applied to the singer. As others who knew him well would often say, he wasn't a nasty person. At worst, he liked his own way and might well have fought to get it, but it was often done with an unavoidable charm you couldn't fail to admire. Some people have star quality etched into their faces and Bon Scott was one. It has to be remembered that as he was older than the other members there was an extra confidence he brought to the band. He had also served his time on the sidelines observing the others in action, and knew exactly what he could contribute to the party. As he himself had predicted, AC/DC was going to be very big with him singing.

"Cause I'm T.N.T. I'm dynamite, T.N.T. and I'll win the fight, T.N.T. I'm a power load, T.N.T. watch me explode."

The charm was evident in the remake of the band's earlier hit, 'Can I Sit Next To You Girl?' with Bon leering like a dirty old man, the glint in his eye almost audible. The album also included a Chuck Berry cover, 'School Days', which was perfectly suited to the their bluesy/rock style.

It was thanks to performances like these that the band began to attract record company attention beyond Australia. After meeting

the group through Carol Browning (daughter of the AC/DC manager at the time Michael Browning), it was Phil Carson who offered them a worldwide deal with Atlantic Records in London. They
signed the papers, which proved to be a wise career move.

Once the people behind the *Countdown* TV programme realised AC/DC might provoke outrage but would doubtless enhance
viewing figures, they renewed their support for the boys and booked
them several times. On one occasion the band performed 'It's A
Long Way To The Top (If You Wanna Rock n' Roll)' on a flatbed
truck driving through the streets of Melbourne. By the end of 1975
AC/DC was truly established as the biggest and most entertaining
act in the whole of Australia. At this time *High Voltage* was certified
triple gold.

After signing their worldwide deal with Atlantic, AC/DC made
another group decision, which was to prove exceedingly shrewd. At
the suggestion of Michael Browning the band knew in order to further its career a move abroad would be necessary. The choice was
either England or America. Given that the members were mostly
of British origin, the choice seemed logical. Though they had been
children when they'd initially relocated, Angus, Malcolm and Bon
were more comfortable with the press in Britain, and felt this was
the place to solidify AC/DC's standing in the music world. They
came to Britain to settle on April 1, 1976.

PEERING INTO THE ATLANTIC

The Atlantic Recording Corporation is one of the most cel-ebrated labels in rock 'n' roll history. Ahmet Ertegun, the son of a Turkish diplomat, formed the company in Septem-ber 1947 in New York City. The name Atlantic wasn't the first choice for the company. Every name Ertegun initially wanted to use had already been taken. Hearing of another record label called Pacific Jazz he decided to name his busi-ness Atlantic.

The very first company office (which doubled as a living room) was in the condemned Jefferson Hotel near Broad-way. To help pay the fees Ertegun rented a bed to his cousin, a poet named Sadi Koylan. The first tracks recorded for At-lantic were by The Harlemaires on November 21, 1947, with 'The Rose of the Rio Grande'. By the end of December sixty five songs had been recorded for the label.

In April 1949 Atlantic had its first major hit with Stick McGhee's 'Drinkin' Wine Spo–Dee–O–Dee'. By 1955 Atlan-tic was in a strong enough position to bid for the contract of Elvis Presley. Ertegun offered Colonel Tom Parker $25,000 but eventually Presley went to RCA. The label continued its success during the sixties and seventies with both popular rock and soul acts. Everybody from Aretha Franklin to Ray Charles, Led Zeppelin and The Rolling Stones, signed to the established company. In later years, it would be the home of artists as diverse as Metallica, Björk and Missy Elliott.

To this day Ertegun serves as chairman of Atlantic Records. At the tenth annual Rock and Roll Hall of Fame Induction Dinner in 1995, it was announced that the museum's main exhibition hall would be named after him. He had already been personally inducted into the Rock and Roll Hall of Fame in 1987.

Chapter 5 – Caught With Your Pants Down

"I have been a reforming influence on Bon. You should have seen the man when I first met him. He couldn't even speak English. It was all 'fuck, cunt, piss, shit.' I introduced him to a new side of life. Sent him home with a dictionary..." Angus Young

"He taught me to say 'Please fuck'. And 'Thank you' after." Bon Scott

Before arriving in England AC/DC had recorded their third album in January 1976 in Australia. This LP, titled *Dirty Deeds Done Dirt Cheap* would be released in Australia in September of the same year. Angus came up with the line, 'Dirty Deeds Done Dirt Cheap' from the cartoon 'Beany and Cecil'. This animated show featured a character called Dishonest John who carried a card that said, 'Dirty Deeds Done Dirt Cheap. Holidays, Sundays and Special Rates.'

The first single taken from the album was entitled 'Jailbreak'. On the b–side was an oddity, a traditional Scottish folk song rearranged by the Young brothers called 'Fling Thing'. It was an incredibly unusual song for the group, something they were never to repeat. Somehow they managed to turn the established campfire tune into an AC/DC styled rock n' roll instrumental. Clearly they were enjoying playing with the expectations of their fans.

AC/DC were something of an anomaly in the music scene of 1976. Punk rock was bubbling into the public's consciousness and the band fell between several genres, none of which were punk. Nevertheless the attitude equalled anything the Sex Pistols could come up with. AC/DC did not have the sense of calculated outrage that kept Johnny Rotten and friends in the headlines, but their live shows communicated a sense of passion that was, in its way, just as startling as the contemptuous cackle of the punks. Who was this bunch of funny looking little Aussie men with a tiny schoolboy playing every note like his life depended on it?

"We have no sympathy for punk bands." Angus Young

"What's a punk band? Hey, who's got beer?" Bon Scott

Sweaty clubs the length and breadth of London were to host the advance guards of the punk rock revolution. The venues were due to become sweatier than ever, given Britain was about to experience its hottest summer since records began. In parts of the West Country the temperature exceeded 32°C for seven successive days, a statistic without parallel anywhere in the British Isles in modern times. Many long–standing records were broken. At Mayflower Park, Southampton, a reading of 35.6°C still ranks as the UK's highest June temperature. To add to the onslaught, the country was about to be hit with a ladybird plague. None of this seemed to disturb the equilibrium of AC/DC however– for one thing, they were used to the heat. Also, playing live with the ferocity and intensity they displayed would always raise the temperatures above bearable levels anyway.

The band's first live performance in the UK was in April at the Red Cow pub in Hammersmith, West London. For their first set of the night there were just 10 people in attendance, but by the time they took to the stage for the second performance, word had spread like wildfire, and the place was packed. AC/DC were to play the venue, as well as The Nashville pub, on a regular basis thereafter. Just as the band had arrived in London, Bon was hit with a pint mug (supposedly by someone with a grudge) as he walked into a pub where he had worked during Fraternity's stay in London. This explains why Bon was wearing shades in photo sessions shortly afterwards.

These shows were followed by other dates at small clubs across Britain. A tour with Back Street Crawler, a band formed by former Free guitarist Paul Kossoff, was to be just the thing the group needed to garner a hard gigging and even harder playing reputation. The tour was originally scheduled to take place in April but, was postponed because of Kossoff's death the month before. In the middle of May, AC/DC took a break, only to learn they had been booked in for a 20–venue tour of the UK. This was sponsored by *Sounds* magazine, and went under the self–explanatory heading 'Lock Up Your Daughters'. When the band played their homecoming gig of sorts, at Glasgow City Hall, the audience destroyed seats during the performance. In keeping with AC/DC's sudden notoriety, the tour sponsors placed Angus on the front cover of the next issue.

"We never care about labels such as punk, psychedelic or whatever else." Bon Scott

Though the crowds would not be the biggest for some shows – partly because the band only had 50 minutes in which to play, wedged between a DJ and videos of other artists – the tour was a success. AC/DC was promoting the U.K. version of *High Voltage*, which was radically different, and rather better value for money, than the Australian original. Oddly, the track listing was closer to the band's second long–player: the whole of side one was actually the same as the *T.N.T.* album, with Side Two including 'T.N.T.', 'Can I Sit Next To You Girl' and 'High Voltage' from the same source. Only 'Little Lover' and 'She's Got Balls' came from the Australian *High Voltage* album.

This UK version of *High Voltage* would become the definitive article: combining the highpoints of the first two albums made creative and commercial sense, although it does make the band's discography a little untidy and confusing. AC/DC now had a solid list of songs comprising their global calling card, and forming the basis for their incendiary live set.

The Marquee Club was a tight, cramped venue that had developed a reputation as *the* place for rock bands to prove their worth. By July of '76, AC/DC had made such a name for themselves they were given a weekly Monday residency at this London landmark. They were in good company, as the Soho–based club had been a key launching pad for the careers of The Rolling Stones, The Who, and The Small Faces. Other bands that played the club in their infancy were The Yardbirds, The Sex Pistols, David Bowie, and later, R.E.M. and U2. Dave Stewart of the Eurythmics remarked in 2002, "You'd walk in and stop in your tracks, because your feet were stuck to the floor with beer and chewing gum". The ambience, in this sense, was similar to the legendary New York venue CBGB's – intimate and grubby.

The capacity of the venue was only 700 but AC/DC would regularly pack the punters in and more than a thousand would often end up paying to see the new Australian sensations. Unsurprisingly, the temperatures would raise beyond an acceptable level, but this only added to the atmosphere. In any case, Angus would turn himself into a Niagara of sweat whether the temperature was 5 degrees or 150, but there is no doubt that having to cope with the unexpected arrival of more fans than the club could hold during a sweltering summer season only helped the group.

The band's shows at the Marquee sparked interest from Rainbow guitarist Ritchie Blackmore who asked AC/DC to come on tour through Europe with him for 19 dates. After the band accepted, Blackmore allegedly came down to the Marquee on a night AC/DC was playing and asked to jam with them. He was rather confused when the guys agreed, but left him on stage alone tuning up while they sneaked out through a back door.

"Style, I didn't think we had any! I just plug in and hit the thing really hard. That's my style... or lack of one!" Angus Young

Prior to playing with Rainbow on tour AC/DC went to Germany where they played three headline shows. The locals were particularly taken with the band. But playing to vociferous audiences in Deutschland was small fare compared to the huge arena AC/DC was about to grace. They were invited to play the Reading Festival in England on August 29, with the crowd that day clocking in at around 50,000. Other names on the bill included jazz–rock combo Brand X, featuring Phil Collins; folk–rockers Sutherland Brothers & Quiver; Southern rock titans Black Oak Arkansas; and primeval axe hero Ted Nugent, probably the closest in terms of sound and attitude to Angus and company. AC/DC's set was described in some quarters as being disappointing, but this may simply have been down to the size of the event. It was the Aussies' biggest show to date, and they were more at home with sweaty, intimate club dates than with gigs in fields.

On tour with Rainbow, AC/DC was playing to a convention-ally 'metal' audience and found it difficult to fit in with standard boogie blues rock or heavy metal. AC/DC seemed to fall between two stools. Again, they had trouble coping with the larger venues. Distance from the audience was a problem for a band that relied so much on interaction with the fans, but if attention wavered, a quip from Bon or a quick moon from Angus was usually enough to pull it back. The show was the most important thing and they made sure the audience did not forget that.

In December 1976, *Dirty Deeds Done Dirt Cheap* was re-leased in the UK. On the British version, 'Rocker' (from the *T.N.T.* album) and the previously unreleased 'Love At First Feel' (which the band would release as a single in Australia in January 1977) replaced 'Jailbreak' and 'R.I.P. (Rock in Peace)'.

"No matter how long you play rock n' roll, songs might change just as long as the balls are there, the rock balls. And that's what's important to us." Bon Scott

Dirty Deeds Done Dirt Cheap is packed with rock goodies. The line "Just ring 36 24 36 0" in the title track led to endless grief for the blameless White family whose number that was, as AC/DC fans delighted in making prank calls. Legal action was threatened, but in the end the number in question was quietly put out of service.

Perhaps the most surprising song on the record is the slow blues number 'Ride On'. In among the frenetic attack of the all–out crunchers like 'Squealer' and 'Rocker', here we could hear Bon's serene and sensitive side sneaking through. He sang of isolation ("But I'm lonely, Lord I'm lonely, What am I gonna do?"), his prob-lems with women ("I ain't too old to cry when a woman gets me down"), and even a need for redemption ("One of these days I'm gonna change my evil ways"), but the need to keep on regardless. The song is fairly straightforward with a pulsing bass line and the odd intricate guitar lick thrown in, not to mention a blues–based solo, which never once outstays its welcome, but rates as a very spe-cial AC/DC recording. You can hear the subtleties in Bon's voice, so often invisible in other more pounding work. It was one area AC/DC would never particularly elaborate on; although in the hands of lesser bands, this style would mutate into the dreaded 'power ballad' so beloved of FM radio stations in the mid–1980's.

Bon would often introduce 'Problem Child' on stage by saying it was all about Angus, although it could well have applied to any of the other band members. With lines like "What I need I like what I don't I fight" and "with a flick of my knife I can change your life" the song was more violent than the band's usual material, although Angus's description of his so–called wayward past was less colourful. "I wasn't really a bad sort of kid," he mused. "I mean, I listened. If I wanted to learn something, my old man used to say, 'Angus do yourself a favour. There's a library down the road, go in there.' When I'd been truant that was the first place I'd head to. It was great. There'd be racks of the magazine *Down Beat* from America, which had articles on Muddy Waters. And I liked reading about that. So I much preferred going there because they didn't sell it at the newsstands. It wasn't part of the curriculum of Australia. In my music class in school I was given the triangle, a little piece of metal, and then they took that off of me because they said, 'you have no rhythm!'"

The irony was not lost on Angus, who by now was developing a fearsome reputation as a guitarist. Not only did he keep his rhythms locked tight, his solos were off the scale. Though he would follow the song itself as closely as possible, there was still a large degree of improvisation evident, as would become obvious on stage. No solo was ever replicated exactly twice, although it would always retain the energy and basics of the original. Angus would claim he didn't really work out his solos. "I never had an ear for sitting and picking out notes," he explained. "I just play it. If you said to me, 'Play someone else's song,' and I did it, you'd go, 'What's he playing?' I can't sit down and pick a note off a record. Mal's got a good ear for hearing things, but me, I never did. I always think it's more the feeling. If you ever got an album where they include a couple of different takes, like an old blues album, and they've got alternative takes, you'll hear it. The one they settle for in the end usually has a different feeling and sounds totally different. No, I never work them out before, unless there's an important part, like if its part of the song. It just has to flow. Solos have got to have continuity."

"When I'm on stage the savage in me is released. It's like going back to being a cave man. It takes me six hours to come down after a show." Angus Young

As guitar bands were developing heavier and faster sounds, Angus in particular began to feel that things were getting a bit over the top. He said: "I just want to add to the song. You don't want to suddenly give a raging solo in a song where really it should be sitting in there. Sometimes it can go a bit over the top. Guys will try and go over the top and get every lick they can get, cover ever bit of space. We just like to go with what the track requires."

As for composition, he claimed that the process of creating a solo was spontaneous. "I mean, there are some things I've played and gone 'how did I do that?' You can sit there and try to figure it out for years and there is nothing to match it. In the early days, if you were playing an A chord, you might play a solo in A; but then again put in progressions or notes in there, that don't sound right. It sounds like you are playing in the wrong key or something, and sometimes it works."

For AC/DC, playing as a unit was the important thing. The five musicians performing together was the 'X' factor that made the band great. The idea wasn't to have any one player standing out from the others. Angus was often the visual focus, because of his costume and his hyperactive scurrying around the stage. But the younger Young never once forgot that he was merely a cog in the machine. For one thing, Angus was convinced that Malcolm was the better guitar player. As Angus put it: "That's the easiest part, the solos. There is no great thing in being a solo artist. The hardest thing is to play with a lot of people together, and to do it right. I mean, when all four guys hit the one note at once, very few people can do that."

This underlined the AC/DC philosophy exactly. Clicking in a group as one giant music–making machine was the most important factor in creating noteworthy music. This solidarity still did not stop

Angus sometimes going out on a limb, especially in a live setting, but he always tried to stay close to the source material, and not improvise his way into a completely different tune. "It's just how you hear it in your mind. You try to stick to it because a lot of people get condemned for not doing it. If you can do it, it's always good to throw something in, but still keep that feeling in there. You don't want the kids to come in and say, 'Aw, that guy is trying to play Beethoven on top of that sound.'"

In October of 1976 AC/DC, went out on a headlining tour of the UK. The vice squad followed them for their entire journey and Angus was threatened with arrest in Glasgow and Liverpool if he dropped his pants on stage. Needless to say, that particular part of the show was censored. It paid off because, not only were AC/DC allowed to travel without further hassle from the law, their live sets were riotous enough musically to please the fans and by November they made their first headline appearance at the famous Hammersmith Odeon in London.

In December, the band flew back to Australia. After eight months away, AC/DC were welcomed by their fans as heroes, but the Australian media were reluctant to offer them credit for their success abroad. When the boys scheduled a tour of their homeland, titled 'A Giant Dose Of Rock & Roll!' local authorities cancelled several dates due to the increasingly obscene image of the group, as portrayed by the Australian newspapers and television. According to the government at the time, AC/DC were a bad influence on the youth of the day and their popularity was something to be feared.

After the tour, the group took a short break for Christmas. They remained in Australia during the first two months of 1977 to record their fourth album at Albert Studios. *Dirty Deeds Done Dirt Cheap* was to be rejected by the US record company. They felt it was too raw and wouldn't sell. It took the label four years to realise they were wrong. The album would eventually be released in the United States on March 23, 1981.

TO PEEL OR NOT TO PEEL

In June 1976 AC/DC recorded a 4–track session for
BBC Radio 1's John Peel Show at Maida Vale Studios in
London. Throughout the seventies, and indeed right up
until his untimely death in 2004, Peel worked ceaselessly
to promote bands through the vehicle of the UK's first
national pop music station. He helped to break several
hundred artists into the mainstream, among them David
Bowie, Joy Division and The Ramones. Equally, Peel gave
exposure to groups who had little chance of real success.
Regardless of an artist's commercial potential, Peel would
simply work with music that he liked himself.

Nevertheless, he maintained an uncanny knack of spotting
talent early on. As with so many other artists, he came
across AC/DC at a vital starting point in their history and
yet he could see the promise in the young rockers. Once
'DC broke both Britain and the United States they didn't
need Peel's support, but his vision early in their career
should not be underestimated.

Given the quality of many of the bands that Peel invited
to play on his show, AC/DC were in esteemed company
and their appearance early on in the band's history gave
an added intrigue to their recordings for the only DJ ever
to gain such a high level of respect from both the industry
and from music fans of all persuasions. Unlike many of
the classic sessions recorded for the Peel show throughout
the years, unfortunately the AC / DC set has never been
released commercially.

Chapter 6 – And the Lord Said...

"We used to think of ourselves as an Australian band, but we're be-ginning to doubt that now; the fuckers won't even let us play here!"
Angus Young (1977)

AC/DC's next album was *Let There Be Rock*. The lyrics to the title track were a clever pastiche of the opening verses of the Biblical Book of Genesis. Bon sang:

'Let there be light', and there was light.
'Let there be sound', and there was sound.
'Let there be drums', and there was drums.
'Let there be guitar', and there was guitar.
'Let there be rock.'

'Let There Be Rock,' written by Young, Young and Scott, Published by E.B. Marks Music Corp

The lyrics more than summed up the AC/DC approach, and the music itself was punishing, three–chord rock at its finest. The album featured tracks that were to be the mainstay of the band's live set for years to come and marked a significant step forward in terms of production and maturity for AC/DC. The music now took on a life of its own. This was not merely kids having fun with updating the Chuck Berry blueprint, it was an act that was developing a new benchmark for modern rock n' roll. *Let There Be Rock* contained no filler material; this was balls–out blues and the only complaint was that it was over all too quickly.

The final track on the album would be AC/DC's calling card for a long time to come.

'Whole Lotta Rosie' was the finest track they had yet pro-duced. Featuring a blistering riff from Angus it was one of their heaviest, yet catchiest, songs to date, and included lyrics only Bon could have written.

'Wanna tell you a story
'Bout a woman I know,
When it comes to lovin'
Oh she steals the show,
She ain't exactly pretty
Ain't exactly small,
Forty–two, thirty–nine, fifty–six
You could say she's got it all'.

'Whole Lotta Rosie' Written by Young, Young and Scott
Published by E.B. Marks Music Corp

"Bon wrote the song about a huge Tasmanian woman he had shared a 'wild time' with in Melbourne," Angus later said. "Interestingly, the band ran into her again in Hobart, Tasmania, but she had lost a lot of weight and Bon was disappointed that she was no longer the '42–39–56' that he remembered. She did know the song was about her, and took it as a compliment." The memory of Rosie was given added status when the band played live. A huge inflatable woman would lie as the backdrop when they performed the song.

AC/DC played a number of gigs throughout Sydney, Melbourne and Adelaide, before returning to the UK in February 1977. Here they embarked on a 26–date tour around the country from February 18 to March 1. The jaunt was immediately followed by a second European tour supporting Black Sabbath. Despite the dissimilar styles of the two bands, AC/DC went down very well with the Sabbath fans and such was the level of their own standing in the rock world now that many fans came specifically to see them. Many believed that the support act blew the headliners off the stage most nights.

Whether this was the catalyst is uncertain but it wasn't long before AC/DC were kicked off the tour. There was allegedly a confrontation between Sabbath bassist Geezer Butler and Malcolm Young but this has never been really clarified. The incident was said to have occurred whilst the two bands were in Sweden as part of the European venture, with Butler apparently pulling a flick–knife on Malcolm, who responded by punching the Brummie in the face. Whatever the reality, the members of AC/DC returned to London.

"There's been an audience waiting for an honest rock n' roll band to come along and put it on 'em. There are a lot of people coming out of the woodwork to see our kind of rock. And they're not the same people who would go to see James Taylor or a punk band." Bon Scott

However there was also tension within the band itself, which came to a head with the sacking of bass player Mark Evans after personality clashes with Angus. His last gig was in Offenbach, Germany, although some sources identify the location as Helsinki, Finland. Evans: "No, we were on our way to Helsinki. And we were planning to fly to America afterwards. There was a problem with the record company in America at that stage; they had chosen not to release *Dirty Deeds Done Dirt Cheap*. The Americans knocked us back as we were really eager going over to promote the album. So, the US tour at that stage was cancelled. We were in Germany with Black Sabbath. We went back in London and we had a month off before Helsinki. That's when the whole scenario happened when I split from the band. I think the main reservation that the Americans had was something to do with Bon. I didn't get the full picture because the band was Malcolm's and not much info came to me. I think that the Americans wanted to change the singer, which seems unbelievable now."

AC/DC found a suitable replacement for Evans very quickly. This turned out to be for the best as the man they found was to prove a mainstay of their future line–up. It was manager Mike Browning who had heard about Cliff Williams from a mutual acquaintance, and immediately made contact. Williams strolled through his audition and the job was his.

The ex–Home and Bandit member would later say: "I got a call from a friend who told me that AC/DC was looking for a bassist and my name was on the list. They weren't satisfied about their current one and the boys in the group thought they would have more luck to find the man they wanted in England than in Australia. I had an audition in Victoria, in a tiny repetition room. The first tracks I played with them were 'Live Wire', 'Problem Child' and, if I remember right, some old family blues. The band's manager told me after a short time I had the job. The idea was that I left London to go to Australia, because we were meant to prepare the recording of the next album, but the Australian immigration service wasn't really good with me. In fact, the guy who had my folder told me: 'I don't know why an Englishman has the job. An Australian would have done it fine.' I answered: 'You fool, you could make me lose my job!' So, I had many problems, but finally I've been able to go to Australia where we have recorded the album."

For Angus, having small arguments were part and parcel of being in a band, but it was growing increasingly important that AC/DC could attain some level of stability. By this time Phil Rudd was becoming a solid ingredient in the group and they just hoped Cliff Williams would prove as permanent.

"It was clear to me it was Malcolm's band," said Richard Griffiths, the band's first booking agent in the UK, and now CEO for Epic Records. "Bon was a great guy. But even then, I sensed, off Michael Browning that he wasn't sure that Bon was the singer to take the band all the way. He was sort of separate from the rest. Phil, he was off on his own, he was actually pretty obnoxious. Angus and Malcolm were thick, obviously. And then Mark, you knew Mark wasn't going to last, he was just too much of a nice guy."

"We squabble, but we come together in the music thing," said Angus of his relationship with his brothers. "We may have different interpretations of what we do, but we both know at the end of the day that it's the result that counts. We'll sit and battle away, but we probably get along better playing than we would if we were simply living together. I wouldn't do that. He would kill me. Mal has always pushed me out there in the front. He has always been supportive of what I do and my playing. He would be the first to turn around and say, 'Ah, Angus can play. He can do that.'"

In turn, Angus was always complimentary of his brothers' playing ability. It seemed to have been purely by default that Angus became the face of the band because according to him, Malcolm is the better player and would easily prove it whenever necessary. "He played solos on four tracks from our first album, when the two of us had traded off", stated the younger sibling. "Mal is a good soloist. He can probably do what I do quite well. He plays lead like he would play rhythm, and that doesn't sound like someone else. When we used to trade licks, it was always the same way. Before AC/DC he would try doing a lot of different solos. He is a very good performer, the heart of the band. I sit and watch him play rhythm, and I go, 'Ah, I'll play that now.' I'll try to copy what he is doing."

It was clear when watching AC/DC Malcolm was indeed the heart of the band. He always kept it as basic as the song demanded; with very little showmanship– yet the performance would always be exemplary. That he managed this so easily was testament to his talent.

"He makes it look so simple," said Angus. "There are people out there who do that, and you look at them and what they make, that is their art. They make the hard look simple. It is like when you saw Hendrix. He would pick up a guitar, and it's like he's brushing his teeth with it. But while he's doing that he's making music. That is an art form. Guys like me have got to put on school suits and dive off buildings to achieve that sort of high ranking!"

The camaraderie the two could achieve was, Angus believed, partly due to being brothers. "It used to be a game, sort of. It becomes an instinct with you. And my other brother George was so quick; you learned a lot when you were with him. Especially when you were 14 or something. He would pick up a bass and hand you the guitar. And you'd think you were incompetent, but before you knew it you were playing with him. He would go, 'G...A...' and you were away. Say you play a song five nights in one key, but the sixth night the singers voice ain't makin' it, you might have to go down a tone or so. George was really used to that, and he got me used to it too."

George was clearly a teacher who knew exactly what was required, and he had instilled these virtues in the guitar happy youngsters who looked up to him. As Angus continued, "He was into some crazy things too, you know. Like he'd tell me the D string annoyed him. The G too. 'Too sweet for Rock N Roll' he'd say. So off went the G string. The last time I saw him with The Easybeats, he had four strings on that guitar. He was never a fan of light strings either, especially when those slinky strings came out. He'd say, 'You can't tune 'em.'"

In July 1977 Cliff Williams made his live debut with AC/DC, and the band organised two secret gigs at the Bondi Lifesavers event in Sydney. They billed as 'The Seedies' the first night and 'Dirty Deeds' the following evening. After this they flew to Texas for three shows supporting the rock act Moxy. They then played shows in Florida with AOR titans REO Speedwagon. The first night the bands played to 8,000 people at the Coliseum in Jacksonville in a co–headlining show. They also performed in front of 13,000 people at the outdoor Hollywood Sportatorium. Afterwards AC/DC played several dates in the Mid–West, alternating headline shows and opening slots for Michael Stanley, Head East, Foreigner, Mink DeVille and albino blues legend Johnny Winter.

"It was pretty strange", said Angus of the first time the group experienced playing in America. "I hadn't even heard of a lot of the music here at the time. I thought it would be more rock. But when we got here it was a disco type thing. When we first came here we toured around in a station wagon. We got put on with Kiss. This was when they had all the make up and everything, the whole hype. They had everything behind them, the media, the huge show and stuff. And here we were, five migrants, little microscope people. It was tough to get into the show with that station wagon. Many a time they wouldn't let us in the venue 'cause they didn't see a limo. 'Wheeah's duh limo? If yaw the rock band, wheeah's yer limo?'"

AC/DC were so 'normal', they looked very much unlike the archetypal rock stars who American security had grown accustomed to. Here was a group who wore their hearts on their sleeves and den- im on their person, completely oblivious to how they a high–profile rock act was supposed to look and behave.

"What was real strange was that although the media was pushing this really soft music", Angus added, "you'd get amazing numbers of people turning out to hear the harder stuff. We were playing big stadiums and getting a great reaction. We would be on the bill with a whole heap of acts, like in Oakland, playing a Bill Graham 'Day On The Green' event. We were on at 10:30 in the morning; the first act. But at 10:30 in the morning there were about 65,000 people. And they knew what we were about when we came on. We were only on for 35 minutes. But in 35 minutes you had to do a lot. It was fun; it was exciting. I would do it again."

What AC/DC would also often do was blow other bands off stage. Angus later confessed: "Sometimes we could be real mercenary. Like if another band was givin' us a bit of stick; the headlining band or something, we'd get on and just sort of say, 'Okay, we'll turn up to 11 here, and let's go.' Blow 'em away; we were good at that too."

As the group's fame spread, some of the notorious perks of rock 'n' roll stardom came their way. AC/DC had their times with the women, groupies in particular. Initially it wasn't the case, however. "In those days, girls were interested in... well, not us," Angus would say. "You met more of that when you started in clubs and pubs. Because, in that time, you got rich people coming to slum it, and other people coming to see what the fuss is about. So those were your times when you could meet some more of those weird and wonderful women. The crazy people. But during those first tours in the states... no. No more than we would be now. Same thing. And we were never that sort of band, anyway. I've never saw a girl out there that would faint over me. Maybe she would look and go, 'Mmmmm, I've never seen someone as ugly as this!' Maybe I'd get some of that. But not a – what would you call it? A fan sort of thing." As he would admit that was actually to the band's benefit. "In a way that's always worked for us. You don't see an audience of young girls screaming for us. So other people say, 'Now that's a real band. That I like. It's real'. Because we aren't the prettiest things in the world. With AC/DC, it's not like we're here to steal your wife and your girlfriend or your daughter. We may borrow them, but..."

The most direct connotation with anything sexual in the band's music was the kind of residual memory their seedy blues could conjure up. Angus: "I guess there is something a bit sexy in the blues element of what we do. That is probably more what's associated with the old strip club routine. I think that's somewhere in the back of people's heads when they hear that sort of music: the strip club image; you know? The smoke filled room and the girl on stage. Well, I would like to believe that."

For AC/DC's first concerts in New York they made a guest appearance with The Dictators at The Palladium and opened for The Marbles at CBGB's. On the evening they were playing with The Dictators the group were even pencilled in for a stint at the CBGB's venue on the same night, which was unprecedented.

The Dictators were very much an institution in New York, having enjoyed success in the 70s with their Bloodbrothers and Dictators Go Girl Crazy! albums as well as their incendiary live shows. However AC/DC would leave a lasting impression on the audience. It was the first time Angus could use his new cordless guitar, introduced to stop him from becoming tangled up in a mess of leads and wires when pacing around the stage. Bon said of the new contraption: "It was amazing to see. Angus had this Cheshire cat grin all over his face and evil thoughts seemed to be going through his brain as to what havoc he could wreak with this evil little invention."

Though fans were incredibly enthusiastic over an act that was virtually still new to them, the Atlantic record company were nevertheless hard to persuade regarding AC/DC's global appeal. Let There Be Rock had received a lukewarm reaction from the powers that be and they were loath to give this dirty little Australian outfit more time than they deserved. However, even Atlantic recognised AC/DC's power as a live act and it was this realisation that prompted the label to house the band in the Atlantic studios for a recorded performance.

The boys made their way to Broadway on December 7th 1977 and performed a live set in front of about 50 people, as many as could be crammed into the studio. The show would later form the basis of AC/DC's first official live recording (If You Want Blood You've Got It). It was a small gig, reminiscent of their earliest live shows in tiny clubs throughout Australia and England. The band were clearly in jovial spirits, Angus in particular, running his mouth off via his guitar, playing extended solos and generally asserting himself as star of the show.

Bon speaks to the audience watching in the sweatbox: "You all come from New York City, is that not true? Then this one's for you, 'Hell Ain't A Bad Place To Be'." He was speaking with tongue firmly in cheek but it was also a subliminal snigger at the American way of life, far at odds with the laidback Aussies (and one Brit) who had invaded its shores some time ago but were still yet to reap the same rewards they had at home. Still, it beat a regular job, as Bon put it himself. In an interview with Sounds he revealed, "It can get to be a drag being in a different hotel room every night and not knowing where you put your toothbrush or a clean pair of drawers. But what's the alternative? It's even more boring being stuck in front of a conveyor belt at some factory every day of your life for the next 60 years, like a lot of the kids who come to see us, which is where we'd all be now if it wasn't for this life. So I'd be stupid to knock it, it's great. And how can you get bored with so many different beautiful women around?"

Bon was exaggerating a little by his own admission in other interviews. Otherwise why weren't the band writing about gorgeous ladies in their lyrics instead of the less than attractive beauties they actually depicted? Apart from 'Whole Lotta Rosie', Let There Be Rock featured a track titled 'Go Down', which was all about a groupie AC/DC had become rather familiar with. Her name was Ruby Lips and she was commemorated in the lyrics:

'Ruby, Ruby, where you been so long?
Don't stop drinking whiskey baby since you been gone.
Ain't no one I know do it as good as you,
Licking on that licking stick the way you do.'

Though Let There Be Rock would become a bigger success much later, it was still good enough at the time for the people of Britain. In November, the album reached No. 17 in the British charts. It seemed that AC/DC had made the right decision in plying its trade in their familiar stomping ground; the Brits loved the band and AC/DC loved them back.

ALBERT RECORDS

Jacques Albert founded the music publishing empire J Albert & Son, now the oldest independent publishing house in Australia. He migrated to Australia from Switzerland in 1884 and set up as a music publisher. When Albert senior retired his son Alexis carried on the business and it would be one of his three sons that would help shape the fortunes of The Easybeats and AC/DC. Ted Albert, the middle son of Sir Alexis, helped form the offshoot record company Albert Productions. Ted set about signing the musical talent of Australia in the early sixties. It was through a friend called Mike Vaughan that Ted first met an up and coming band by the name of The Easybeats. First impressions of the outfit stirred Ted and he promptly snapped the band up. When that group lost its appeal, Ted Albert brought Harry Vanda and George Young back to Australia in 1973. The two wrote a song called 'Pasadena' and in 1972 John Paul Young scored a hit with the tune. Thanks to the success of the song the two then ran their own recording studio for Albert records. Unfortunately, Ted Albert passed away in 1990 following a fatal heart attack.

Chapter 7 – Power To The Max

"This guy from a film crew got hold of me and Bon and asked what kind of show it was gonna be. Bon said, 'you remember when the Christians went to the lions? Well we're the Christians!' Then he asked me and I said, 'if they want blood, they're gonna get it!'"
Angus Young

In early 1978, while recording their fifth album proper, AC/DC also taped some of their concerts. Though they had first intended to fly to Australia for a short tour, the band's English road crew, as well as Cliff Williams, were refused a work visa by the local authorities. So the band stuck to the territory in which they were increasingly comfortable. They travelled to Glasgow to play the renowned Apollo venue, and recorded the show, which was to become legendary. The album would be called *If You Want Blood You've Got It* and the cover featured a guitar piercing a bloodied Angus. Subtlety was not exactly AC/DC's style, but even by their standards this was a particularly nasty record sleeve.

The live album was meant to cramp the style of bootleggers who had been increasingly active, recording virtually every AC/DC show, and then selling the tapes and vinyl to rabid fans anxious to hear each note of every gig they had played. While it did not manage to slow trade down in any way, the album was at least a serious piece of work, showcasing AC/DC's strengths as a live act. Before the LP was released the group played throughout the United States with many rock greats. Among their touring partners would be Alice Cooper, Molly Hatchet, Ronnie Montrose, Aerosmith, Foreigner, Van Halen, Pat Travers, Alvin Lee, Rainbow, Savoy Brown, Ted Nugent and Cheap Trick.

"I'd like to do a whole string of concerts headlining as big as this one is today. The more people they can give us upfront the harder we play." Bon Scott, Newsbeat 1978

If You Want Blood You've Got It became a very good promotional tool for the band's latest studio album, *Powerage*. The record, again produced by Vanda and Young, was arguably AC/DC's most accomplished to date, and followed up the promise implied by *Let There Be Rock*.

While it would only peak at #133 on the US Billboard charts, by the end of their US tour, *Powerage* had sold a quarter of a million copies in America. This was partly due to playing such prestigious shows as the Day On The Green outdoor festival in San Francisco during August. The band performed over a hundred dates throughout the States during this period. They also made an appearance on ABC's *Midnight Special* (hosted by Aerosmith and Ted Nugent), where they played 'Sin City', taken from *Powerage*.

"I like the album" said Angus of *Powerage*. "I think because it has got a good mix for me. You've got rock tunes, but you've got a few things in there that are different. I always thought that album set us apart from a lot of other bands. I know a lot of people judge success on numbers. For us, that was always a great record."

Though it was not as well received initially as it would finally become, Angus's views on the album would ring true for most fans eventually. It is, perhaps more than any other, the purists' favourite AC/DC record. The front cover finally brought the electrical connotation in the group's name to the fore. The sleeve pictured Angus plugged into the mains supply, with wires sprouting from his jacket sleeves in place of limbs. "I suppose I look a bit like a Christmas tree," joked Angus. "Plenty of balls, but without the fairy on top!"

The lettering of the title and the band logo were both deliberately cheap and broken. Here was no–nonsense rock n' roll, epitomised equally by the photo on the back sleeve. Angus takes centre stage, tie out of place, and manic grin on his face. Bon lurks next to him with a sly fox smirk, all teeth and hair. In the background is the familiar shape of Malcolm, thumbs in pockets, seemingly bored with the shoot. Phil Rudd and Cliff Williams complete the package, confident, cool and very much part of a successful rock group.

"I've got holes in my shoes, and I'm way overdue," sings Bon on the second song, 'Down Payment Blues'. The song was a tale of struggle as a rock 'n' roller on welfare, lyrical evidence that AC/DC were not exactly raking in the bucks at this stage.

Despite featuring three of the band's subsequently most famous tracks in 'Riff Raff', 'Rock N' Roll Damnation' and 'Sin City', *Powerage* was more a complete recording, short, sweet and very much to the rock n' roll point. Nowhere was this more evident than on the pumped up blues of 'Riff Raff'. This song, as much as any that had preceded it, was AC/DC defined by audio proportions. It had everything, Bon's shrieking lyrics, bubbling bass holding Rudd's airtight drums together and some barnstorming blues guitar from the Young brothers. Malcolm kept it in the pocket while Angus went off on several tangents, not once losing sight of the tune itself. All this burst out from a simple riff, but one only the likes of Angus or Malcolm Young could have created.

'Sin City' was always destined to become a live favourite. It had a gently shrugging groove, which could so easily be prolonged for sing–a–longs for audiences the world over. The lyrics were about nights out on the town, of which Bon had ample experience. "Bring on the dancing girls and put the champagne on ice," sneers the singer.

The opening track from the album, 'Rock N' Roll Damnation', became a surprise inclusion on many US radio play lists, and it was this song which gave AC/DC the break they deserved in the States. Perhaps inevitably (especially given their new found acceptability in American circles) some critics considered AC/DC to have gone 'commercial' after *Let There Be Rock* and as a result gave *Powerage* a less than positive review. After the raw noise of their earlier work, some felt cheated by the band's stronger songwriting. But clearly these critics were not only in the minority; they had got it entirely wrong. AC/DC were just improving as a unit, buoyed on by a permanent, settled line up as well as hundreds of road miles covered together. The resultant record simply showcased the hard nights and months of roadwork while demonstrating increasing confidence in the group.

'3, 2, 1, Nuclear energy is dead, the neutron bomb can kiss my... AC/DC's newest blast to the rise, Powerage. Powerage, the ultimate AC/DC album.' An advertisement for Powerage.

Bon told *Sounds* magazine: "Our writing comes from life on the road really. Whatever comes into my brain when we're on the road I jot down on a tape recorder, in order not to lose it. Usually I'm in a drunken state; when I listen back to it the next morning I think, 'hey did I say that? Did I think that?' But out of it you can usually get some pretty good road stuff." "Our albums and music will never get orchestrated or ballady or that kind of mush," added Angus. "Our musical ambition is to put down the whole album like it was done by Little Richard back in the '50s, no double tracking or anything. We may be little but we make a lot of noise!"

The tape machine Bon spoke of was something he would perpetually carry with him. During the bands tour of 1979 he lost it. There were also other troubles for Scott, including a situation where he had to try to convince venue staff at the Glasgow Apollo he was actually a member of AC/DC after he had stepped out for a few minutes to catch a breath of fresh air. "I went around front and they wouldn't let me in until I found a t–shirt vendor who attested to my identity", recalled the singer. "By that time, ten minutes had gone by, and everyone was saying, 'Where is that son of a bitch?'"

The design of the *Powerage* tour programme featured the same cover art as the eventual *If You Want Blood You've Got It* album. The live set reached No. 13 in the UK charts and broke into the US Top 50 for the first time. A maxi single, available on both 7" and 12" formats, was issued by Atlantic shortly after the LP. It combined live renditions of 'Whole Lotta Rosie' and 'Hell Ain't A Bad Place To Be'.

"Bon joined us pretty late in his life, but that guy had more youth in him than people half his age. That was how he thought, and I learned from him. Go out there and be a big kid." Angus Young

Early 1978 produced a scenario typical of Bon at the time. As he explained, he had been frequenting an establishment with a lady he had met. "We had been drinking in the airport bar for about ten minutes when I says, 'don't you think it's time we caught our plane?' And she says, 'What do you mean our plane? I'm staying here.' I run back and the fuckin' plane has gone. Anyway she takes me to this black bar and she's Mexican and I start drinkin' and playin' pool. I had a good night, beatin' every bastard. After about two hours playin' this big–titted black chick and beatin' her too, I happen to look and the bar is goin' 'Grrr.' I think, 'Uh oh, Bon,' I give her another game and lose nine to one. 'Anyone else want to beat me?' I say. So I escapes with me life, only barely and I made it to the gig in Austin."

This kind of environment was one Bon revelled in, never feeling out of his depth. As ex–bassist Mark Evans admitted: "He was a tough son of a bitch. If he went off – shit it was fuckin' scary! Not sort of hitting people with chairs but fist–beating people. He was the best street fighter I've ever seen, bar none."

An Atlantic Records employee found this out the hard way. When finding himself standing next to Bon relieving himself in a urinal at one venue on AC/DC's US tour, he asked the singer whether he was 'AC' or 'DC'. Accordingly Bon replied, "Neither, I'm the lightning flash in the middle!" BAM! Bon punched the employees' lights out. Though Bon himself would never confirm or deny this story it seems highly plausible and was never denied in the Atlantic camp either. Bon's quick wit and bravado was certainly too much for most people to handle. If he was approached with respect he would return the gesture like a gentleman, but come at him with sarcasm or hostile intentions and he would return the nastiness ten fold.

In Philadelphia, the typically clueless record company staff mixed up AC/DC with British rockers UFO. An employee strolled up to UFO vocalist Phil Mogg (after his band had played their set before AC/DC's) and said, in front of the members of AC/DC: "Bon, what a great show!" Luckily said employee managed to escape with all but his ego intact. Both Mogg and bassist Pete Way described touring with AC/DC as being great for both acts. As Way put it, "We drew a hardcore audience who weren't into hit singles bands, but wanted the sort of hard rock music that both bands delivered."

There were problems when playing with another British outfit in America however. At one show, playing alongside Ritchie Blackmore's Rainbow at the Calderone Theater in Long Island, Angus found himself in hot water. As he later described: "I had a bit of a punch–up that night. I got the fright of my life. The guy hit me with an orange. And he had been spitting on me and throwing things and giving me a hard time. And Mal doesn't like me disrupting the show. His big advice to me was, 'just ignore it, Ang.' But that night I just had enough. So I put the guitar down and I went for him. The trouble was when I hit him he kept going! I mean, I was sort of staring at this guy's ankles. I prayed."

Angus described AC/DC's secret of live success to *Sounds*, "When the kids come to see us, they want to rock– that's it. To be part of this big mass thing with the band. You watch, I'll hit a chord on the guitar and right down there at the front there will be a hundred kids hitting it right along with you, going through the motions like they were up there onstage with you, which I guess is where they would be if they could. They're really no different to us."

The empathy between band and fans is understandable: after all, when AC/DC started they were little more than kids themselves. "Back in Australia we were like your average kid into rock n' roll from a small town sort of background," continued Angus. "We were like the outcasts or whatever, always getting into trouble with the cops and picked on because we had long hair and didn't dress like them. But we made it onto the stage and the fans are still trying to get there, or at least dreaming and fantasising about it. We haven't forgotten what it was like and we are definitely on the kids' side."

The constant tour–and–record syndrome had afflicted AC/DC and its members so much that for the last few years finding a permanent dwelling was not exactly an option. "None of us have had our own places to live for the past two years," said Bon. "I rented a flat for eight months but I was only there for six weeks. All we've got is our parents' homes in Australia. We live in hotels, and don't say at the end of a gig, 'I'm going back to the hotel'. We've got the habit of saying, 'I'm going home'."

Angus added that the group "live like the Mafia. Bon's always been of no fixed abode and I'm in the flat above. If you're really wealthy, maybe you can afford to say, 'Whammo, I'll have that block of apartments there.' I suppose I'll buy a place sometime, but I'll probably end up with one of those police boxes at a city crossroads so I can be in the thick of it. At the moment I'm quite at home in these motels. I'll go to my parents at Christmas and after a week I'll check into a hotel. I mean, I've got brothers who bring their kids round and at six in the morning they'll fucking jump on you, yelling, 'He's home!' In a hotel I could complain about the noise and change rooms."

"The shows go so quick. You're on and you're off and you have to go back to how you are as a person. That's the hard part, because once you go into being the schoolboy, it's pretty hard to come off it. It's two different people...I've been up there playing and thinking, 'What are those feet doing?' I'm watching them to see which way they wanna go! That's all I ever do, follow the feet and the guitar."
Angus Young

AC/DC's live album had, to some extent, signalled the closure of a particular period of their career. This is not an uncommon phenomenon; the live album often captures a certain era of an act's progress, which is subsequently saved for posterity, enabling the band to move on to the next stage.

There would be other changes before the next release. Atlantic considered the production team of Harry Vanda and George Young to be out of touch and too close to the group to truly take them much further, despite the assistance they had already given. AC/DC were fighting a losing battle trying to retain the services of their additional members and friends and eventually came around to the idea of finding a new producer. It hardly bothered George Young, who was perpetually busy and in his own view had only been lending a helping hand to his siblings. Eddie Kramer (producer for The Rolling Stones and Jimi Hendrix among many others) initially seemed perfect to handle their kind of material, but the fantasy was quashed when things just didn't seemed to flow properly. "The guy couldn't produce a healthy fart," Bon wrote home in a letter to ex–Fraternity pal John Ayers. AC/DC therefore turned to a more considered choice as George's replacement, Robert John 'Mutt' Lange, who was sharing a flat with Mike Browning at the time.

Along with a change in producer, the band also found a new place to record, moving into the Roundhouse Studios in Chalk

Farm, London. As well as this they also had a more powerful world management taking over from Mike Browning. Peter Mensch of the New York–based Leber and Krebs organisation would now handle AC/DC's business affairs. The whole period was one of necessary change and it led to a new way of working for everyone involved. This was the first time the group had recorded outside Australia. Previously they hadn't spent more than three weeks working on an album, but they spent six months in the Roundhouse Studios with Lange. The result was a life–changing recording that would truly underline AC/DC's new standing as the hottest prospect in rock.

A MAN CALLED MUTT

*Robert John Lange was born on November 16, 1948 in Mu-
fulira, Northern Rhodesia (now Zambia) and moved to South
Africa as a teenager. One of the most successful record producers of all time, Lange would eventually work with the
likes of Def Leppard and Bryan Adams as well as his future
wife Shania Twain.*

*Lange was given the nickname 'Mutt' at a very early age
and grew up listening to country music predominantly. Mutt
started his first band in high school, where he played rhythm
guitar and sang backing vocals. He married Stevie van Kerk-
en (aka Stevie Vann) and moved to England where, in 1970,
he formed a band called Hocus in which Stevie also sang.*

*Mutt began to work as a producer in 1976, when he sat at
the controls for Graham Parker's Heat Treatment album as
well as the first recording of City Boy, whom he would later
produce regularly.*

*Mutt Lange's breakthrough came with his work on AC/DC's
Highway to Hell. He would reunite with the group a year later for Back in Black, followed in 1981 by Foreigner's huge
selling opus 4, which earned him a Grammy nomination as
'Producer of the Year'.*

*That same year, he also worked on Def Leppard's High 'n'
Dry album, his first collaboration with the Brits. But it was
the 1983 hit Pyromania that made Leppard a resounding
success worldwide. Lange even co–wrote some of the albums
most popular tracks including 'Photograph' and 'Rock of
Ages'. During this time Lange also wrote Loverboy's 'Lovin'
Every Minute of It' and Huey Lewis & the News' 'Do You
Believe in Love.'*
*After his next huge hit, The Cars' 1984 album Heartbeat
City, Lange would again join up with AC/DC on 1986's*

Who Made Who before working again with Def Leppard for 1987's Hysteria, one of the best–selling albums of all time. He then moved into other musical areas, working with soul singer Billy Ocean, before teaming up with Bryan Adams' for his 1991 album Waking Up the Neighbours, which included the smash hit single '(Everything I Do) I Do It for You.' Lange gradually worked less as he became more successful, though a year after Adams' world smash he produced Michael Bolton's The One Thing album.

In the late '70s, Lange produced two albums for the band Clover, which featured Huey Lewis on harmonica and Alex Call on lead vocals. Call explains Lange's production style: "Mutt is a real studio rat. He is Mr. Endurance in the studio. When we were making the records with him, he would start working at 10:30, 11 in the morning and go until three the following morning, every day. He is one of the guys that really developed that whole multi, multi, multi track recording. We would do eight tracks of background vocals going, 'Oooooh' and bounce those down to one track and then do another 8, he was doing a lot of that. A lot of the things you hear on Def Leppard and that kind of stuff, he was developing that when he worked with us. We were the last record he did that wasn't enormous, and that's not his fault, he did a really good job with us. Mutt is famous for working long hours. In the story I heard about one of the Shania Twain sessions, he had Rob Hajakos, who is one of the famous fiddle session men down here in Nashville. Rob was playing violin parts for like seven or eight hours and finally he said, 'Can I take a break?' And Mutt says, 'What do you mean take a break?' Rob goes, 'Have you ever held one of these for eight hours under your chin?' Mutt really loves to record, he loves music and he's a real perfectionist and an innovator. An unbelievable commercial hook writer."

Chapter 8 – Highway To Sell

"The bottom line is still very much hard rock, but we've used more melody and backing vocals to enhance the sound. It's possible there is a more commercial structure to the music, without going the whole way. In the past, it's just been a total scream, so I worked on it a lot more this time." Bon Scott

The recording of AC/DC's new album would be fraught with difficulties and many hardships had to be overcome. Before they had even begun to work with Mutt Lange, Eddie Kramer suggested they cover the Spencer Davis Group hit 'Gimme Some Lovin'' for guaranteed airplay, but the band refused point blank. They were good at making a tune their own but it's difficult to imagine Bon carrying off the lyrics of the song with any real conviction. It wasn't a surprise when Kramer was fired after just three weeks' work, without a new AC/DC track to show for it.

Mutt Lange's policy when he took over as producer was to let AC/DC behave exactly as they wished, simply offering his expertise to make the songs sound the way the group wanted them. It is possible Eddie Kramer had been pushed into changing AC/DC's sound by the record company, but Mutt was not about to be persuaded.

It wasn't long after working with AC/DC that Lange would team up with British rockers Def Leppard. In this instance, the sole purpose of teaming producer and band was to crack the American market. Leppard gradually became softer and more radio–friendly, so it was evident Lange had those capabilities and enjoyed working with more melodic rock music. Despite AC/DC's penchant for a great song they were certainly more raw and gutsy than Def Leppard, or indeed many of the other acts with whom Lange would work in the future.

Mutt couldn't have softened AC/DC even if he'd been inclined to try. The Aussies were resolute that if they were to crack America it would be on their own terms. When they came to name the album, the horror of touring the United States was uppermost in their minds, and *Highway To Hell* seemed an appropriate response. This tongue–in–cheek rebellion against the mundanity of the arena conveyor belt would cause serious trouble for the band. Angus didn't think much about appearing on the front cover sporting devil horns and a tail, but it would give fuel the arguments of religious fundamentalists convinced that any musician noisier than Little Jimmy Osmond was in league with Beelzebub.

Bon even wore a chain with a pentagram on it, but despite the fact he was laughing during the photo shoot, some assumed he was genuinely an evil magician! Indeed, it didn't matter that Angus was dressed in school uniform or that the rest of the group looked decidedly normal, what many took to heart was the use of the word 'hell', along with AC/DC's 'evil' logo. It was hard to convince the cynics that the logo was taken from an electrical device and it did not represent any of the definitions those searching for Satanic or sexual overtones had suggested. Someone close to the band even countered the evangelicals' claims by stating that AC/DC stood for 'Altruistic Christians/Doing Charity' to soften their image!

While recording the LP AC/DC had trouble with others who were behind the controls in the studio. "The engineer had all these strange ideas of what he wanted," explained Angus. "Every day you'd come in and play and he'd go, 'I don't want to hear that shit!' One day he said he was off horse riding, showing us these photos of his missus and his horses, and Bon said, 'which one's the horse?' It was that kind of relationship. So he took the weekend off, and we wrote most of *Highway to Hell*. He came in and got the cassette to hear what we had been up to, and his kid pulled all the tape out. We were in a total panic, but Bon got a pencil and managed to get it back together, thank God."

That one of the finest records in rock history might have been lost in its original form was typical of the disorganised way things in the AC/DC world would work. They'd often have innocent intentions only for something to blow up in their faces at a later date. One of the songs on *Highway To Hell* was to have that effect eventually. Written as the last track for the album, and placed at the end, 'Night Prowler' was creepy in its lyrical content and quite unlike anything Bon had written before.

"As you lie there naked like a body in a tomb,
Suspended animation, as I slip into your room...
I'm your Night Prowler, break down your door,
I'm your Night Prowler, crawling 'cross your floor,
I'm your Night Prowler, make a mess of you, yes I will.
Night Prowler, and I am telling this to you,
There ain't nothing you can do".

Despite the spooky lyrical theme, the sinister tone is typically undercut by Bon's penchant for zany humour. As a tribute to Robin Williams, Bon declaims 'Shazbot, Nanu Nanu!', the phrase Williams' character Mork used to end transmissions to his home planet in the sitcom *Mork and Mindy*.

It was Bon's way of ending an otherwise heavy and serious song where his vocals required greater effort than usual. Elsewhere on the record, Bon is in more jovial lyrical form, especially on the upbeat paean to 'his' girl, 'Girl's Got Rhythm'. He talked of travelling the world seeing "a million girls" but that not one of them had what his lady had got. The chorus culminates by clarifying exactly what Bon meant by 'rhythm': "The girl's got the rhythm, She's got the backseat rhythm."

The sound of the *Highway To Hell* album was one of a band at its peak in terms of both confidence and execution of ideas. It was their strongest batch of songs to date, and the production of Mutt had wrought extra power from a group already strong on energised guitar based rock n' roll. Angus had an even clearer tone to his guitar parts and Bon's raw vocal style hadn't changed, but received the gloss it deserved.

The entire LP throbbed with a pulse that didn't falter for over forty minutes. AC/DC had seemingly invented a new form of rock music that would develop further during the eighties. Essentially this was simply a clever twist of an existing genre. The blues–based rock littered throughout the album was basic enough, yet the style with which it was executed turned the hard rock genre on its head. Nowhere previously had any band combined the melodious sensibilities such as the Young brothers song writing, with a heavy, pounding background. From 1979 onwards many acts would attempt to reach the levels of *Highway To Hell* for sheer catchiness and raw power, though arguably no one group would ever be able to match AC/DC's prowess. Mutt had brought out the best in them, although the songs would have been strong whoever produced them.

'Touch Too Much' was the epitome of Bon's canny lyrical prowess and vocal histrionics with sublime back ups from the rest of the lads. The lyrics concerned the dangers of excess, with which AC/DC was by now more than familiar. They were becoming notorious for their wild parties and general debauchery, with girls and excessive drinking. A live version was released as a single in the UK.'

The additional advantage with the upfront production was the way the songs had been placed so close to each other. As one track ended, another began, leaving the listener barely time to recover from the first blow to the head before being assaulted with another. This was a production technique quite ahead of its time in rock music. In the early nineties the Slayer and Red Hot Chili Peppers producer Rick Rubin would use this technique to maximum effect and make a reputation based on his method of working, but it was Mutt Lange who had initiated this form of aural battery.

Even the order of songs on the album was perfect. 'Girl's Got Rhythm' ends its swaggering beat and moves straight into the sultry beginning of 'Touch Too Much'. As that song finishes, it moves into the even heavier 'Beating Around The Bush' but the track starts with a lingering guitar lick, giving time to reflect before the beat comes in.

Canadian writer Martin Popoff had this to say of the record: "Without a doubt, more alcohol has been consumed and subsequently returned orally to the earth to the distorted strains of this record than any other release in history. The party album from the party band, one of the largest expressions of electric jubilation ever harnessed."

According to other reviews, this was the AC/DC you knew and loved and they had not exactly changed their sound in any way. It was indeed the same old guitars, bass and drums based on the blues. Yet, the group had inarguably refined their sound and honed it finally to stake a claim to be the greatest rock outfit operating at the time. The only track, which did not sit so well with the band members, was 'Love Hungry Man' of which Malcolm would say, "The overall thing was a lot rougher on our original demos. In the studio it didn't happen right. We had to settle for it. But it doesn't mean the band have to like it or listen to it."

Though they would always stubbornly pledge allegiance to the blues and little else, the release of *Highway To Hell* would mark AC/DC's association with heavy metal, for better or worse. The front cover had helped. Though true heavy metal (progressing from early acts such as Black Sabbath and Led Zeppelin, through to heavier and more defiantly "metal" outfits like Iron Maiden and Judas Priest) was in its early stages, those seeking something over the top and preferably blasphemous from loud guitar music just needed to check out the diabolical overtones (however tongue in cheek) of the cover art. The band's logo also seemed to suggest some kinship with their contemporaries (such as, again, Maiden and Priest). However, AC/DC never felt comfortable being lumped in with metal acts.

As metal progressed into a genre of its own, AC/DC felt it was false, and contrary to the spirit of rock music. They abhorred the clothes, the bravado and what they saw as meaningless lyrics. Heavy metal would soon move even further down this road, and AC/DC would be tainted by their associations – however unfair – with the genre.

Released on July 27, 1979, *Highway To Hell* quickly became 'DC's first UK Top 10 album, peaking at No. 8. It was also their first US Top 20 entry, reaching No. 17. In Australia, it climbed to No. 24, making it the first AC/DC album to chart there in nearly three years.

For the remainder of 1979 the group toured the United States and Britain, though still not Australia. In the States, AC/DC played a handful of headlining shows while opening other concerts for the likes of Cheap Trick, UFO and long–time touring associate Ted Nugent. This time however, acts they had played alongside previously, such as Foreigner and Van Halen, decided not to play with AC/DC and turned their offer of a tour down. It is not difficult to see why, given the band had overshadowed them on previous occasions. Despite playing regularly in America, 'DC were still yet to succumb to its allure on a personal level. "I'm happy playing, when I go on-stage, I'm happy," said Angus. "America…I don't like the TV and things like that, the food I don't like, it's all fake. And I don't like the fact that every time you turn on the TV there's some guy running for president."

In Britain, the group played with Def Leppard, fellow clients of their producer, Mutt Lange. The bands were different enough not to step on each other's toes. Even though Leppard were still rough around the edges, and had not yet found the lush harmonies they would later employ, they still played a harmonic, radio–friendly form of rock. They were perfect as a warm–up act, but the real deal was still AC/DC.

Playing with another British outfit, AC/DC discovered a new audience. Their biggest show in the U.K. to date was a support slot for The Who on August 18th 1979 at Wembley Stadium. The gig was actually part of a festival, called 'Who And Roar Friends', which also included Nils Lofgren and The Stranglers. AC/DC were un-lucky to experience sound problems, when the PA broke down in the middle of their set. They persevered like the true road warriors they now were, and managed to complete the concert, to rapturous applause from those in attendance.

This response from the band and their ability to turn a poten-tial banana skin into a great gig won respect from The Who, and the legends took AC/DC out with them for further outdoor European dates. The Aussies had by now developed the ability to play a con-cert regardless of the size or venue. They could cope with the un-predictability of outside arenas, but still excelled at playing indoor venues, whether they held 20 or 2,000 people.

After a Christmas break, AC/DC headed back out on the road with more European shows. They sold out the Pavillion De Paris twice, filming the second show, which was later released as the movie *Let There Be Rock*.

In January 1980, AC/DC made an appearance at the annual Midem music industry convention in France, at which they were presented with several gold and silver discs for sales in France and Canada. They also played dates in Newcastle and Southampton to make up for shows that had been cancelled on the previous British tour. They even appeared on the UK Television show *Top of the Pops* to promote their current UK single 'Touch Too Much'. By this time *Highway To Hell* had been certified Gold in the United States, with sales reaching 500,000 units.

But the group was about to be plunged into its biggest crisis to date. On January 27, 1980, though nobody knew it at the time, Bon Scott appeared for the last time onstage with the band.

THE LONG SPELLBINDING ROAD

Barry Taylor was a roadie with AC/DC and he found God while working on the band's Highway to Hell tour. He later wrote a book about his experiences called Singing In The Dark – A Rock N' Roll - Roadie Steps Into The Light. He is currently completing his Ph.D. in Postmodern Studies at Fuller Theological Seminary in California. Songs from his album Love Songs for the Underdogs are featured in Agnieszka Holland's 1999 film The Third Miracle. He also scored the Bui brothers' Green Dragon (2001). Taylor is of the opinion that the Austin Powers movies have profound theological meaning.

Chapter 9 – R.I.P. – Rock In Peace

"He couldn't have recorded albums and stuff if he'd been in the condition they said he was in. When we were touring there may have been six months of the year when he was as dry as a bone and if we got one night off then he was entitled to a drink. Bon was not a heavy drinker." Angus Young

During early February 1980, Bon worked on lyrics for AC/DC's next album. He also attended the wedding of Angus Young, who married his long time Dutch girlfriend Ellen. On Tuesday February 19th Bon visited 'DC tour manager Ian Jeffrey' house where he had dinner. At about 6:30pm the two left to attend London venue The Music Machine (later known as The Camden Palace and currently Koko). It was a place frequented by musicians and a general 'hang out' for the music industry, much like the Rainbow Bar and Grill in Los Angeles. It was somewhere Bon felt rather at home.

He had also made plans to meet up with UFO's Phil Mogg and Peter Way, but neither of them turned up. Bon remained in the venue after it was clear the two were not coming, and mingled with various locals, hangers on and groupies. One of the friends he encountered was a man named Alistair Kinnear (a musician, apparently a bass player) and the two left together at around 3am.

Kinnear drove Bon home to the singer's London flat, but when he tried to wake him he had no luck. Bon was looking somewhat immovable and so Kinnear jumped back in the driver's seat and took Bon back to his own flat in East Dulwich. He hoped that by the time the two reached his home, Bon might have woken, but that didn't happen. Instead, Scott was seemingly in a deep sleep. Unable to carry the booze–sodden frontman out of the car and up the stairs to his flat, Kinnear decided it would be better to leave him in the back. He covered Bon with a blanket and went up alone, leaving him instructions how to get there when he awoke.

This particular evening was bitterly cold and regardless of any drink consumed, it would not have been a sensible option for anyone to sleep out in a car in the dead of winter. This was especially true on this occasion, as Kinnear himself passed out for almost 15 hours, making it well into early the next evening by the time he went out to check on Bon. By this time, when the singer still wouldn't wake, Kinnear began to panic and realised there was something seriously wrong. Bon was curled around the gear stick. Kinnear drove him to King's College Hospital in Denmark Hill, close to his Dulwich flat. Bon Scott was pronounced dead on arrival.

This sequence of events is the recognised version, it has been repeated many times by AC/DC themselves and additionally has appeared in many previous publications.It does however leave many questions unanswered, it is inconsistent with other details which have emerged since and in general it simply doesn't sound completely believable. My own research has opened a lot of new doors in the search for the real truth about that fateful night, but alas, it has raised as many new questions as it answers old ones. What it does achieve however, is to prove incorrect some of the previous theories which have suggested that Alistair Kinnear was in fact a pseudonym for someone very close to Bon Scott, but who, for their own reasons, was unprepared to reveal their true identity.

Three days after Bon Scott died the coroner recorded a verdict of death by misadventure, with acute alcohol poisoning cited as the cause. According to Kinnear, who appeared at the inquest, Scott had consumed "at least seven double whiskies" and this had caused him to pass out later in the evening. In the London newspaper, the *Evening Standard*, John Stevens recorded Kinnear's recollections. According to Kinnear he met with Bon before visiting The Music Machine, rather than meeting him in there. Kinnear told Stevens: "Bon was pretty drunk when I picked him up. When we got there he was drinking four whiskies straight in a glass at a time…I just could not move him, so I covered him with a blanket and left him a note to tell him how to get to my flat in case he woke up. I went to sleep then and it was later in the evening (of 20th February) when I went out to the car and I knew something was wrong immediately."

Angus young picked up the story when speaking to the press a short time later. "I received a panic phone call from Kinnear's landlady explaining how Bon had been rushed to King's College Hospital and declared dead on arrival. I immediately phoned Malcolm, 'cos at the time I thought maybe she's got it wrong, you know, and just thought it was him. And Ian Jeffrey, our tour manager, said it couldn't be him 'cos he'd gone to bed early that night. Anyway, the girl gave me the hospital number, but they wouldn't give me any information until his family had been contacted."

Malcolm took it upon himself to give Isa and Chick Scott, Bon's parents, the bad news. "We didn't want them to be just sitting there, and suddenly it comes on the TV news, you know," explained Angus. "Peter Mensch, our manager, got to the hospital as soon as he could to find out exactly what had happened and identify him, because everyone was in doubt at the time. At first I didn't really believe it, but in the morning it finally dawned on me. It's just like losing a member of your family, that's the only way to describe it. Maybe even a bit worse, 'cos we all had a lot of respect for Bon as a person because, even though he did like to drink and have a bit of a crazy time, he was always there when you needed him to do his job and things. There were times you could say he lived on the edge, but I was still pretty young. He himself was not an old guy and I suppose in those times you think you're immortal."

It is generally accepted that Bon just had a bad reaction to a night of heavy drinking. Angus certainly thought this version of events was entirely plausible. "As a band, it's your history and you reflect back on it, and sometimes you laugh. Sometimes you're somewhere and you remember something. What he did – he could be an adventurous type of person."

Ex–manager Mike Browning said: "Bon always used to say that he was pretty sure he wouldn't live beyond 40. So I think in some ways everybody kind of expected it to happen if he was left to his own devices."

The former AC/DC bass player Mark Evans didn't think Bon's lifestyle was destined to lead him to an early death but he did "remember being with him a few times where he sort of had a few drinks and passed out, due in part to him being heavily asthmatic

Though it was a shock when it did happen, certainly after the dust had settled it was no surprise." Though Evans refers to Bon being asthmatic, this seems to be a new revelation, with little or no mention of this in other accounts of the singer's life.

A writer who researched Bon Scott's life and death extensively, Clinton Walker has stated "a lot of people thought it was remarkable Bon lived as long as he did."

"Nobody was more hurt than the AC/DC boys at the time, because they lost a great friend and a fine singer. A lesser band would have collapsed, but they came back and went on to make so many more huge records. Bon was an awful hard man to replace." Jimmy Barnes

The death of their frontman shocked AC/DC to the core. Bon was older than the rest of them, but he was still only 33. How was it possible he had joined the catalogue of rock stars who'd checked in before their time?

But notwithstanding this, the band decided that Bon would have wanted AC/DC to carry on. Before his death the group had been planning their next album together and songs were already written. It was agreed they would have to find a new singer and continue where they had left off with Bon. "It was my brother that picked me up a bit from his death" Angus admitted. "And he said to me, 'Let's get together and just continue what we were doing.' We were writing songs at the time Bon died. He said, 'Let's continue doing that.' It kept you going and was good therapy, I suppose."

Angus remembered the last time he saw Bon alive "Me and Malcolm were in a rehearsal studio in London. He came in and said, 'Oh you'll be needing a drummer,' so the last time we ever played together Bon was on drums." Bon did indeed play along to the initial songs that would eventually comprise the *Back In Black* album as a drummer rather than a vocalist. Of course on the actual album Bon is not present in any capacity, with the drums being re–recorded by Phil Rudd.

"I was at home in Sydney at the time," remembers Vince Lovegrove of the day he found out about Bon's death. "I got a phone call at about three in the morning from his ex–wife, Irene, a good friend of mine at that time. She told me the news and I freaked. From then on until dawn I was besieged by the media, asking for quotes and all that shit. You know, was it expected? Did he deserve it? All the stupid questions that the media asks at a time like that. I don't know what it was like overseas, but in Australia at that time it was over-whelming. He was the first real rock star from Oz who died, and so nobody there could believe it, almost as if we were immune from the tragedies of rock. Nobody could believe an Australian rock star could die, especially under those questionable circumstances.

"Anyway, I cried and cried about the loss of a mate, and all the things you do emotionally when someone you love leaves for-ever...you know, anger, regret, sorrow, pain, the full tilt boogie, but it was not a surprise. I am never surprised when someone from the rock world dies. It really is part of the deal; it is a life on the edge, and everyone plays it to some extent at some time, some get out, some go under. He was troubled, I saw him in Atlanta, Georgia in 1978, and we raved and got fucked up until dawn, and he told me then he'd had enough. He said he couldn't stand the touring lifestyle anymore but that he had to keep going because the big money hit was just around the corner.

In many ways, Bon was not suited to be a pop star, in other ways he was. But he longed to get out, settle down, have kids and just write and sing music, that is for sure. No matter what anybody else says, he wanted out, but the addiction of it all was too much, he was hooked like we're all hooked on music. It's just a matter of how hooked, what we do about it, and under what circumstances we try and let it and its side effects take over."

WHAT IS REAL?

"Cause I ain't too old to die but I sure am hard to beat." 'Ride On'

On Wednesday, February 23, 2005, the following statement was printed in the *The Guardian* newspaper's corrections and clari-fications column, following an alleged error in a previous edition of the newspaper a few days earlier.

"In this story, it was suggested that the name Alistair Kinnear might have been a pseudonym used by one of Scott's associates. That was incorrect. Alistair (not Alasdair) Kinnear is the name of Bon Scott's former friend and neighbour. We have been asked to make it clear that Mr. Kinnear reported finding Bon Scott immediately on his discovery. Scott was then taken to King's College hospital in Camberwell, where he was declared dead."

The journalist responsible for the story was Richard Jinman. After the correction I called him in an attempt to discover the source of the correction. Mr. Jinman was most helpful and told me, "It's an interesting one. After the article ran I was contacted by Alistair's son who lives in London. He told me his father was alive and living in Spain. I had no reason to think he wasn't telling the truth. He told me he had a huge amount of detail about the night Bon died, but said his father would not want to talk about it and was not in good health. It was a shock obviously because people like Clinton Walker have been convinced that Alistair Kinnear was a made up name, apparently, he was very real."

With Mr. Jinman's assstance I managed to get in touch personally with Daniel Kinnear – Alistair's son – who it would appear is indeed living in London. I told him about the planned publication of this book and my desire to set the story straight once and for all about that fateful night.

I asked him whether his father would speak to me about the events that have become so muddled over the intervening years. Daniel told me he would contact his father but repeated that his father was not in the best of health and may wish to avoid dragging up unpleasant memories. He did however clarify the following via e–mail:

1. Alistair Kinnear is a real person.
2. He was a close friend of Bon Scott's.
3. He was with him on the night he died and did indeed take him home. When not
being able to get him out of the car, he drove him to his flat in Overhill Road, South London.

4. Sadly, Alistair left him to sober up in the car and upon his return the next morning found him dead.

5. Alistair immediately reported his discovery and Bon Scott was taken to King's College Hospital.

6. Alistair experienced considerable grief and a sense of "if only I'd..." which he has spent a long time coming to terms with.

Clearly Daniel Kinnear had known for a long time about his father's connection with Bon Scott and the night he died and admitted that "Although my father resides in Spain, I did ask my mother of her recollections of that date (note that I am 32 and do not recall anything). She stated that it was a traumatic time and that Bon Scott was indeed a very heavy drinker of Scotch Whiskey. In fact, it was noted at the inquest that his drinking had so seriously damaged his physical well–being that there was a heightened probability that he would have died shortly afterwards anyway. Being aware that many people within the industry at that time experimented with various 'other' drugs, I asked my mother whether that could have been a factor in Bon Scott's death.Her recollection of Bon Scott was that although he may have experimented, he wasn't a habitual user, his medication of choice being whiskey."

Although Daniel Kinnear's intentions appear to be honourable in attempting to set the story straight, and the facts he has repeated – a carbon copy of the 'offical' version – are of course entirely plausible, there are still many areas of ambiguity regarding these events that require some explanation. Many fans and journalists are of the opinion that there has always been more to this story than has been fully divulged. I include myself among that group.

The most common insinuation is that Alistair Kinnear never existed, that this name was a pseudonym for someone close to the band who was himself with Bon the night he died. It is interesting to note here that tour manager Ian Jeffrey is named in the 'official' version as the man who went with Bon to the music machine on the night in question. As mentioned above Jeffrey's was later to state that 'It couldn't be him, he'd gone to bed early that night'.

Bon Scott biographer Clinton Walker claims, in his book 'Highway To Hell – The Life and Times Of Bon Scott', that he has spoken to the very person who used the name Alistair Kinnear deceptively. This theory has, however, always appeared far fetched. Would anyone risk using a false name to not only report a death but to also attend an inquest, and undergo a police interview certain to lead to some personal investigation. And, let's be realistic, wouldn't the police have seen through it in five minutes flat? If this theory had been the truth, whatever the perpetrator's reasons were for such an elaborate hoax, they would pale into insignificance compared to the likely repercussions. While it's a nice story, it has the ring of 'conspiracy theory' about it and this writer, at least, never believed it.

There will be those who claim that it could be just as likely that Daniel Kinnear is a pseudonym as Alistair Kinnear. Well a quick check on the Friends Reunited website does reveal that one Daniel Kinnear was a student at a school close to the stated address where Daniel claimed his father was living at the time of Scott's death, and the other information given on the site fit in with details Daniel told me about himself, such as his line of work and qualifications. Daniel's emails come from a place of work that completely checks out and his name is in the address.

But there were questions still needing answers. How did Alistair and Bon know each other? How close were they, and did Alistair know the other members of AC/DC? In what sense were they 'neighbours' – at the time Bon lived in a flat in central London's Victoria and Alistair in the South East Dulwich area – a good 30 minutes drive even at 3 a.m. Hoping that Daniel was about to approach his father on my behalf, I put these questions to him and asked if he would forward them, or, if he knew any of the answers himself, let me know. The questions were put politely and with no indication of any underlying suspicion, I was therefore surprised that I received no reply. I left it for a few weeks then emailed again but still received no response. As deadlines were tight I emailed one more time, telling Daniel this and making it clear that if he and his father did not wish to make further comment, that of course would be respected, but I asked him if he would be good enough to confirm this either way. Again nothing came back.

Although I have never believed that Alistair Kinnear did not exist, I still felt that, while we may have the truth, we don't necessarily have the whole truth, nor nothing but the truth. My remaining questions were many.

I should make it clear at this point that I am not suggesting Daniel Kinnear has attempted at any time to mislead either Richard Jinman or myself, but whether Daniel is actually in contact with his father remains questionable. At no time has he stated that he is, and indeed he has claimed that all his knowledge of these events came from his mother, being too young at the time to remember them personally (he would have been approximately 7 years old when Scott died). Daniel told Richard Jinman that he had a wealth of information regarding the night Bon died, yet while claiming he was keen to set the record straight he did not appear willing to answer even the most pedestrian of questions, nor indeed to respond to me in any way other than giving me the standard take on events.

The coroner's report gave 'excessive consumption of alcohol' as the cause of death. This seems a little strange as Bon was a huge drinker, a fact confirmed by virtually everyone who had ever known him. So, while it is more than plausible that the 'excessive alcohol' alone killed him, it should also be considered whether any other factors contributed to the tragic event. On the 19th February 1980 he was, after all, allegedly only doing what he did virtually every other night at this point in his life.

Other rock stars who have died under similar circumstances – Keith Moon and Jimi Hendrix come to mind – were in many cases not killed directly by their regular 'poisons'. It is thought that Moon overdosed on drugs which, ironically, were supposed to help him refrain from alcohol, and Hendrix choked on vomit induced by his excesses.

It has been suggested that Scott also was asphyxiated by vomit, but if this were the case, surely it would have been diagnosed during the post mortem.

Certainly, suspicions have been expressed by some who knew him, and many who didn't, that Bon was indulging in harder substances than just drink. There is evidence Bon had tried heroin, but whether he went further than just dabbling is less certain.

It has previously been reported that on at least one previous occasion, Bon almost died of a heroin overdose. In Melbourne in early 1975 he was mixing with the kind of people who would experiment with any type of narcotic. Much like Jim Morrison of The Doors, Bon was also keen to try anything at least once. Vince Lovegrove talks of snorting speed with Bon when they had first become friends. The two would meet in breaks from work and go to a pub and quickly sniff a shot of amphetamines before going back to the daily grind.

In his autobiography *Scar Tissue*, Red Hot Chili Peppers vocalist Anthony Kiedis reveals the perils of his own drug addiction: "I was getting more and more into shooting cocaine, drinking lots of alcohol and taking lots of pills. I didn't see it happening, but the wheels were falling off of me. The horribly ironic cosmic trick of drug addiction is that drugs are a lot of fun when you first start using them, but by the time the consequences manifest themselves you're no longer in a position to say, 'Whoa, gotta stop that'. You've lost that ability and you've created this pattern of conditioning and reinforcement. It's never something for nothing when drugs are involved."

Clinton Walker describes the following episode in 1975, involving Bon's girlfriend of the time, Judy King. King was a heroin addict who spent all her money on smack, earned from working in a 'massage parlour'. King's sister Christine was also an addict and one night when Bon came to Judy's apartment he found the two in their usual narcotic haze. The sisters kept on at Bon to try the heroin, suggesting he might like it. Initially he was sceptical and had certainly never envisaged himself as some strung–out junkie like his current squeeze. But with the constant badgering from the two women to just have a taste, Bon eventually agreed.

Bon pulled up his sleeve and let Judy tap his vein with the syringe, shooting the smack into his body. For a short period Bon felt the rush, the elation of the drug, but then he turned a deathly blue/grey colour and fell into his chair. Judy suddenly became very frightened and it was left to Christine to act quickly. She struggled to find a vein, but managed to inject him with amphetamine in an attempt to counteract the heroin. She then gave him mouth–to–mouth resuscitation and massaged his heart, and he let out a whimper. Judy called an ambulance and eventually Bon was revived.

If Walker's story is accurate it is clear Bon was no stranger to smack. Whether this incident had been enough to put him off for life though, is another matter. He did not feel quite the elation that some do when dabbling in their first fix, but who is to say he didn't want to try again at some point in the future?

The main reason that any suggestion of drug use on the night he died has been so readily dismissed, is largely because there was no mention of any such substance in Scott's blood at the inquest or in the subsequent report. That said, it should be noted that back in the early 1980s it would not always have been standard procedure during an autopsy to undertake a toxicology report, which requires a different process of testing than the one used to detect alcohol, and if an excessive amount of alcohol was found in the blood stream of a victim, it was then customary to presume that that was the cause of death, rather than looking for other 'clues'.

"Bon said 'Vinnie. I really am getting tired. I love it, you know that. It's only rock n' roll and I like it. But I want to have a base. It's just the constant pressure of touring that's fucking it. I've been on the road for thirteen years. Planes, hotels, groupies, booze, people, towns. They all scrape something from you. We're doing it and we'll get there, but I wish we didn't have these crushing day after day grinds to keep up with. Rock n' roll, you know that's all there is. But I can't hack the rest of the shit that goes with it.'" Vince Lovegrove

The above quote was made to Bon's close friend shortly before his death. There has also been odd lines from unused lyrics published, which equally point to a mild depression or at least some disillusionment with the life he was leading. However, while some journalists have suggested that Bon may have been suicidal at this point in his career, there really is no evidence to suggest that he took his own life, and again some light would have been shed by the coroner.

As is the case with all deaths when the reason is not immediately apparent, Bon Scott's London flat was searched very shortly after he was declared dead, but nothing of significance that would shed any light on the tragedy, appears to have been found, neither any illegal drugs nor a suicide note. Clinton Walker is also of the opinion that someone, other than the police, ransacked Kinnear's residence. If this was indeed the case it would point to some questionable circumstances, however Walker's source for this information is not substantiated.

In the late 1970s members of AC/DC were close friends with the British rock band UFO. It was no secret that this heavy metal four piece were big drinkers and regular drug users. At one time, AC/DCs manager, Peter Mench, was even heard to comment that the British group were a bad influence on his charges. Bon's personal friendship with guitarist Paul Chapman and bassist Peter Way was strong and there have been those who blame these two musicians for the spiralling of Scott's excessive behaviour.

Bon's death affected Pete Way in particular. "It hit me hard. And it's funny it took his death to wake the world to AC/DC. It was like, something special. Punk rock almost made it but AC/DC made it to the max. Bon launched AC/DC's career into stardom. You can't buy a Bon Scott. When we were on tour in the US with them, every night I watched Bon and Angus and I thought 'Wow!' It was like a hurricane. It was much better than UFO and we had to go and follow it."

In a *Classic Rock Magazine* article, commemorating the 25th Anniversary of Bon Scott's death, Peter Way claimed that he used to buy heroin from an Australian man who would visit the band with Bon Scott in tow. He also states that on many occasions he 'jacked up' in Bon's presence. When asked whether Bon had ever used the drug in front of Way, he was vague and non committal.

In the same article he stated that he first heard about Bon's death via a phone call from Paul Chapman at 10.30am on the 20th February . As it has always been claimed that Alistair Kinnear discovered the body at 7.45 pm, this counter–claim does suggest some inconsistencies. However it must be remembered that both Way and Chapman were regular users of heroin, a drug not known for it's memory enhancement.

Paul Chapman's recollections of the night Bon died however are really quite staggering when compared to the 'script' that has been readily accepted for so many years. While, of course, some details may be incorrect, there would seem little point in him making up such a story in its entirety.

According to Chapman, on the evening of 19th February, he met up with Bon Scott and an Australian called Joe King, and invited them both back to his flat in Fulham, just off the Wandsworth Bridge. King apparently had changed his name by deed poll, being previously known as Joe Bloe. Chapman claims that King was his guitar technician at one time and worked for UFO for around six months, the pair having first met at King's Hammersmith flat, where he lived with his girlfriend Silver Smith, an old flame of Bon's. Apparently a dealer in heroin also lived at the flat.

Paul Chapman further states that once back at his flat, Joe told him he didn't have much smack left (indicating therefore that King was also a user), which allegedly prompted Bon to go off and find some for them. After waiting hours for him to return, King decided he had to leave himself and return to his own flat. It would seem at this time Joe was living with Bon at the Victoria flat. Joe King left the Fulham flat around 7am and made his own way home, having turned down Paul's offer to call him a cab.

If King walked the distance between the two apartments, it would have taken him between 45 minutes and an hour, an uncomplicated journey straight down London's fashionable King's Road.

Paul Chapman goes on to state that at about 10.30 am the same morning, he was awoken by the telephone. It was Joe King who told him that Bon Scott was dead.

King had returned to the Victoria flat apparently, but it is not clear how he knew at that time in the morning that Scott had died. Chapman states that King told him that he had contacted other members of AC/DC to tell them the news. One final point of interest in Chapman's account is his insistence that Bon was intending to go to Dulwich in order to 'score' the heroin. Whether the heroin Bon was intending to purchase that night was solely intended for King and Chapman, is not clarified. Chapman has claimed that he never once saw Bon use any drugs whatsoever, although, "he drank like a Wildman".

The two contrasting versions of events, from Alistair Kinnear and Paul Chapman, have many connections that would suggest there is some truth in both of them. In the Kinnear version, Bon and Alistair were intending to meet up with two members of UFO that night at The Music Machine, but those named were Phil Mogg and Peter Way, no mention of Paul Chapman. It was stated that Way and Mogg didn't show. But perhaps Paul Chapman *was* at the venue and Bon met up with him, and subsequently got invited back to the Fulham flat. Another parallel between the two versions is Paul Chapman's insistence that Scott intended to go to Dulwich to score the drugs. The only link previously made between Bon Scott and Dulwich is via Alistair Kinnear.

But if Bon was picked up on the 16th February at around 6.30pm and taken to The Music Machine, and there he met up with Paul Chapman, went back with him to Fulham, and then left to head to Dulwich, what happened to Alistair Kinnear during this part of the evening?

There only seems to be two possible scenarios that could fit in – somewhat at least – with both stories. First, and more probable, is that Bon had left The Music Machine with Chapman, then returned later, met back up with Kinnear, got seriously drunk, and at closing time the pair left together. The other possibility is that Kinnear was with Scott, Chapman, and King, and that Bon and Alistair left the Fulham flat together, and went back to Dulwich in Kinnear's car. Chapman had made no mention of Kinnear being in the party, but the passing of time can of course make memories less lucid.

Both of these scenarios would indicate that heroin was expected to be available in Dulwich that night. It should be noted too that Alistair Kinnear saw fit to drive a car on an evening he was out on the town with Bon Scott. And although the drink driving penalties in the UK in 1980 weren't as severe as they are today, and the chance of being stopped by the police were not as high, anyone even vaguely trying to keep up, would surely be in no fit state after 8 hours of partying with Bon Scott, to get behind the wheel of a car.

Alistair may of course have been tee total. Perhaps he was high on life itself.....

In the post–Bon universe, the band closed ranks. Protected by the guiding hand of hardened professionals such as Peter Mensch, the management did a fine job in avoiding the musicians being linked with hearsay, gossip or speculation. Ever since February 17th 1980, the original members of AC/DC have retained a dignified silence with regards Bon Scott's death.

Angus, Malcolm and the others like to talk of the times they were lucky enough to share with Bon as do the many others whom he came into contact with. He was only in AC/DC for just over five years but he gave them their rock n' roll wings, enabling them to fly on long after his passing.

"I've been on the road for fifteen years and I have no intentions to stop. We meet a lot of people, we drink lots of stuff and have lots of fun." Bon Scott

Without Bon, AC/DC might never have progressed beyond being a small club band – he brought the character a front man so desperately needs to make an act great rather than good. Geoff Barton of *Classic Rock Magazine* thinks: "He could make a pub feel like an arena and an arena feel like a pub." With his clever vocal phrasing, distinctive singing voice and undeniable stage presence, AC/DC became a band capable of transcending their humble back alley roots. It was the subtle interplay between Bon and Angus which lent the group an appeal that would see them become bigger with every album they released.

Bon was only in AC/DC a short while but he sang on some of their most memorable records. The likes of *Highway To Hell* and *High Voltage* are classic rock records of the 1970s and Bon was integral to their success. His lyrics brought the music to life and his voice gave the songs their longevity. There are few frontmen who can compare to him.

Rose Tattoo vocalist and fellow Australian Angry Anderson, remembers Bon as "A gypsy, a vagabond, a buccaneer. He was a bad boy and a rock n' roll outlaw. He was truly a street poet documenting in lyric and performance all that he thought felt and cared about life. Life from his point of view." It would appear, from the testimonies of hundreds of friends, colleagues, fellow musicians and even people who met him just once, that Bon Scott was a genuinely decent human being .

"Bon was one of the nicest guys I ever met. I really mean that. If he was an asshole I'd tell you. I'm not just saying that because the poor guy is dead. He really was a lovely guy... It was a great loss..."
Ozzy Osbourne

Angus Young said of Bon: "Often he would trail off with fans who came backstage after a show and go off with them to a party or something. He judged people as they were and if they invited him somewhere and he was in the right mood to go, he went. It didn't matter to him whether they had a name or were a 'star', he just went with them. We used to call him 'Bon the likeable'. We could be somewhere where you would never expect anyone to know him, and someone would walk up and say, 'Bon Scott!' and always have a bottle of beer for him. It was uncanny."

Of course Bon Scott had a rogue mentality and he was not the devoted family man it sometimes appeared he wished to be. However, it seems possible that he may have turned into such had he lived. As he had mentioned to Bruce Howe, it was starting to concern him that he had not found the right woman to settle down with. Perhaps, above all else, true love and family life was what Bon really desired. The success of his career in music was a welcome distraction from apparent upset in his personal life, but not enough to steer him into complete contentment.

Angus Young felt positively about the upcoming album they were due to record with Bon. "Malcolm and I were really looking forward to getting him into the studio and doing the next album more than we've done with any album before, because after the success of the last one, it was going to be a really big challenge. That was the sad part of it all because perhaps it could have been the best thing he'd ever done on record. That would have been the crowning glory of his life."

The music media, of course, pulled their usual trick; creating yet another rock 'n' roll martyr. As Angus put it, "When he was alive, all people would say about him was that he was this creature straight from the gutter; no one would take him seriously. Then after he died, all of a sudden he was a great poet. Even he himself would have been laughing at that…"

We will probably never know the true sequence of events that caused the premature passing of one of the greatest and most charismatic rock vocalists of all time. But we have the records and we have the memories. And that is what's really important.

A MEETING OF MINDS

Paul Di'Anno, the first permanent singer for Iron Maiden, recalls meeting his hero. "I'd skived off school with a mate – like you do – to go and see AC/DC. They were playing a club in London and we just went along. They played a great show, and we managed to meet them in the bar afterwards, when we blagged our way in for a few underage beers. Get this – the person who bought me my first ever beer in any pub, anywhere, was AC/DC's singer, the late, the great Bon Scott; legendary singer, womaniser and general hell–raiser.

Talk about an honour – I was just overwhelmed by the guy and his wild man reputation. Years later he came to be a huge influence in my life, not just for his music, but the way he approached everything, just taking it as it comes and living for the day. We both lived life to the full, and aside from a shared appetite for pussy, drink and drugs, we also shared the same down to earth attitude and sense of humour, which got us through all the craziness which surrounded us.

There is a terrible coincidence relating to the day he died. That day, myself and the guys in Maiden were making our debut appearance on Top Of The Pops, when I became the first singer to perform live on the show for almost a decade. We'd refused to mime, so they bent the rules for us. So there I am, riding high as a rock singer, and there was Bon, my idol, lying dead in a car, a few miles away across London."

Chapter 10 – The Boys From The Black Stuff

"Forget the hearse 'cause I never die
I got nine lives
Cat's eyes
Abusin' every one of them and running wild.

'Cause I'm back
Yes, I'm back
(Well) I'm back in black." 'Back In Black'

On March 1st 1980 Bon Scott was buried in Fremantle, Australia. The funeral was a quiet affair with only close friends and
family in attendance. Bon's family had always quietly admired and
respected his bandmates. Where some might have cast blame upon
the band for its hard living lifestyle, Isa Scott was smart enough to
understand Bon had been heading that way of his own accord for
a while. When he visited his parents a short time before his death,
they saw at first hand how that his behaviour was out of control
– and this was at a time when the other members of AC/DC were
nowhere in sight.

Isa knew that there had been nothing she could do to persuade
her headstrong son to stop drinking. She had raised him to be independent; stubbornness was therefore inherent in Bon's personality.
A rock 'n' roll death was, if not inevitable, then certainly on the
cards.

Isa also understood the band's need to carry on without Bon,
rather than calling it a day. "Go out there and find a new singer,"
she told them. "You have to do it. Bon would have wanted it that
way". This endorsement, given so soon after his death, reassured the
Young brothers that they would be doing the right thing in carrying
on with the group. They already had a phenomenal back catalogue
to draw upon, but as Bon had hinted to his mother in early 1980,
this next album could be the one to propel AC/DC to even greater
stardom. It is unclear how much of the resultant album Bon had al-

ready written. The band has never confirmed exactly what scraps of paper he had left lying around, containing lyrics that would be sung by a man with a seemingly impossible task. How do you replace someone like Bon Scott? The names considered early on did not seem to have the 'X' factor AC/DC would need to continue Bon's legacy appropriately.

"I didn't join a band to be a casualty. There's a romantic myth that you should live fast and die young, the James Dean thing. AC/DC are here to disprove all that. We're hoping to get a pension." Angus Young

Among the candidates were Stevie Wright (ex–Easybeats), Alan Fryer (of the Australian band Future Heaven), Terry Wilson–Slesser (formerly of Back Street Crawler), Brian Johnson (previously in British hard rockers Geordie) and also Gary Holton (ex–Heavy Metal Kids). When Fryer auditioned, the Youngs and their comrades felt that he was too similar to Bon. Wright was ruled out almost by default; AC/DC didn't want to go backwards by taking the easy option and fitting in a friend from their past. Londoner Gary Holton had the cheeky charm of a true front man and his down–to–earth demeanour would have fitted in well against the buzzing backdrop of the AC/DC musicians. In the end, however, the group felt Holton would be too difficult to tame and could well turn out to be another Bon, in the sense of going off at the deep end.

In retrospect, it seems that the Youngs made the right decision in not hiring Holton. He was a great singer and entertainer, and had further success as an actor, appearing in the highly popular British TV series *Auf Wiedersehen Pet*. However, his private life was sadly marked by drug and alcohol abuse and he died at the age of 33. Holton had previously suffered a brain haemorrhage, which left him temporarily paralysed, blind and unable to speak, but he later recovered. He also had a near–fatal heart attack seven years before his death, but it was announced his death was down to heroin and alcohol ingestion.

For AC/DC, the job of finding a new vocalist wasn't easy but they narrowed down their choice of singers to a shortlist of two:

Terry Wilson–Slesser and Brian Johnson. The latter had been front man with Geordie, from the Northeast of England. A fiercely proud Newcastle native, Johnson, born on October 5th 1948, had enjoyed reasonable success with his band, especially in Britain. At the time of AC/DC's interest he was attempting to resurrect the outfit, who had split up in 1976.

Geordie had started under the name U.S.A. but the members soon gave themselves a moniker far closer to home. "I just wanted to be in a band," Johnson would say of his time with his fellow Tynesiders. "They were famous when I joined them. They were a great rock band at the time, but they let themselves be turned and twisted by the record company into a pop band. You know, all those big platforms shoes, all the silly shit I had to wear. And the trousers, I could've put a small African village in there. It was just terrible. But the songs, I knew I had a rock voice, and I just let go with the flow. I really didn't have much to say in the songs. When I looked at the lifestyles the boys had, it was just great. When I heard the stories, I went just nuts."

Geordie released several albums, including: *Hope You Like It* (1973), *Don't Be Fooled By The Name* (1974), and *Save The World* (1976). During this time, they gained popularity throughout Europe but gradually lost their footing as other, more glamorous looking acts hogged the spotlight. Geordie went the opposite way; Brian in particular sought to wear street clothes on stage. They would soon disband but after a few years, just before the interest from AC/DC Brian would go it alone with a new line up. He released the album *Geordie Featuring Brian Johnson*, which had new adaptations of several Geordie classics. To supplement his income Brian ran a vinyl car roofing business until 1980 as Geordie weren't always completely solvent and he had long had an interest in cars.

"In Geordie we would get up at 5 in the morning and follow the milkman around. We used to look in the window at Indian restaurants and wait for people to leave a half eaten meal just so we could run in and steal it. Jesus, the things we'd do. We never saw a penny from the records." Brian Johnson

It was an AC/DC fan that introduced the band to the talents of Brian Johnson. The ardent devotee from Chicago, Illinois posted the Leber–Krebs management a tape of the Geordie album *Hope You Like It*. The anonymous fan believed that Johnson's voice would suit AC/DC, and Peter Mensch thought Brian was at least worth an audition. Johnson tended to use the lower range of his voice with Geordie, and his performing style with the two groups is very different. Indeed, although both Geordie and AC/DC were loosely labelled as rock acts they were in fact rather different.

The tape from the fan was not the first occasion that Johnson had crossed the AC/DC radar. Geordie had once toured with Bon Scott and Fraternity, travelling throughout Europe together in 1973. Bon was impressed with Johnson's vocals, despite the Geordie singer being on less than top form. As Brian later explained explained: "We were in this horrible place up north on a horrible cold night and I had appendicitis. He was watching with his then band, Fraternity. I was in agony, I got carried out." Allegedly Bon also told Angus to give Johnson the job of vocalist if anything should ever happen to him.

Shortly before he died Bon happened to see Brian singing in a club, performing Little Richard covers. Angus remembered, "Bon played me Little Richard and then told me the story of when he saw Brian singing. And he says about that night, 'there's this guy up there screaming at the top of his lungs and then the next thing you know he hits the deck. He's on the floor, rolling around and screaming. I thought it was great, and then to top it off – you couldn't get a better encore – they came in and wheeled the guy off!'" Angus continued: "Bon had pointed Brian out, especially to me. Bon and me were great rock n' roll fans. Bon would always come in and give me a record of Jerry Lee Lewis or Little Richard, something that he bought in a record store and if I saw one, I would pick it up for him. Late at night, if we had a little get together, we always had on those records. He always told me the story of when he first saw Brian on stage."

"Bon loved being in this band. He said it gave him the chance to be himself for the first time in his life. And sometimes, even now when

we're recording, I do a double take because I can feel something, that Bon edge. Hopefully he's still plugging in and hearing what we're about." Angus Young

When Angus spoke about auditioning Brian, he did not mention the 'fan's tape' story, which suggests that it may be something of a rock myth. "Brian's name came up right away. The guy who was managing us at the time said, 'What do you wanna do? Are you gonna continue?' He suggested a list of people. At the time I said, 'Maybe check out this guy Brian and see what he's doing.' Maybe in hindsight, it was Bon's way of saying 'it'll never happen to me.'"

"I hadn't known about AC/DC long enough to have a pre-conception of them," Brian later said. "I was up there in Northern England and it was just six months before I auditioned for them that I first heard them. Malcolm Waley brought back an album, 'cause he'd seen them at the Newcastle May Fair and he said, 'You gotta fuckin' hear these! Fuck!'"

Brian came across AC/DC after witnessing the punk phenomenon. "I fuckin' don't get it. I know everybody's ranting and raving about it but I didn't like it at all. So with the boys there was something out there that was at least decent. You could tap your foot to it."

"At that time he is talking about the mid–seventies and we were giving punk a good name", Angus chipped in. "Because that was the word to describe us, a 'punk' band. They would get the wrong idea. We weren't a punk band but they would put us on the same bill as punk bands. They sure got a shock when they started spitting and we spat back. We were never ones getting tagged into a title or filed under: A, B, or C. We started as a rock n' roll band. That's what we play; that's what we do best. We never claimed to be anything else. And then, in the 1980, they would slump us as a heavy metal band. Even before that they had other things: power pop. Crap!"

"For ten years I've not only had the burden of carrying my wife and family, but also having people saying all the time that I've been wrong . So it's nice at the end of the day to turn around and say,

'well I might be a little bit late, I'm not exactly an overnight sensation, but...'" Brian Johnson

The pure rock n' roll ideology of AC/DC summed Brian up as much as it did the other members of the group. On the subject of musical trends, his response was: "You put all the names together and it spells bullshit." Angus concurred, "It's true. I mean, okay, the word 'blues' conjures up something definite. You know where you're going it says. But the heavy metal thing? I immediately think of men in armour. And then there's that split leg routine. You know what I mean? There's more to playing guitar that being able to do the splits while wearing a pair of tights. The heavy metal thing offended me more then the punk thing 'cause I thought, 'Jesus what have they conjured up now?' Then just because you call an album *Highway to Hell* you get all kinds of grief. And all we had done is describe what it's like to be on the road for four years, like we had been. A lot of it was bus and car touring with no break. You crawl off the bus at four in the morning, and some journalist is doing a story and says, 'what would you call an AC/DC tour?' Well it was a highway to hell. It really was. When you're sleeping with the singer's socks two inches from your nose, that's pretty close to hell." It was a Saturday night, less than a week after Brian auditioned with AC/DC, that Malcolm called him and told him he had the job. In fact, Angus had made the first call but Brian told him where to go, as he thought it was someone winding him up. With the singer in place, the band immediately set to work on their eighth album, flying to the Bahamas along with Mutt Lange in order to record at Compass Point Studios. It took them just six weeks to complete the recording of *Back In Black*, an album that was dedicated to Bon Scott. Everyone in AC/DC agreed the title was perfect. They also wanted a completely black front cover out of respect to Bon. Unfortunately the record company would not allow it. They did not care for sentiment or tribute; they simply decided it would be ludicrous to have an album cover without a title or the band's name on it. But a compromise was reached whereby the cover would be black apart from white outlines on the lettering of the AC/DC logo and title.

A decade later Metallica sold more than 15 million copies of their eponymous 5th album, housed in a sleeve virtually black all over.

Chris Gilbey remembers that just after he had joined the Alberts Company in 1973 he was to represent the Red Bus catalogue, and that included Johnson's band Geordie. "The band has changed – Brian made a big difference," says Gilbey. They got tougher – and perhaps more 'stadium'." Remembering those early days he recalls, "I helped arrange a tour for the band (Geordie) in Australia later that year – so it's a small world. And I met Brian before any of AC/DC's members had even heard of him or them, and certainly before he had heard of them."

While AC/DC were in Nassau recording their album it seemed simply enjoying themselves in a tropical setting wasn't an option. On the contrary they had to guard all equipment with six–foot long spears, which everyone in the group had for protection. "At the time they were having problems in Nassau," remembered Angus. "A few tourists had been killed on the beach and then we got robbed. We were all out there in these little huts... And the lady who used to come round who looked after the place, she had a big machete. She used to say, 'Listen, if anyone sticks their head through that door and you don't know them, chop it off.'" The tense atmosphere of a country in turmoil did not dampen AC/DC's enthusiasm. Despite the sad circumstances of his arrival, Johnson's presence had revitalised the band. By his own admission he was belting his lungs out for the chance to be in the famous group and he was clearly enjoying every minute of it. As for going to the Bahamas in the first place, Angus explained, "There were a lot of different reasons for us finally deciding to work out there. Tax was one of them, and another was the actual availability of studios. We wanted somewhere in England because the country has a great working atmosphere. We didn't really want to go over to Europe since most of the stuff from there tends to be disco. There was one in Sweden that Led Zeppelin used, but that belongs to ABBA, and at that point they themselves were using it. But we didn't want to hang around waiting, we just wanted to get on with it." The atmosphere in the Caribbean was hardly conducive to work, however. "It's actually very slow at Compass Point", continued the guitarist. "I mean, the studio itself is very good but the lifestyle is such that you tend to spend half the day lying around on the beach and having to work at night. But we didn't do that. Once we start working we want to get on." Suddenly finding himself among palm trees, sun and sand was quite a culture shock for the new singer, coming as he did from a humble background in chilly Newcastle upon Tyne. "I didn't like it," he mused, "and the lads hated it as well. And trying to do a rock n' roll album there…plus the fact that half the songs were half written and I'm sitting there thinking, 'Is this gonna work out right? If it doesn't work out right, I'm gonna be the biggest scapegoat the world's ever known.' If it didn't work out well, they could have just said, 'That was a waste of time', thrown it in the bin and said, 'Let's try with someone else.' That was all running through my mind because I didn't realise what I had taken on."

Brian need not have worried. As soon as the Atlantic management heard the material, all fears were alleviated. "I was so relieved at the end when the first phone call came through from the manager saying, 'Oh, great, brilliant'", remembered Brian. "And Atlantic phoned up and said, 'Fantastic, it's gonna do the business.' For three days when I came back from the Bahamas, I just sat in the chair at home and didn't move."

Even though Bon was absent, his spirit suffuses the album. It opens with the tolling of a huge church bell (a clear tribute), before the band kicks into 'Hells Bells'. Later, when this song became a live favourite with fans, AC/DC would add a two–ton bell to their stage show. Another homage to Scott was 'Have A Drink On Me', which some considered a little tasteless, considering the circumstances of Bon Scott's demise. However, it surely represented the sort of attitude that Bon would have appreciated, an attitude shared by his successor. "When I first joined the band, I came from Newcastle, and we are big drinkers up there" explained Brian about one of his favourite songs. "And the first thing I said to the lads was 'Come on, have a drink on me'. And the boys got the title from there. It's just my philosophy, if I meet new people; it always seems to be the best way to get to know them…'Come on lads, let's have a drink'. It just breaks barriers, anywhere in the world."

"The amazing thing about the older stuff is that when we do a song like 'Let There Be Rock' onstage, sometimes it seems like Bon's ghost is right up there with us. It's a very strange feeling. But we're sure that Bon would have wanted us to keep playing those numbers, and when you see the reaction from the fans, you know that they want us to keep playing them too." Brian Johnson

'You Shook Me All Night Long' was to be the first single lifted from the album. Johnson came up with the line "She was a fast machine, she kept her motor clean" when he decided that cars and women were very much alike – they go fast, let you down, but then make you happy again when you see a spruced up model. It became the first AC/DC song to make the US Top 40. When Johnson explained the meaning of the song, he compared his and Bon's songwriting styles. "I think Bon's songs were more like documentaries. They were very true to life. Mine were just instances of life put together. I mean the line from 'You Shook Me All Night Long'... 'knocking me out with the American thighs...' I hadn't been even in America at the time. But we were in the Bahamas and I had seen couple of American girls, they were just so beautiful. They were blond, bronzed, and tall... I'd never seen anyone that beautiful before. So I was just using my imagination, what I would do if I could. But Bon had done it all."

The title track of the album would become a defining moment for AC/DC, including one of the most memorable riffs in hard rock history. "Malcolm came to me once when we were on the *Highway to Hell* tour and said, 'I've got this riff and it's driving me nuts'" recalled Angus. "It's three o'clock in the morning and I'm trying to sleep and he's saying, 'Well what do you think of this?' I said, 'sounds fine to me.' And that was 'Back in Black.'" The band had already thought of the title before any of the music was actually written.

As for the lyrics, Brian would be the one given the responsibility of writing most of the words to accompany the increasingly catchy music the Young brothers were creating. Bon had several lyrical ideas strewn here and there but it was decided to begin again, or so the story goes. Former AC/DC manager Ian Jeffrey claims to have a folder containing lyrics of 15 songs written for *Back In Black* by Bon. But Angus would counter the insinuation that AC/DC used Bon's old lyrics, one of which had allegedly been 'Rock N' Roll Ain't Noise Pollution'. "A lot of people like to scrape barrels and take whatever they can when someone dies but we don't want that", Angus insisted. "It would be like using his death as a means to gain something. If we'd done things in the studio with him, we would possibly have used them, but it's probably best for him too that we won't. There's some stuff of his left, songs off other albums, 'cause we rejected them then and it would be just scraping the barrel. And that's possibly the worst thing that could happen."

A friend of Brian's in Newcastle thought his range of singing was too high on the album. Brian laughed later, "I'd taken my first copy of the album back home and his exact words were, 'They've ruined you, you're singing far too high'. My mate, my so–called fucking mate!" Of course he wasn't to know the album would become AC/DC's best selling and an absolute classic in the realms of rock music. Defying any particular category and keeping it breathtakingly simple yet effective, *Back In Black* was a supreme return and the most fitting tribute to Bon Scott. It is easy to imagine Bon singing most of the material on the album, even though he didn't even get a chance to hear it, but that's not to take away from Brian Johnson's ascendancy from his role as a 'bar band' singer to becoming frontman of one of the biggest rock acts of all time. With Johnson in place, *Back In Black* would eventually seal AC/DC's place in rock n' roll folklore but like many of the best products; it took time for everyone to come around to its charms. For some, Bon was always going to be impossible to replace. Brian Johnson gave the group a new sheen; he was completely different to Bon in terms of personality and sound.

For some, he was too different to be acceptable. Phil Sutcliffe of *Sounds* said: "Essentially I just don't like him. I don't mean anything personal against him. I'm not saying he's a nasty chap and he's obviously tried very hard to fit the bill, but I think his assessment of AC/DC's needs were wrong. It's quite a tribute to the rest of them that *Back In Black* remains a genuinely excellent AC/DC album."

Sutcliffe wasn't alone in his dislike for the new singer. It was too hard for some to overcome such a huge change in personnel. However he was among many journalists who completely under-estimated the Geordie vocalist. *Back In Black* could not have been a 'genuinely excellent' album if it were not for the talents of Brian Johnson. Yes, he screeched like a strangled cat and lent a gravel–voiced bark to even the subtlest of musical backings but he was an awesome carrier of a hard rock tune. Even Angus coined the phrase, "He sings like a truck is driving over his foot!" But Angus also knew that Brian's voice was melodic as well as loud, an advantage he probably had over Bon.

Johnson's impossible task was to replace the irreplaceable, a man who would always remain the archetypal AC/DC vocalist to many fans. It was not so much the existing fans of the group who became excited about *Back In Black*, but new listeners who had heard the story of the legends and become interested in how a New-castle singer wearing a flat cap, jeans and a tight vest was going to overcome the odds.

The catchy nature of the new material duly enticed poten-tial listeners to AC/DC's party and the sound had been refined fur-ther still by another Mutt Lange production special. Johnson had a stronger voice than Bon, and in many ways he turned AC/DC into a more powerful group. It wasn't long before even the non–believers were silenced as 'Jonna' took to his second unenviable task, replac-ing Bon Scott on stage. On July 1st 1980, Brian Johnson made his debut appearance in a live setting with AC/DC at Namur in Bel-gium.

"I remember the first night after we played," he said. "I'm not an emotional person by any stretch of the imagination. But the kids had this forty–foot long banner right across the audience, which read 'The king is dead, long live the king.' And it was smashing. It was great. And then we went to England and the kids were chanting because they knew how I felt. They knew I was scared."

He found out just how accepting the AC/DC fans really were. "Everybody's been dead nice," he affirmed. "I was expecting a few people to maybe say something bad, but nobody has…from the first gig – and you've got to remember we were doing tracks off *Back*

In Black and nobody had heard them – the reaction was great. It was nice that as the tour progressed, the album went straight up the charts, and people started to know the songs."

'DC soon filmed promotional video clips for *Back In Black* which were shot in Breda, Holland. The purpose of the films was simply to show Johnson and the band performing together. The videos were short on visual stimulation but the music covered up for the lack of finesse in the presentation.

From July to October the group would embark on their first major tour with Brian Johnson. Travelling across the United States and Canada was a blunt initiation into the AC/DC world. Johnson not only had to contend with working on a much larger scale than he had been used to with Geordie, but dealing with the expectations of fans who worried he might not live up to Bon Scott onstage. On every one of the 64 dates Johnson proved he was the right choice and a logical replacement. AC/DC were supported by the likes of Streetheart, Gamma, Humble Pie, Def Leppard, Nantucket, Krokus, Johnny Van Zant, Blackfoot and Saxon. For the last time, when playing in Toledo, Ohio they played as support act to another band, when they went on before ZZ Top.

"I like the bell 'cos it makes a brilliant sound and it was fitting for the time we went through after Bon's death and Back in Black and so on. It was part of the situation at the time. Those cannons I'm not sure about. If it was a real cannon out there and we could blow everyone's brains out, then that would be great." Malcolm Young

Back In Black was released worldwide on July 31 1980. Within a couple of weeks, it was top of the UK charts and it stayed at number 1 for two weeks. In November, it reached number 4 in the American charts and remained in the top ten for over five months. In Australia, it reached number 2.

Towards the end of the year it was Europe's turn to experience the newly inspired AC/DC. The group sold out every one of 24 UK tour dates; this included six shows in London with three at the legendary Hammersmith Odeon. They then played a further 24 dates covering Denmark, Norway, Sweden, Germany, France and Switzerland. For this tour they were supported by the increasingly popular Whitesnake, as well as Midnight Flyer vocalist Maggie Bell. Soon AC/DC would throw a party at London's 'Cockney Pride' pub in Haymarket to celebrate the mammoth achievement of reaching the 10 million mark in albums sold worldwide. By the end of the year, all AC/DC albums had been certified gold in France. *Back In Black* was certified platinum and sales had totalled 2 million in France alone. It was a remarkable triumph for the band to have overcome such hardship and in defiance, create a rock masterpiece. They had received their fair share of ups and downs already in their short career but bounced back to begin a new era, with *Back In Black* the catalyst and Brian Johnson the master of ceremonies.

But perhaps the most lasting achievement of the album was the way Johnson had been accepted and nurtured by AC/DC. "They're a great band and a great bunch of lads," Brian would state in 1982. "I know what they were going through when Bon went, wondering about going on and all that – it's only natural. And they are people; you don't just walk away and forget that sort of thing. But they never made me feel left out."

BACK IN BLACK FACTS

The album has sold over 40 million copies worldwide.

Bon originally played drums on the demo tracks, 'Have A Drink On Me' and 'Let Me Put My Love Into You'.

AC/DC played the song 'Back In Black' when they were inducted into the Rock And Roll Hall Of Fame by Steven Tyler of Aerosmith (he sang the song with the band) in 2003.

It is not uncommon for the album to be given to strippers and lap dancers when they first enrol in a club to perform. The title track tends to be used often in strip acts.

The Hollywood movie A Knight's Tale features the track 'Back In Black' playing over the end credits.

The Beastie Boys sampled 'Back In Black' on their 1985 single 'Rock Hard'. AC/DC refused the New York trio permission to release the song on their 1999 Sounds of Science compilation.

The Atlanta Falcons American football team used 'Back In Black' as their theme song for a while.

Chapter 11 – Twenty–One–Gun Salute

"We're just a battery for hire with a guitar fire
Ready and aimed at you.
Pick up your balls and load up your cannon
For a twenty–one–gun salute.
For those about to rock – fire...We salute you"

It was always going to be difficult for AC/DC to follow a landmark album such as *Back In Black*. They did it they only way they knew how, by heading out on the road and then, at the end of their massive tour (which concluded with 14 dates in France, Spain and Belgium) going back into the studio. In every country the band visited they converted fans to the Brian Johnson live experience. He could never replace Bon but nobody knew that better than the Geordie fellow himself. Such was AC/DC's sensitivity regarding Bon Scott in fact that at one stage the issue of songs to avoid performing was addressed. Initially the musicians did not want to play songs like 'The Jack' with any singer other than Bon. As Brian explained, "We thought it was a bit too personal, the way Bon sang it and the personal connotations it had for him. But then about two weeks before we left America, we started to do it and nobody seemed to mind at all. And we did it in England and nobody seemed to mind, and that was it. We thought, 'From now on there's nothing that we can't do because the kids will accept it.' They're just pleased that AC/DC have kept going. It's been too easy actually."

The whole experience with the band had been easy, according to the new singer. After time with a group like Geordie, joining an outfit as laidback as AC/DC was always going to be "easy as piss", as Brian put it. "It's the easiest band I've ever joined. In other bands it always took time to get to know people. But in this band, it was always just like going out to the pub and having a drink with a few mates. All that shit about joining a band after somebody else had passed away was just something that anybody would have had to deal with in that situation. I'd be a real wimp if I said, 'Oh, I can't take the pressure. I can't go on.'"

Backstage, the scene was hardly one of debauchery, as it was in the old days of the group. Whether Johnson's influence or Bon's unfortunate demise had calmed things down, there was no excess or substance abuse behind closed doors as far as AC/DC was concerned in 1981. In fact, the worst possible extravagance was a spot of gambling. As Brian Johnson explained, "You've got the old dartboard, in the bar. The great thing is when you go backstage first of all, and you're playing darts; those 5,000 or 20,000 kids waiting for you don't seem like such a threat any more. Because you're worrying about getting through to the next round of the darts final…at ten dollars a head, why that's two hundred pounds. It's good because it makes it feel a little bit like home."

Talking of road life Johnson went on to admit: "The pace does really start to cripple you, you start not being able to go to sleep until seven in the morning. Your whole life is just totally knocked on the head. You snap out of it when the curtains open; you hear the crowd starting to go crazy, you realise this is for real. And you've got to get down to some hard work."

"It's like AC/DC, they've become successful but they've still managed to remain honest, regular sort of guys. They're our sort of group, a sort of no–nonsense, get–down–and–do–it group. Like us, they're down to earth. And I'm gonna make sure we stay that way"
Paul Di'Anno (of Iron Maiden, 1981)

The tour ended in late January. When they performed at the Brussels Forest National venue they invited Atlantic Records' Phil Carson to play on 'Lucille', where he took over from Cliff Williams. This would be the only time a guest musician would share a stage with AC/DC. The band was gaining momentum, travelling to places they had only ever dreamed of playing, such as Japan. But the tour was to be remembered for all the wrong reasons. After a show in Brisbane, at least one car, possibly more, was set on fire by fans. The problems followed AC/DC to Melbourne. After the gig at the Myer Music Bowl there were 23 arrests made after a riot, which lasted around half an hour. The following day, once more after the gig over 60 people were arrested. 30 suburban trains and dozens of trees around the bowl were damaged. About 50 youths fought each other at the Princes Bridge Station. Hospitals were packed with people who had suffered drug overdoses, broken limbs and lacerations.

In amongst the mayhem, the members of AC/DC were developing a new version of their trusty sound. The album that would become *For Those About To Rock...We Salute You* was an updated form of the original Acca Dacca blueprint. The songs were becoming more boogie–orientated and even more humorous. There was no insinuation that AC/DC was not a serious band any longer, but they seemed to be having a looser time on record and having more fun creating their material. Some would even cite the material they recorded in the early 80's as throwaway, as the boys struggled to maintain the momentum of *Back In Black*. It is inarguable that *Back In Black* was an incredibly strong record, and one that deserved its huge sales figures. In fact, AC/DC was in a difficult position in having to follow it. Their task was even more impossible than having to follow Bon's departure because they had already proved it could be done, but they did it to such a degree that following the greatest rock album in decades would be almost unattainable.

"Whatever I did on Back In Black I want to keep on doing it. It sold 12 million albums and I'm chuffed to bits! But with the new one, you can never be complacent. You can't sit back and say 'hey the last one worked.' It's still up to the kids whether they buy it or tell you to piss off and try again. Don't try to bullshit us. But I've done my best." Brian Johnson

AC/DC started recording the sessions at EMI Pathé Marconi studios in Paris, but after two weeks decided to move to a rehearsal studio, called H.I.S. just outside Paris. The backing tracks were laid down in the Mobile One Studio. "We came to Paris and went into Pathé Marconi, which must be a good studio 'cos a lot of bands use it, but it just wasn't right for us," explained Johnson. "We went in thinking it was okay, but when we tried to get that live sound we wanted on an album, it just didn't happen."

Mutt Lange had decided after a fortnight that the group was "missing the point" and the normally laidback proceedings had become too much like "hard work." The vocals were recorded at Family Sound Studio later. The sessions for *For Those About To Rock...We Salute You* lasted until September. Just before the band finished recording the album, they parted company with manager Peter Mensch, but remained with the management firm, Leber–Krebs. Mensch would go on to even greater success as co–manager of Metallica.

The previous year had seen the inaugural Monsters of Rock festival at Castle Donington in the East Midlands of England. It was such a huge success that the format was revived in 1981. By this time AC/DC's standing in the rock world was such that the band was asked to headline the prestigious event. The show would attract 65,000 fans, and featured the increasingly fashionable Whitesnake as well as Slade, Blue Oyster Cult and Blackfoot. The compere was Tommy Vance, presenter of the *Friday Rock Show* on BBC Radio One. "Sometimes it's frightening", Angus said when being asked about playing to a huge Donington audience, "But you've got to psyche yourself up a little bit. Being older, Malcolm's the best person to give me a kick. He'll just say to me 'Those feet look a little slow tonight'. Usually once I've got the uniform on I'm okay. I'm on edge, nervous, but I'm not in a panic. At least I don't have to put on make up. I sport my own pimples!"

The title track of the band's new album would be a defining feature in their future live shows, giving them an opportunity to indulge in mini–pyrotechnics. They would let off two cannons and fireworks as Johnson screamed "Fire!" In fact a cannon would be the main focus of the album cover art, backed by the AC/DC logo. It wasn't the most inspiring of sleeves, but then AC/DC did not need to be too elaborate, as the album and song title explained, along with the lyrics. "Hail hail to the good times, 'cause rock has got the right of way, we ain't no legend, ain't no cause, we're just livin' for today," sings Brian. This was a humble statement, a response to the critics and fans who suddenly defined the group as 'legends' after *Back In Black*.

Certainly the members of AC/DC did not see themselves as legendary; they were playing rock music pure and simple. *For Those About To Rock We Salute You* is therefore a relatively simple and straightforward rock n' roll opus. It is almost deliberately so, given the hype surrounding the band at the time. Brian Johnson was now settled into the group and could inject more of his own personality into the lyrics and the delivery of his vocal lines, which in turn made the album far rawer than its predecessor. Despite the unrefined aura, Mutt Lange's production somehow managed to keep the record ticking over with a metronomic efficiency and a cool commercial sheen.

"Punk and all that was just an image that ripped people off. Johnny Rotten is a wanker, and that's all there is to it." Brian Johnson

Angus said of writing basic rock music: "People have said we've hung around long enough! Some bands fade when they try to adapt to what is current. We play rock music. It's a little too late for us to do a ballad. Rock is what we do best. Sometimes I'm asked if I want to play music other than AC/DC. Sure, at home I play a little blues, but after five minutes I'm like, 'Sod this!' and I'm playing hard rock again."

The album title itself was somewhat historically based. "We had this chorus riff and we thought 'Well this sounds rather deadly,'" Angus remembered. "We were trying to find a good title and there's this book from years ago about Roman gladiators called 'For Those About To Die We Salute You'. So we thought 'For Those About To Rock…' I mean, it sounds better than 'for those about to die'. Actually that song's got a lot of meaning to it. It's a very inspiring song. It makes you feel a bit powerful and I think that's what rock n' roll is all about."

The band's interest in matters historical was spilling over into their songwriting. Brian Johnson was fascinated by military history, and 'Night of the Long Knives' refers to the night of June 29/30, 1934, when Hitler authorised the liquidation of upper echelon of the SA (Sturmabteilung, also known as the Brownshirts), a paramilitary group associated with his Nazi Party, as well as other figures who has incurred his displeasure. After this date, Heinrich Himmler's SS became the dominant uniformed group in German politics. In the song, Johnson sings: "Who's your leader, who's your man? Who will help you fill your hand? Who's your friend and who's your foe? Who's your Judas, you don't know?"

The song was something of an anomaly; elsewhere on the album, the lyrics revolved around women, sex and rock n' roll. Much closer to the standard AC/DC template was 'Evil Walks', about a woman who had not endeared herself to Brian Johnson. He sings: "Black widow weavin' evil notions, Dark secrets bein' spun in your web, Good men goin' down in your ocean, They can't swim 'cause they're tied to your bed."

Perhaps the most impromptu moment comes in the line "I sometimes wonder where you park your broom," which Johnson reels off as if it were unplanned, giggling manically.

"As the name says, evil walks – it's everywhere!" Angus said of the inspiration behind the song. "When we were playing it at the beginning I said, 'those chords sounds dead evil.' And that's how we do it, just sitting around and nattering and jamming away. And someone says something like 'evil walks' and that's it."

Powerful rock n' roll was exactly what AC/DC were all about. So much so, that they were actually referred to as 'heavy metal' in the very first issue of *Kerrang!* Magazine, which hit the shelves in June 1981. Initially the magazine was intended to be a one – off heavy metal special produced by the music weekly *Sounds*. It quickly became a monthly publication in its own right, and is now a weekly, thriving long after its original parent publication bit the dust.

"We never thought of ourselves as a 'heavy metal band'. We've always regarded ourselves as a rock band. The big difference is we've always thought we had a lot more feel for rock, we always went out for songs, not riffs or heavy, heavy sounds. But every now and again it does come on like a sledge hammer." Angus Young

Readers of the magazine had voted for their top 100 heavy metal tracks of all time, and as AC/DC were clear winners for their

'Whole Lotta Rosie' track, editor Geoff Barton decided to place Angus Young on the front cover. From then on the group would be termed 'heavy metal' more than rock n' roll. It's not difficult to see why readers didn't see too much distinction. Loud rock n' roll was essentially the basis of heavy metal, and AC/DC fit the remit of long–haired, angry sounding, sweaty oiks who liked nothing more than playing as loud as was possible.

This meant that the band was popular throughout the top 100 poll, scoring hits with 'Walk All Over You', 'Hell's Bells', 'Highway To Hell', 'Touch Too Much', and 'Let There Be Rock'. They even topped the tracks that were 'bubbling under' the hundred, having three songs in the 10. These were 'Back In Black', 'Shot Down In Flames' and 'Sin City'. Angus for one was not initially flattered at making the magazine front cover however. As he recalls, "When I saw the first edition of *Kerrang!* with my picture on the cover I thought the magazine was a piss take. A lot of people call me Ang, you see…"

It is clear that in 1981 many defined heavy metal in a markedly different manner than they would in the late '80s and the '90s. For instance, Lynyrd Skynyrd, Queen, Pink Floyd, Hawkwind, Free and even The Beatles were in the top hundred chart. Metal was simply considered to be the dirtier end of rock music, and many would shy away from it because of its connotations (music played by sweaty men wearing denim). It was perhaps this image that dissuaded a number of loud rock bands from embracing the label. Even the likes of Rush, Led Zeppelin, ZZ Top and Meat Loaf would have had a strong argument against being labelled as heavy metal.

Those happy to be included in the genre, and also on the list, included Iron Maiden, Black Sabbath and Diamond Head. The lines would later be blurred by *Kerrang!* in a bizarre fashion, as the magazine would eventually produce issues with the likes of Prince and Phil Collins on the front cover!

By the turn of the century *Kerrang!* would successfully update itself to become less of a metal and hard rock publication and associate itself with garage, punk, hardcore, indie, and even pop bands. AC/DC seemingly never fitted into any category but they always had their dedicated fans. If a poll were constructed in 2005 of the top metal tunes, it would certainly feature a far broader list of entrants but would doubtless still include Iron Maiden and Black Sabbath. Perhaps there might not be a place for AC/DC; but if one were to produce a list of the greatest heavy rock songs ever, the band would flood the chart as they did in '81.

"AC/DC are the best at what they do. It's as simple as that. I wouldn't say that I like everything they have done, but in their own way they are as classic a band as Led Zeppelin or Deep Purple..." Tony Iommi, Black Sabbath

In December 1981 AC/DC played their first ever headline concert at New York's Madison Square Garden, completing a superb two years of productivity and a final clarification that they had truly made it in America. Johnson was by now established as their vocalist and had now co–authored 20 songs. Things were looking good.

However, this was the same month in which a line from 'Dirty Deeds Done Dirt Cheap' came back to haunt the band (see Chapter 5). A couple from Chicago tried to sue the group for $250,000, claiming harassment in the form of obscene phone calls. Luckily the band was acquitted; how was Bon to know it was a real number and, furthermore, whose number it was?

THE MEANINGS BEHIND *FOR THOSE ABOUT TO ROCK WE SALUTE YOU*

"We're never going to win any Grammy awards. We're never gonna win any respect from the squeaky clean mob and Rolling Stone or everybody like that, because we don't give any messages out that they think are important." Brian Johnson

'Put The Finger On You' – Angus: "That's basically a gangster line, like they do in the movies. We're not putting the finger on anyone in particular, it's always the other way round!" The title came about after Brian had been watching an old James Cagney film one early morning. In a scene, Cagney turns to Humphrey Bogart and says, 'Watch it buster, or I'm going to put the finger on you.'

'Inject The Venom' – Angus: "That's a power thing. It's rather like the title track; it means 'Have it hot.' Do it once, do it hard and good or you're finished. It's a real rock and roll line." Brian: "There's a line that says 'If you inject the venom it will be your last attack', which is like a snake. Once it bites you, it's got nothing left."

'Snowballed' – Angus: "Meaning, you've been conned, fooled again. And we figured we've been tricked enough in our time, so we came up with that. It could be the woman you're paying alimony to, anything."

'Let's Get It Up' – Brian: "Filth. Pure filth. We're a filthy band!"

'C.O.D.' – Angus: "Most people think of. C.O.D. as 'cash on delivery' or 'cash on demand'. I was sitting around trying to come up with a better one, and I came up with 'Care Of The Devil.' But we're not black magic Satanists or whatever you call it. I don't drink blood. I may wear black underwear now and then but that's about it."

141

'Spellbound' – Brian: "It's about when you get one of those days where it's like a trance. It's hard to describe really but that's 'Spellbound'. We set it to a man driving a car, blinded by a bright beam. But it could be any situation. I'm sure there's some deep Americans who can tell you what we're talking about!"

Angus: "That's a tricky one. It's a slower one for us but we liked it anyhow. It's one of those moody ones. It's so simple; it's like being naughty. Like peeking through the keyhole at somebody changing their knickers or something. Nothing bad. We're just pranksters more than anything. You're having fun and that's all there is."

'Breaking The Rules' – Angus: "It's like when someone says, 'you can't do that.' They were always saying that to me at school. You do it anyhow."

SOUNDS, KERRANG! AND THE NEW WAVE OF BRITISH HEAVY METAL

Many have argued it was the Sounds Heavy Metal Special that propelled heavy metal into the mainstream, at least in the United Kingdom. For the first time, the metal scene was covered in a glossy mag that was on the shelves of main- stream newsagents throughout the country. Although it was planned as a one–off, it spawned Kerrang! magazine, which is now approaching 25 years of existence.

However the editor of Sounds (and original editor of Ker- rang!), Geoff Barton almost missed the boat in terms of cov- ering a specific offshoot of metal. Indeed the 'Heavy Metal Special' was primarily a focus on the New Wave Of British Heavy Metal (more commonly known as NWOBHM) but as a movement this had all but died out by 1981, the year the magazine was produced.

The peak period for NWOBHM was 1979–1981. In the late 70s, disco was the dominant musical genre in Britain, but punk rock was also at its height. Inspired perhaps by the DIY punk ethic and the idea that you could learn how to play your instrument as you went along, many heavy rock bands began to form throughout Britain at this point. Buoyed by the success of homegrown talent such as Status Quo, Thin Lizzy, Led Zeppelin, UFO, Nazareth, Judas Priest and Black Sabbath, many outfits began to form, mostly in the larger cities of England. Though they were often influenced by im- ported bands such as Aerosmith, Kiss, Rush and indeed AC/ DC, the groups who formed in Britain were unmistakably British in both appearance and sound.

Bands who had formed in the mid to late seventies were given the opportunity to reach a nationwide listening audi- ence every week when the BBC gave a slot to Tommy Vance and his Friday Rock Show at the tail end of 1978. The show was a haven for rock and metal acts. Vance played current and classic rock vinyl, but the real success of the show for groups and listeners alike came in the form of specially recorded sessions, featuring a mixture of new and established acts.

Due to the show's success and the burgeoning presence of homegrown acts such as Def Leppard, Iron Maiden and Girlschool, towards the middle of 1979 certain journalists picked up on an exciting time for British rock music. It was Geoff Barton who coined the phrase 'NWOBHM' but the movement was all but over by the time he did so.

The scene itself hit a peak and was relatively short lived; however there are many acts that continue to play a style most commonly linked to the NWOBHM. The term itself has become much broader in meaning, and much British guitar –based music owes something to the genre. This is the reason many cite 79–81 as the prime period for the scene, as simply at this time there was less cynicism surrounding the marketing of a 'scene' and it was generally a more exciting time for British rock.

Like many trends, the NWOBHM burned itself out, with too many bands all vying for a piece of the action and as many began to play the style of music for the sake of it, all but die-hard devotees became jaded.

Only a small minority of bands that were identified as part of NWOBHM made it to any level of mainstream success, to the extent that some purists decided they were no longer 'true NWOBHM'. These acts included Maiden and Leppard, as well as Saxon and Samson.

As far as AC/DC were concerned, both the punk and NWOB-HM scenes were helpful to their career. In essence, the group were certainly not part of either movement, yet their sound intrinsically contained elements of both and thus appealed to fans of each genre. They were closest to NWOBHM in many respects but the fact they were not entirely British meant they were never likely to assume a role in the scene. Doubtless many would like to have included AC/DC as part of the genre yet geographical sticking points and a refusal to bow to any 'trends' marked them out for a different role altogether.

There is also the assertion that, due to 'DC's already successful career they had inadvertently taken themselves out of the running by the time they moved to England. In many respects perhaps there was an element of snobbery at work, with some fans claiming AC/DC as their own whilst being too proud to contend they could really be part of a New Wave Of British Heavy Metal. Effectively, the band were thriving when they made the move whereas acts like Iron Maiden were gradually working their way through the small bars of East London. Indeed AC/DC were themselves performing in tiny pubs as well, but their Australian success and adopted nationality gave them the ability to negotiate current fads. This in many ways is part of the reason 'DC managed to become a sensation in Britain on their own terms, and remain popular in the country for years to come.

THE MEANING OF METAL

'Heavy metal' is now a well–established term and most seem to think they understand its connotations. The origins of the musical movement stretch as far back as early blues.

However, a few key artists and recordings are generally identified as pioneers of the genre. Steppenwolf's 'Born To Be Wild' containing the line 'heavy metal thunder!' is often labelled as the Rosetta Stone of metal, although the phrase itself was probably borrowed from the writer William S. Burroughs in his 1962 novel The Soft Machine. Others see the heavy guitar playing behind The Kinks' 'All Day And All Of The Night' and 'You Really Got Me' to be indicative of the shape heavy rock music would soon take. Even the likes of The Beatles, with 'Helter Skelter' were considered protagonists. In fact many heavy blues–based rock bands have a stake in the terming of metal: The Yardbirds, Cream and Jimi Hendrix have all, at some stage, been identified as being metal role models. There is also an argument for American acts such as Blue Cheer, The Stooges and MC5.

Most would agree that the first bands to base their careers around what might be described as heavy metal were the likes of Led Zeppelin, Deep Purple, Uriah Heep and of course, Black Sabbath. However, there is little in common between the bands, other than long hair and prominent guitar players and vocalists. Though in their own ways, Zeppelin, Heep and Purple ripped into some serious heavy rock during their long careers none were deliberately aiming to be heavy metal and it was an area the groups merely dabbled in. With Black Sabbath however, the term would finally come into its own and create a true meaning to heaviness within rock music. The innovative guitar playing of Tony Iommi, with immensely weighty riffs and structures, along with the whiny, sombre singing of Ozzy Osbourne brought Sabbath roaring out of record players throughout the U.K., and soon the world. Thanks to Sabbath's originality and unexpected commercial success there were soon large swathes of musicians eager to follow their lead, with many prompted to mimic the Iommi guitar style in particular.

While bands such as Motorhead and Venom certainly added new slants on the heavy form of music, injecting greater speed and harsher vocals, they followed much later than Black Sabbath. Perhaps more importantly, Motorhead in particular, much like AC/DC, sought to distance themselves from metal, claiming instead to be a rock n' roll band. It was merely an offshoot of their energy and intensity that they could claim to have influenced thousands of straight heavy metal bands who were to follow.

Metal has inevitably spawned any number of variants over the years. There are many similarities with hard rock and many bands have been classified under both headings; for example, Aerosmith, Whitesnake, UFO and Uriah Heep. In the end, 'heavy metal' and 'hard rock' defy short and simple definitions; it is probably most useful to list a selection of bands, and to pinpoint where in the spectrum they stand, at least as far as this book is concerned.

HEAVY METAL: Black Sabbath, Judas Priest, Metallica, Megadeth, Pantera, Machine Head, Anthrax.

HARD ROCK: Kiss, Van Halen, Aerosmith, Poison, Motley Crue, Skid Row.

As far as AC/DC are concerned, they probably belong in neither genre. They are simply a rock band. In fact it is difficult to come up with a convincing argument as to why a band that insists they are not heavy metal, and have not been influenced in any way by the bands within the genre, should be considered part of it. To generalise, metal tends to be based around minor chords, distortion pedals, the harsh realities of life and most of all, aggression. While AC/DC have dab-

bled in all these prerequisites, it is certainly not essential
to their work as a group and, as they have all individually
stated over the years, 'DC is simply not part of heavy metal.

Chapter 12 – The Wright Stuff

"The biggest bonus about being in this band is the fact that I can get into their gigs without paying for a fucking ticket, honestly! Now and again I've forgotten I'm singing and I just stop and watch the band because I think they're just fucking great!" Brian Johnson 1982

In New Haven, Connecticut on the *For Those About To Rock* tour, AC/DC were forced to drop the title track of their latest album from their live set after warnings from the police. The band's road crew, as well as tour manager Ian Jeffery were handcuffed whilst the authorities decided whether or not to arrest the members of the group. The apparent problem was the explosion AC/DC were due to create at the appropriate point in the song. To make things smoother they at first agreed not to play the song at all. When they realised the crowd would have been baffled at the absence of one of their most important songs they thought of a compromise. And so Ian Jeffery operated a Prophet Synthesizer to simulate the sound of cannons in any venues where the firing was restricted.

Playing in America had plenty of upsides for the road crew, and for one or two members of AC/DC, but Brian Johnson for one, was not about to be caught with his pants down with any groupies, whose numbers were increasing in direct proportion to the rising popularity and success of the band.

His response to female attention was dismissive to say the least. "You never fuck them!" he told *Sounds*, "You leave them alone. There are nasty diseases going around America. You shake hands and that's it. That's for the crew – they're the ones with back-stage passes, not us! We have good clean fun you know – a quick game of cards and all that. I'm saying nothing. Me, I'm married with two kids… thing is, though, these gigs in America. The boys were sitting around the dressing room last week and saying that this is the first time they've actually heard girls scream at them. Because in England it's nearly all lads. Most of the audience is fellas in

America as well, but since we started this tour there's been a lot of girls. I don't know; I think it's because we're on the radio so much. I don't think it can be my good looks…"

He may have been on the right track concerning radio audiences in America. After all, their previous touring partners Def Leppard were to break the country on the back of extended radio play, finding more lingering females than they could count because of their popularity on the airwaves. Perhaps Brian Johnson was right, as it's possible some came along not knowing what the band even looked like!

"I don't think any bastard knows who I am anyway, so I never have any trouble getting mobbed off stage. And look at Brian; do you know what some hotel cleaner said to him the other day? She asked him if he was Neil Diamond or his twin brother." Malcolm Young

"That was the final bleedin' insult! Kevin Keegan I wouldn't have minded, but bloody Neil Diamond…" Brian Johnson

"Funny thing is, we've been going great on this tour," continued Brian. "All the gigs have sold out, real big places too. Last time we played Indianapolis we played to about 4,000. Tonight what is there, 17,000? And it's brand new audiences. But it's funny here tonight playing songs like 'Sin City', because it shows in their faces that they don't know what the fuck it is! The only albums they've bought so far are *Highway To Hell, Back In Black* and *Dirty Deeds Don't Dirt Cheap.*

In June of 1982 AC/DC played Japan for the last time, giving the fans four dates on which to catch them. Just after this the band left their management firm Leber–Krebs. It was tour manager, Ian Jeffrey who took over as the group's personal manager. Come September AC/DC gave their thanks to the United Kingdom with a tour across the U.K. and Ireland, comprising 19 dates. This included four sold–out shows at the Hammersmith Odeon and two dates, also capacity, at Wembley Arena. Towards the end of the year, continuing their friendship with French band Trust, and their special affiliation with Paris, AC/DC were present at the group's show at the Rose

Bonbon Club in the capital and Angus even joined them on stage for an impromptu jam.

At the end of 1982, *Kerrang!* published the results of their readers' poll. AC/DC were voted 'Top Band', Angus was 'Top Guitarist', Cliff was 'Top Bassist', the band were voted as having produced the 'Best Live Gig' and 'For Those About To Rock' was the 'Best Single'. Brian was third top male vocalist, Phil was second best drummer, 'Let's Get It Up' finished sixth best single and Angus was, bizarrely, in second place in the 'Male Pin–Up' category. Never mind that *Kerrang!* was still basically a heavy metal magazine, AC/DC were clearly top of the readers' requirements however the music was actually defined.

"Once you're on stage you can't go back, even when things go wrong people expect you to stay there and entertain them. When all else fails, you've got to try tap dancing." Angus Young

At the beginning of 1983 the band took a well–deserved break. They did not even begin to compose any new material for several months before finally reconvening to start work on the follow up to *For Those About To Rock...We Salute You*. They again travelled to the Bahamas to begin recording sessions in the Compass Point Studios in Nassau. It was at this point that the drug problems, as yet unknown to the world at large, of drummer Phil Rudd were becoming problematic. On the 'Cannon And Bell' World tour promoting *For Those About To Rock*, Rudd had been hallucinating and claiming that there were strangers hiding in his room waiting to attack him. He also had become embroiled in a personal spat with Malcolm and eventually the two traded blows, before Rudd finally received his marching orders. After leaving AC/DC, Phil Rudd started a flying business in New Zealand while continuing to play in a private studio. Angus commented to *Kerrang!* in 1990, "He's not sheep farming – sheep shagging maybe! Nah, someone told me he's flying choppers. He put some money into a helicopter business. He passed on a message to us through George that he was thankful that things worked out the way they did. He would have gone the way of Bon and I think he was grateful for his sanity."

Regarding the exact reasons for the split with Rudd, Angus would say with some understatement later, "Well, he liked a good time, that's for sure. Phil could have his crazy stages but the biggest change I saw in him was when Bon died. He couldn't take it so well because, as a band, things had been that tight between us, it was pretty thick. We had done a lot together; lived in a house together, set up all the gear together, slept with the same women – at the same time! When Bon died it hit him harder than anyone. He really thought that I in particular wouldn't be doing it any more. So when we carried on he thought that the early thing, the tightness, had gone, which wasn't the case. He was going for the high life and I think it caught up with him in the end. If he hadn't have stopped he could have gone overboard and done something drastic either to himself or someone else. I mean if you ever got in a car with Phil it was close to the edge, that's the kind of person he was."

Angus always gave Rudd credit for his role in AC/DC. "He was a great drummer," said the guitarist. "You couldn't get Phil to do a drum roll and that was his charm. He'd just sit there going, 'Wham! Wham! Wham!' That was his style. I think he's one of the great rock drummers."

Former Procol Harum drummer B.J. Wilson was asked to help finish the album the band were working on but his parts were actually never used. All in all 'DC recorded 13 tracks for the record, which would be called *Flick Of The Switch*. However the actual release only contained ten songs; the other three were left aside, and have not since been released in any form. For the first time AC/DC themselves would man the production controls, although they were assisted by Harry Vanda and George Young.

"We don't know what people are saying about us. We just like being in the womb of the road. That's the greatest thing for us; going from gig to gig...we don't even hear ourselves much on the radio. Every time I turn on the radio, I hear some band like Styx, and I quickly turn it off. That's not rock n' roll; that's show business."
Angus Young

The result was a strong album; some even felt it was more solid than its predecessor, and it contained several songs that would become classics in the band's repertoire. The cover was classic AC/DC schoolboy high–jinks; a drawing of Angus about to pull down a huge lever, presumably preparing to unleash the 'Rising Power' of the sturdy opening track. 'This House Is On Fire', 'Nervous Shake-down', 'Bedlam In Belgium' were all steadfast 'DC numbers and the production was just as heavy as before. It appeared the group's decision not to use Mutt Lange for *Flick Of The Switch* had been fully vindicated; what they had yearned for was a stripped down sound.

They were aiming for the raw and spontaneous edge of their early work with an additional few years of experience and know–how. It seemed to ooze from the speakers on every track. "The album is a really good rock album, that's all it is," reckoned Brian Johnson. "We weren't trying to do anything else, we just wanted another album that would burn! It's a little different this time, because we didn't have a producer, but that turned out to be an advantage. It was like, we had our own thoughts and there was no outside influence to stop us. It was a struggle at times to produce ourselves but that was half the fun of it. We found ourselves getting trapped by producers who wanted something different from us, so this time we thought, 'Bollocks to 'em. We'll do it ourselves!'"

The title had been changed from its original, which was *I Want To Rock* (surely too simplistic even for AC/DC) according to *Kerrang!* magazine. After *For Those About To Rock* surely they would have been more creative? Nevertheless, *Kerrang!* were not able to avoid some kind of hoax. Indeed they again got it wrong when in July they announced a possible replacement for Phil Rudd. It was supposedly Roxy Music and Angelic Upstarts' drummer Paul Thompson. In fact, after answering an advert in *Sounds* Magazine (the ad read 'Heavy Rock drummer wanted. If you don't hit hard, don't apply') and playing with the band at an audition in Nomis Studios in London, the new sticksman was named as Simon Wright.

He was 20 years old at the time but was already an experienced musician and he could certainly hit hard. Born in Manchester, he remained in the North–West of England with a band named Tora

Tora, who released just one self–financed single, 'Red Sun Setting' on the Mancunian Metal label. In 1980 Wright hooked up with AIIZ and recorded the live *Witch Of Berkeley* LP for Polydor. It wasn't long, however, before the group split, having just released one more single, 'I'm The One Who Loves You'. ·

This prompted the drummer to move to London in the hope of joining a bigger act that sought stardom and wouldn't split up for anybody. At the end of 1982 the powerfully built Wright found himself in the NWOBHM outfit Tytan. The band had already released an EP called *Blind Men And Fools*, and was in the process of recording their debut album titled *Rough Justice* for Kamikaze Records when Wright took over from drummer Les Binks, formerly of Judas Priest. In the end Wright played on three tracks on the finished record. During the summer of 1983, after financial problems Tytan were forced to split before they had even released their second record. It was just as Simon Wright was bemoaning his unfortunate luck when a friend of his persuaded him to answer the AC/DC advert. By October 1983, he had made his live debut with the group in Vancouver, Canada.

"Most bands have ups and downs. With us things just stay the same." Angus Young

Flick Of The Switch entered the US Billboard charts in September of 1983 and would eventually peak at number 15. The album reached No. 4 in the UK charts. Despite their previous good showing in *Kerrang!* magazine in the readers' poll, AC/DC did not top any category in the listings for the end of that year, ending up as fifth top band. They were even labelled as the eighth biggest disappointment of the year. During the winter, AC/DC toured throughout the United States and Canada. On August 19, 1984 they became the first act to return as headliners at the fourth 'Monsters Of Rock' festival at Castle Donington. Other groups on the bill included Van Halen, Ozzy Osbourne, Motley Crue, Gary Moore, Y&T and Accept. After Donington, the band embarked on a series of dates in Europe, which included more at the 'Monsters Of Rock' series of gigs. Even bigger things were to come in January when AC/DC joined in the very first Rock In Rio in Brazil, playing two successive nights at the festival.

"People can go out and hear R.E.M. if they want deep lyrics; but at the end of the night, they want to go home and get fucked! That's where AC/DC comes into it." Malcolm Young

After Rio, 'DC enjoyed a lengthy hiatus. It was a chance to recharge their mental and physical batteries, although Angus, for one, seemed to get most of his exercise on stage. "I've never worried so much about the health," he said. "If I go along with the music, I'm fine. If I concentrate on that, the rest comes. I don't have to worry about the training or running or being in good shape. No one ever told me you had to be a weightlifter to play guitar. People like it when you're sloppy. People like to see that more than, say, someone who is pretty plain and worked out his dance steps. I don't even know one." His tips for staying in good shape essentially boiled down to avoiding eating pizza! "I just try to take it easy and relax a lot," he continued. "If you don't relax, you could be going all the time, which could damage your health. If you're feeling tired or ill you have to think 'well, it could be worse. I could be in some club doing three shows,' or you could be working. The only time I've noticed myself getting weak is when it's been an incredibly hot building. If you are playing in a place like New York in the summer the place is all humidity. There is no air conditioning, and the lights are pouring up there. At the end of it you can barely walk."

Brian Johnson spoke with admiration about Angus's tenacious commitment to going on stage no matter how sick or otherwise damaged he was. The singer respectfully said he "liked that kind of thing" when talking to British television show *Raw Power*.

Angus admitted he had often been hurt during the course of duty on stage. "Sure. I've lost teeth. I mean I don't go out there to hurt myself. But when you're on the road for that length of time, you're bound to twist and ankle or something. I once had splints on my fingers. I soon learned to play slide with them on, Hah! I've jumped off amps and fallen ass over tit and made a complete fool of myself. I've also had my pants fall off. All of a sudden my wedding tackle was there for all to see. You know, I've even had my shorts stolen a couple of times."

Soon AC/DC decided they should write more new material; it was a quick turn around, just like the old days. Again during this period they changed their manager, appointing Crisping Dye, a former Albert Productions executive in Europe, as their new representative. The band travelled to Montreux, Switzerland to record at Mountain Studio, and Angus and Malcolm Young took sole responsibility for production duties.

"Usually I start a few weeks after we've gotten off the road. I'll tell everyone not to bother me because I don't want to know anything about rock and roll for a while. But after about two weeks, I find myself drawn to the same old battered SG that I've been playing for years, and I start to play certain chords. Before I know it, a great deal of a song is written. That's when Malcolm or Brian will come in and help me finish it off. It's really a very simple process. I guess you could say I write most of the songs out of boredom." Angus Young

The album was to be titled *Fly On The Wall* and by the time it was released on June 28, 1985 AC/DC, it was claimed, had chalked up worldwide album sales of an estimated 30 million units. The new album reached No. 7 in the UK charts, but the first single taken from the album, 'Danger', only made it to No. 48. It was a strange choice for a single, very slow, without the buzzing, bristling swing of a regular 'DC track. Indeed it was almost too slow, sounding forced, as if the group weren't sure what to do next, and much of the rest of the album appeared to bear this out. 'Shake Your Foundations' was evidence that AC/DC still had what it took to pen a memorable rock song. With its pounding chorus, where Brian squeezes out the 'Aye, aye, oh, shake your foundations...Aye, aye, oh, shake it to the floor' lines, the song was set to be a new favourite for many fans. 'Sink The Pink' was another brash AC/DC sex anthem. But the choice morsels on *Fly On The Wall* were more sparsely distributed than on previous albums. 'First Blood' and 'Send For The Man' would have been better suited as b–sides or archive tracks; appearing on a fully–fledged AC/DC album they just sounded like filler material.

The record was the rawest sounding that the group had ever released. The title track had gang vocal back ups which were typical of the AC/DC style yet it sounded almost like a 'DC covers band – such was the brutal, basic sound. It was an almost audible reaction to being accused of plying a commercial route on *Back In Black* and *For Those About To Rock*.

"The critics might not like us, as Angus said the other day, 'We put out the same record every year with a different cover!' But the kids still like it and that's all we're worried about." Malcolm Young

Even the strong riffing that Angus and Malcolm were known for, which illuminated the likes of 'Playing With Girls', was let down by a lacklustre mix job which saw Brian's vocals relegated to the background. Perhaps the Young brothers had too much to deal with in just writing and playing the music, without having to oversee the sound of the album as well.

As ever the riffs managed to retain a memorable quality and Angus gave credit to Malcolm for this. "I can churn out hundreds of riffs" said Angus, "But he'll come up with one and once you hear it, you'll go 'shit.' He has that classic guitar feel like in a song like 'Back In Black' or 'Fly On The Wall'. A lot of people don't appreciate what rhythm guitar is."

Rock writer Martin Popoff described *Fly On The Wall* as a "Confused wank of a record which tries desperately to recapture wasted youth, yet the material for the most part is cookie cutter AC/DC, spewed forth with a strange lack of control that resembles a hurried, held back jam, kinda hysterical, thrashing wildly about for something to believe in. Brian's awkward vocals are mixed quite far back, possibly because he's sounding raspier and more incoherent than ever."

It should be noted Popoff is a fan of the band and still sees fit to grant the album a score of 6 out of 10 in his *Collector's Guide To Heavy Metal* book. It might be a poor album in the general scheme of AC/DC's work, but compared to most other acts it is still a solid rock album. Later, Brian Johnson would admit that it would have been better for the group to spend longer in the studio, in order to focus properly on the sound.

Despite this, the music trade magazine *Billboard* acknowledged in their June 1985 survey that AC/DC was the world's best selling hard rock act, with sales of between 25 and 30 million albums. But it was their back catalogue that was keeping the cash registers ticking over.

Flick Of The Switch album had sold just under a million, but *Fly On The Wall* was to fare worse for the 'DC boys, reaching a disappointing 500,000 mark worldwide. Angus shrugged his shoulders at this drop in album sales. "Everybody goes up and down," he reasoned. "We just try to play our music and not worry about anything else. *Back In Black* is our most successful album in the States so many of our fans base their expectations on that. But we were around long before *Back In Black.* In America people tend to associate wealth with success, whereas in other parts of the world success has more to do with making something that satisfies you."

Though AC/DC would often be trapped in the pleasures of success, surrounded by 'yes' men at hotels and gigs, they weren't about to act like rock stars. They hadn't succumbed during the glory days of *Back In Black* and stardom was less likely to go to their heads now that sales figures were slacking off. Brian Johnson was one of the most down to earth people you could hope to meet, despite being one of the most successful rock stars of the eighties. "After you've been in the first limo it's just a thing you know," was his theory. "Because it's not yours, it doesn't belong to you, and you know that in two months time you could be back in your little old Ford Popular. Success is such a fickle thing and the good thing about AC/DC is that they treat it as such."

Despite the lukewarm response to *Fly On The Wall*, a 28 – minute video was released, including the tracks, 'Danger', 'Sink The Pink', 'Stand Up', 'Shake Your Foundations' and the title track. Thoroughly eighties in its presentation, the entire thing dated quickly yet is still somewhat entertaining 20 years on. The band played a set of songs in a fictional New York bar (actually the World's End Bar in Alphabet City). There was a cast of characters who played their parts throughout the performance. AC/DC managed to get a dig in at the paparazzi, nicknaming one character (attempting to take photographs for a newspaper), Super Snoop. There was also a humorous jibe at the eighties phenomenon, the archetypal yuppie. Dressed in suitably decadent attire, the character playing the DJ at the venue, Decadent Dan tries hard to attach himself to a number of women at the club (known as The Crystal Ballroom). As the characters establish themselves, and the band plays on, an animated fly begins to bother everybody in the building. Soon the place begins to fill up and everyone, yuppies included, starts to enjoy AC/DC. The group itself ignores any attention good or bad as they prance around the stage like their lives depended on it.

By the time they are finished everyone in the club begins to chant for their return, and 'DC oblige, launching themselves into 'Shake Your Foundations'. The suits go crazy and Decadent Dan finally seems to find success with the opposite sex. However, as AC/DC gets louder and louder the building itself starts to crumble and every audience member vacates the venue. The band keeps going however, right until the end, at which point the fly – who has often taken centre stage throughout the presentation – zooms off into the distance. Overall the video was an enjoyable romp through some of the contemporary AC/DC material and made a comical advertisement for an otherwise lacklustre album.

AC/DC ACCORDING TO EDDIE VAN HALEN

"Our 'Panama' track was kind of AC/DC inspired. We had just done a tour with them the year before. It was us, Motley Crue and AC/DC in '83, in Europe, and just the power of those guys blew my mind, the constant 'Boom, boom, boom.' They play the same song over and over, but it's a great song. AC/DC was probably one of the most powerful live bands I've ever seen in my life. The energy...they were just unstoppable. I'll never forget our first big tour. It was a theatre–sized tour, 3,000–seaters. We headlined a bill featuring Ronnie Montrose and Journey. We were supposed to do 60 shows, but we left early because we had an offer to do 'A Day on the Green'.

I think Aerosmith and Foreigner were co–headlining. We had our own trailer, and next door to us were AC/DC, who were also playing that day. Anyway, they went on before us, and I was standing on the side of the stage thinking, 'We have to follow these motherfuckers?' They were so fuckin' powerful, but I remember feeling that we held our own. I was really happy. It blew my mind. I didn't think anybody could follow them."

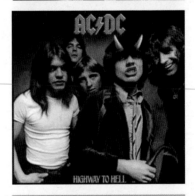

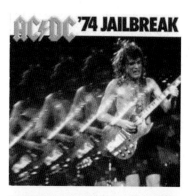

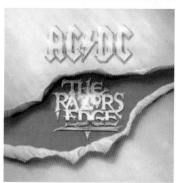

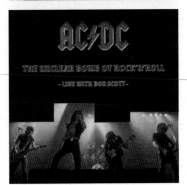

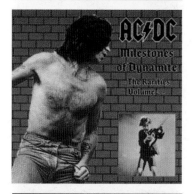

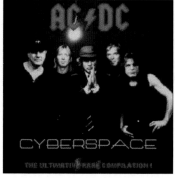

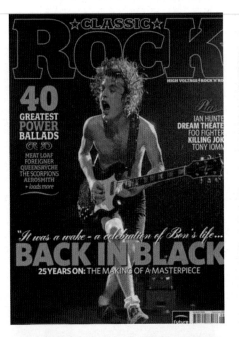

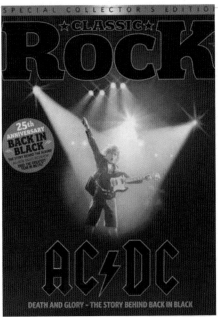

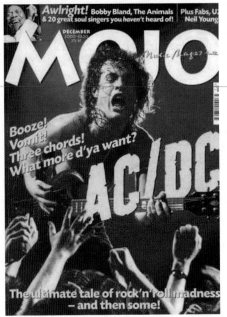

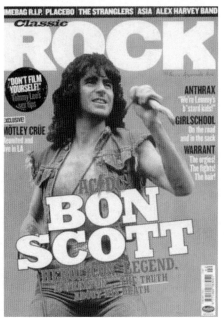

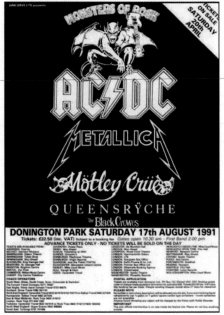

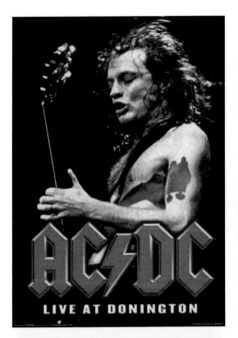

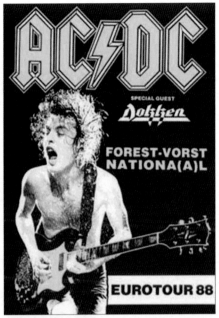

FOR THOSE
ABOUT TO ROCK:

Please DON'T
stand on the chairs
and DON'T trash
the building.
We want to play
here again.
It's up to you.

Have a great time!

AC/DC

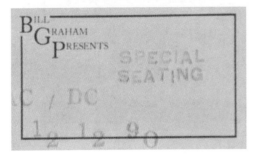

Chapter 13 – High Fault–age

"If a kid thinks he's being naughty by singing 'Highway To Hell', great, because all he's doing is singing or chanting or putting his arms in the air. It's not meant to harm anyone. It's not like I'm coming out with my personal views and this individual meaning to life. If you do that you're in the same game as those religious fanatics who hop on any cause just to get themselves a bit of publicity."
Brian Johnson

In September 1985 AC/DC signed with yet another new manager, this time Stewart Young and Part Rock Management. However, the most tenacious minders in the history of rock would have been unable to divert the controversy that was erupting around the band at the time.

Since the election of Ronald Reagan to the US presidency in 1980, conservative Christian groups had become increasingly loud, proud and powerful. They were constantly targeting the louder, hairier breed of rock act for condemnation, and AC/DC were in their sights. For a start, it was the considered opinion of many people in these organisations that AC/DC stood for either 'Anti Christ/Devil's Children', 'Away (from) Christ (the) Devil Comes' or 'Anti Christ/ Devil's Crusade'. For anyone who understood anything about the group, renowned for their commitment to do little else but 'rock', the insinuation seemed ludicrous.

AC/DC had chosen a name that could conjure up a number of connotations, but in their case it referred to nothing more controversial than electrical power, (unlike the American heavy metal band W.A.S.P. who had deliberately abbreviated its name as a shortening of We Are Sexual Perverts). This didn't hold much water in the American Bible belt however.

"Even before we'd been to America they'd started protesting about us", said Angus. "I wondered who these guys with the full robes on were at our gigs. We pulled up at one gig and this guy tapped the window. I rolled it down and he said, 'Take these.' They were all these pamphlets about this Satanic crap. I went, 'Sounds like a good show, mate'."

"All they want to do is get a little bit of attention," argued Brian Johnson, regarding the religious extremists who handed out leaflets at the group's shows. "In Detroit recently we had a leaflet which said 'The Bible says the word of the devil is evil, and so is rock and roll.' The Bible says rock n' roll is evil? I don't remember the Bible mentioning rock and roll!"

Angus continued, "There are a lot of people who genuinely believe in it and that's all right; that's up to them. But I don't really like people coming bothering me. I had one idiot trying to blast away my ear hole and he started with, 'Do you believe in God?' And I said, 'I've no interest in it so leave me alone.' Their main beef is songs like 'Highway To Hell'. But they are just titles. It's only a song."

Brian: "Those fucking God–botherers mention the devil more than we do. I mean they're trying to scare people. At least ours is all in good fun. When I'm singing it and the lads are playing it, you know that it's just rock and roll, a way to put it across. You've got to go right over the fucking top. Like everything – big gear, big lights, big fucking sound, that's how it is. No need to tread carefully. The big idea with us isn't Satanic messages – it's to get one line to rhyme with the fucking next!"

The attention of fundamentalist busybodies was annoying, but things were about to get really serious. Serial killer Richard Ramirez (real name Ricardo Leyva) aka 'The Night Stalker' claimed that AC/DC's track 'Night Prowler' had driven him to carry out his crimes. When detectives found an AC/DC baseball hat in Ramirez' house, it was time for the media witch–hunt to kick off. *Highway To Hell* (the album upon which 'Night Prowler' appeared) had already aroused the wrath of 'family' campaigners for such lyrics such as "Hey Satan, look at me…I'm on my way to the Promised Land".

25 year–old Texan Ramirez had committed his spate of killings in the Los Angeles area, creating an atmosphere of terror throughout the city, before the police finally captured him. When he was arrested, Ramirez was wearing an AC/DC shirt and an acquaintance confirmed to the police that they were one of his favourite bands.

Police believed that the lyrics of 'Night Prowler' were conducive with the ways Ramirez carried out his crimes, which included murder, rape, mutilation, and robbery. Upon his arrest, Ramirez, was charged with 14 murders and 31 other crimes. A 15th murder in San Francisco also hung over his head, with another potential trial in Orange County for rape and attempted murder. Along with Ramirez's fascination with AC/DC, he was obsessed by Satanism and was a regular user of both cocaine and PCP. His belief was that the Devil would protect him as long as he carried out his evil deeds.

"It's hard to believe that rock songs and marijuana alone would turn a misdirected youth into one of the most heinous serial rapists and murderers in modern history." Anthony Bruno, True Crime Writer

In a *People* magazine article of September 1985 a frightening misinterpretation of heavy rock music was published. The critique illuminated the dangers of the genre. "Rock n' roll is turning too often to sex, Satanism, drugs and violence for its major themes and corrupting the values and views of unwary young people. The lyrics of the last few years of the 1980s have continued on a downward slope. Rachel Matthews, an artist and repertoire representative for Capitol Records, recruits new groups for her company. Her comments regarding a newly signed band reveal what she, as one individual representing the music industry, is looking for in a band: 'I was just going, "Oh shit! I've never heard anything like this!" I've heard plenty of metal and speed metal, but it was just so intense and out of control, just like this caged psychosis going on. I loved it, because you could actually understand the lyrics. And even if they're morbid and gruesome, it's really cool that you could understand what they're saying. It just makes it twice as evil. I like that.'"

The piece then went on to identify dangerous new forms of rock such as "Trash (sic) Metal". It pointed out the primary focus of this kind of music, played by groups such as Megadeth and Anthrax was "violence and death". Apart from the basic error that the genre is more generally known as 'thrash metal', the author also neglected to mention that the two named acts were more apt to compose lyrics about the environment and politics. If that meant the same thing as "violence and death", it was hardly the fault of the bands.

The breathless expose continued: "The third type is known as 'black metal' and is overtly satanic. The lyrics encourage such activities as incest, necrophilia, rape, torture, and human sacrifice. Black metal is represented by groups like Venom and Slayer. King Diamond is perhaps the most Satanic of all 'black metal' groups. He openly professes Satan and incorporates a large amount of satanic activity into his performances."

While this kind of material was clearly written to sell magazines at a time when concern regarding links between metal and Satanism was at its frenzied height, it was not only inaccurate, but also failed to mention exactly how AC/DC could be involved in similar Devil worship. Other than the title of *Highway To Hell* itself, and Angus's devil horns – nothing you wouldn't encounter in your average Shakespeare production – evidence of the band's Satanic message was a little thin. However, this did not stop campaigns by religious and family groups, and attempts to ban the group from playing in certain towns. There was also a concerted campaign for all AC/DC records to be banned and removed from sale.

There were gatherings of concerned parents in some towns, and heavy metal albums were burned and broken in defiance. AC/DC's *Highway To Hell* was among the records consigned to the flames: others included Iron Maiden's *Number Of The Beast* and several albums by Black Sabbath.

"We were a scandal in Australia. They love scandal there. Mums tugging their kids away from us on the street. 'Ooh look, them!'"
Malcolm Young

Author and crime expert Katherine Ramsland, Ph.D, is far more sensible about the factors behind Ramirez and the time of the Satanic phenomena in America. "To understand Richard Ramirez and his passion for the devil, we need to examine more than just his life; we must also look at the times" she says. "Ramirez committed his murder spree in 1985, in the midst of the 'Satanic panics' that swept the country throughout the decade. Anxiety over Satanists and evil conspiracies mounted on a cultural scale, and narratives told by people in therapy about ritual abuse by secret satanic rings showed many common elements, and no evidence. Whole masses of people developed similar physical symptoms that were primarily emotional in origin, and the idea of ritual abuse was heavily promoted by journalists, therapists, physicians, drug companies, and whoever else might find some stake in them. Serial killers, too, adopted satanic robes. During that decade, Robert Berdella killed six men in Missouri for Satanic purposes, Antone Costa killed four women in Cape Cod in rituals, Thomas Creech admitted to 47 Satanic sacrifices, and Larry Eyler buried four of his 23 victims under a barn marked with an inverted pentagram. A teenager who wanted to follow the devil murdered his parents in their beds.

"Also during the 1980s, a former associate of John Wayne Gacy named Robin Gecht inspired a group of three other men known as the Ripper Crew in killing an estimated eighteen women. They would murder a victim, sever her left breast with a thin wire, clean it out to use for sexual gratification, and then cut it into pieces to consume. Ostensibly, they were worshipping Satan, and eating the flesh was a form of demonic communion. The Night Stalker had the same devilish persuasion. He would creep up in the night, dressed in black, and enter homes surreptitiously. Sometimes he removed the eyes of his victims, as if for a ritual. He bludgeoned two elderly sisters and left Satanic symbols on the thigh of the one who died in the form of a pentagram. He also drew pentagrams on the walls in lipstick. When he was arrested, Ramirez reportedly said he was a minion of Satan sent to commit the Dark One's dirty work."

During his trial, Ramirez flashed the "devil sign" (made with his index and little finger as if to imitate horns), in common with many metal bands eager to stir up a little quasi–Satanic controversy. Katherine Ramsland states that he "Took his cue from the song, 'Night Prowler,' noting how the person who made others afraid was the one in control.

"As Ramsland notes, other killers, such as John Wayne Gacy, were also to find a link with metal bands and artists. The likes of Acid Bath would use Gacy's creepy artwork of clowns and children to adorn their records; Marilyn Manson and his bandmates took the surnames of killers, including Gacy and Ramirez. It seems that heavy metal will always be seen as having links to the dark side, although the 80s also saw the arrival on the scene of a number of Christian heavy rock bands. These so–called 'white' metal acts were to prove that metal was all about the music and that bands could therefore sing about Jesus as well as Satan; the result would be the same. This was borne out in the success of bands like Stryper, whose members would throw Bibles to the audience.

1985 saw the birth of an organisation intended to give parents help in assessing whether their children should be buying particular records. Everything from Prince to Sheena Easton was prime for censorship but the main reason the PMRC (Parents Musical Resource Center) formed was to stem the popularity of heavy metal. Their prime objective was to prevent the records being released at all but when this seemed unachievable they sought to sticker records with potentially offensive content; thus the 'parental advisory' sticker was born.

One metal act to come under particularly heavy criticism and censorship was American outfit W.A.S.P. Their first single, 'Animal (Fuck Like A Beast)' had been withdrawn from sale in 1984 and in the UK a cover of *Kerrang!* magazine, featuring the band drenched in blood, was withdrawn from many newsagents. Front man Blackie Lawless remembers, "The story goes that Tipper Gore was walking down the hallway in her house and her twelve year old son's got 'Fuck Like A Beast' blasting out on his stereo and she's thinking 'We're not having that!'" Tipper was the wife of Senator Al Gore, later to become Vice President of the United States, and she was therefore in a strong position to make her presence felt.

Just as AC/DC did, Lawless and W.A.S.P. dealt with the situation via humour, "We were laughing our asses off at everything," recalls Blackie. "There were people coming at us with fiery torches like Frankenstein's monster on top of the hill." Much the same as AC/DC, Lawless' band came in for a rough time that seemed as if it wouldn't ever stop. As the singer remembers, "There was a four or five–year period there where it was really bad. I had death threats and there were bomb scares and I got shot at three times." What the PMRC did not seem to realise was the majority of potential buyers for heavy metal were going to be more interested if they thought a record was going to annoy their parents or was risqué enough to be 'banned'. "Well, it did make us household names," says Blackie, speaking not only for W.A.S.P. but also for countless other rock and metal acts, "But we found that while someone's grandma in Newcastle may have known who we were, that same grandma didn't go out and buy W.A.S.P. records." Also in the metal world, in the same year the case of two suicide victims in Nevada brought further negative attention, this time for British act Judas Priest. The case went to court, with the families of the boys suing the group. Eventually, with the members themselves giving evidence the case was thrown out. Supposedly, Priest had planted several backwards messages on their *Stained Class* album which suggested the listener should 'do it', supposedly a reference to suicide.

Most significantly, AC/DC did not want to be associated with heavy metal whatsoever. They had earlier expressed their distaste at the genre and felt completely distant from the other types of bands within its confines. This was perhaps to divert early negative attention surrounding *Highway To Hell*, as much as their inherent dislike of metal music per se, but unfortunately this did not convince many parents.

"I'm an out and out basic man and AC/DC are one of the best rock n'roll bands in the world, doing things just to the basics, you know."
Brian Johnson

AC/DC would play their US tour as scheduled throughout October and November. City officials in Springfield and Dallas tried unsuccessfully to ban them from playing in their cities following the Ramirez controversy. Malcolm Young explained, "We were due to play at the Springfield Auditorium in Illinois when we heard that these religious fanatics had managed to get us banned by complaining that we were Satanists or whatever. So we spoke to a few people about it and found that these loonies were not allowed to do this kind of thing and we could take them to court about it so that's exactly what we did, and we won." There were still problems ahead however. "The only thing was that the people who run the hotels in the area refused to let us stay in any of the local hotels so we ended up having to spend the night before the gig about a hundred miles away and drive into town on the night of the show." "We've had a lot of shit thrown at us in the States, and that episode with the Night Stalker didn't help," Malcolm told *Kerrang!*, "Some kid was done for murder a couple of months ago and there was a mass of publicity about it. Now, this kid had an AC/DC shirt on, which immediately put the focus on us, and of course the religious fanatics, who've always followed us around over here, put 'Night Stalker' and 'Night Prowler' together. What they can't see is that 'Night Prowler' is just about creeping in at night on a couple of old girlfriends and doing the business, having a bit of fun you know? It's not about raping and pillaging... The whole thing came about because he had an AC/DC shirt on when they pulled him in and one of his friends said he was AC/DC mad. So what? Some loopy loves your band and wears your t–shirt while he's bumping off people – we're not telling the guy to do it!"

"To survive, you have got to have a good sense of humour," Angus reasoned. "What always makes me laugh are the people who expect a rock and roll band to have answers to today's problems and issues. Some of the greatest minds of the century couldn't figure this stuff out."

Brian Johnson agreed: "The worst part is some of these fuckers actually sit there and try to answer these questions. I'm just sitting there going, 'Shut up! Don't talk. Pick up a guitar. Go get some strings.' They sit there until they're so embroiled in it, and then a year later they suddenly realise how foolish they are because they keep getting their fingers burned. They're musicians, for fuck sake. They're not politicians. We talk about politics in the studios. But we certainly don't wanna go run out onstage and spout our fucking opinions."

"The only image we've ever had is what we really are. We never cover up anything." Angus Young

Essentially, AC/DC laughed off accusations of devil worship of any kind. The nearest they came to consorting with the forces of darkness was Angus's occasional predilection for black underwear. "It is easier to take a swing at someone that is singing about sex and rock n' roll, but that's all part of life, and it's all in fun," continued Angus rather jovially. "We're not the ones telling people what to do. I don't like it when people tell me what to do, even teachers. When I was a kid in school, as soon as a teacher starting spouting at me, I would go off to the toilet to have a smoke. I didn't want to be sitting here having to listen to this guy telling me stuff that was no use to me. I would think, 'How can you do that, knowing full well that I'll be out of here at 15 working in a factory somewhere? Learn me something that may improve my lot. There is no way in the world I am gonna get a job as a university lecturer.'"

The band members often deflected attention away from the red herring of Satanism simply because they thought the whole insinuation was ridiculous; they were just five blokes playing rock music, and that is all they had ever wanted to be known for. Richard Ramirez, like many before and since, saw something that did not actually exist in the group's music. He took what he wanted from it, but anything could have given him the 'power' he received from AC/DC. If they had not been around something else would undoubtedly have triggered his behaviour whether it was a movie or another band.

"You know, the first thing Angus and Malcolm said to me when I joined this band," Brian told *Kerrang!* "They said, 'Do you mind if your feelings ever get hurt?' and I said 'Why?' And they said, 'Because if you're going to join this band you're going to be expected to take fucking stick. Because we've been slagged off by every fucking reporter since we left Australia.' And I said, 'Well I'm going to have to take stick anyway, taking this lad's place.' But luckily these guys are so much like a fucking family that you never get the chance to feel alone; like you could just sit by yourself in your hotel room and feel like shit. The lads say to me, 'Just fucking ignore them.' We're good in our field. We just out and out don't give a fuck. We play what we play and that's it. And the good thing is, no one else can do it as good as this band. The band is the fucking best!"

In a later interview, Angus and Brian were asked about their political opinions and whether their lyrics should be the subject of disgust; specifically the way the words often reeked of sexism. "Brian, myself, and Malcolm were out of school at 15," replied Angus. "Your education is limited when that happens. And you don't worry about what's going on in the news and who is running for public office." Brian paid tribute to the political savvy of his late father, whose politics could be summed up as: "I'll vote for the fucker that gets me a job so I can feed my family."

Brian made light of questions about his supposedly misogynistic lyrics. "There was a Swedish journalist who said to me, 'Do you think it is amusing for women to be treated the way you treat them in your songs? How would you like to be tied up and humiliated like that?' And I said, 'I'd fucking love it. Tie me up in a car and get my fucking brains fucked out by some wild rampant tottie.'"

He expanded the argument: "Of course we're sexist, but life is sex. That's why we're here. Sexism mixed with humour is a wonderfully funny thing. We say things with a big tongue in the cheek. And it's not supposed to be just for men, it's for women as well. Women are horny buggers – there's a lot of them about who want to tie you up and use your little body, you know!"

Malcolm, when talking about the band's most lurid days of sexual depravity, would soften the image, saying, "It was more bravado really. It happened more when we were young and inexperienced, of course, but as far as lyrics are concerned we've always used sex for inspiration. We never have a problem with sex in the words. It doesn't embarrass us. The reality is that there were a few stories to tell back then, and now they're just good memories."

"We've got the basic things kids want. They want to rock, and that's it." Angus Young

Overall, AC/DC were still successful and able to play to their own fans, which for them was the whole point of going out on tour. And living the road life for over a decade had not dimmed the Youngs' enthusiasm. Malcolm: "It is hard sometimes but the minute you walk onstage and you hear the kids cheering and you see all the smiling faces, the hairs on the back of your neck stand up, and all of a sudden you're alive and ready to rock and roll all night. Having Brian in the band keeps us all amused! He's a real joker, he's always laughing and fooling around – so how can we get fed up with him around?"

THE NIGHT FALLER

At a preliminary hearing of his defence, Ramirez flashed a pentagram that he'd had tattooed onto the palm of his hand. When he was convicted his lawyers informed him that he might receive the death sentence he replied, "I'll be in hell, then, with Satan." As the newspapers continued to cover his case he realised all he had to do was flash the pentagram or talk about serving Satan, and he would be endlessly quoted in the papers. He also began to wear sunglasses to augment his air of secrecy. In addition he seemed to embrace the idea that he was a 'monster.'

During his trial, one juror was murdered, and this caused the other jurors to suspect Ramirez may have summoned demons in order to have the person killed. They were fearful that he might also attack one of them, especially as he would often stare directly and threateningly at jurors during the court case. He was sentenced to death and placed on Death Row in San Quentin, where he still resides. When talking to police officers, he was quite curious as to whether there would now be books about him as there were about Ted Bundy and Jack the Ripper. He loved the idea that someone had made a movie about him ('Manhunt: Search for the Night Stalker').

On October 3, 1996, Doreen Lioy, 41, married Ramirez, 36, in a simple ceremony in San Quentin's waiting room. They had been engaged since 1988 but the wedding was delayed due to prison regulations.

Chapter 14 – Playing With Expectations

"We've never been current. But there comes a time when people want to be entertained. They want to be happy. And we always look at rock and roll as that happy link. That will never go away." Malcolm Young

During their 1985 American tour, AC/DC were approached by horror writer Stephen King, a huge fan of the band, who asked whether he could possibly include some of their old material for the soundtrack of his forthcoming movie *Maximum Overdrive*, starring Emilio Estevez. He also suggested 'DC record some new tracks exclusively for the film.

At the end of the tour, the group accepted King's offer and as well as carefully chosen highlights of their career to date, they recorded three brand new songs for inclusion. These were 'Who Made Who' (also the title of the album), 'D.T.' and 'Chase The Ace', and they were completed in two weeks. It was to mark a return for Harry Vanda and George Young, as the group realised negative comments regarding their 1985 material were, to an extent, justified. "I always think that we did the great rock tunes when we worked with my brother," explained Angus of the decision. "I like what we did with him better than the stuff we did with Mutt Lange. Mutt was very conscious of what was popular in America but with my brother…if it was a rock n' roll song, he made sure it rocked!" For the recordings, AC/DC travelled once again to the Compass Point Studios in Nassau.

The song 'Who Made Who' saw AC/DC in melodic mode with some clever guitar interplay from the Young brothers. The sound was captured to mark the times, audibly eighties in terms of its construction, yet brought the group into newer sonic realms. They also filmed a video for the title track at the Brixton Academy in South London, featuring hordes of headbangers (fan club members and radio competition winners) dressed to look just like Angus, and wielding cardboard guitars.

The songs picked to represent previous material were 'You Shook Me All Night Long', 'Sink The Pink', 'Ride On', 'Hells Bells', 'Shake Your Foundations' and 'For Those About To Rock (We Salute You)'. This partial compilation is the only time the band has ever had a compiled set of studio material released. The songs were deliberately picked to keep the Brian Johnson era as the main focus, but they couldn't resist tacking on Bon's plaintive road song, 'Ride On', which quietly paid tribute to him and also showcased the group's 'other' side for any potential new fans.

In early 1986 'Shake Your Foundations' was released as a single and this became 'DC's most successful '45 since 'For Those About To Rock', when it reached No. 24 in the UK charts. On May 3, the *Who Made Who* album followed and was equally well received. It peaked at number 11 in the UK charts and number 33 in the United States. Many were disappointed that the album didn't entirely consist of new material, but they were placated by the strong new tracks, which included the band's first instrumental pieces since 'Fling Thing', the b–side to 'Jailbreak'.

"I like rhythm n blues, I like Rock n' Roll. AC/DC, I like a lot: very loud!" Stephen King

The film revolved around the earth passing through the tail of a mysterious comet, a as machines on earth suddenly come to life to terrorise their creators. There is a scene in the movie involving a ferry bridge, and in the background a van can be seen with the AC/DC band logo painted on it. The movie was remade for cable television as 'Trucks' in 1997.

As Simon Wright remembered: "Doing the instrumentals was a bit strange. We had these TV screens which showed us the relevant parts of the movie, and we had to fit the music to the action." Though the instrumentals were almost out of place on a compilation of vintage AC/DC songs the whole package seemed to gel rather well. It also marked a successful venture for the band, but one that they had no reason to revisit. They would not record another soundtrack album, nor would they attempt any more instrumental tracks, making the appearance of two vocal–less tracks on the *Who Made Who* album all the more precious.

To celebrate the welcome their new album had received, AC/DC hit the road for a US tour (supported by US prog metal combo Queensrÿche and Japan's self explanatory Loudness) in July 1986 and stayed out until November, two months later than they had expected. Every show of the tour was completely sold out, and all this was achieved while the concert industry was undergoing something of a recession. America just could not get enough of AC/DC. After their triumphant live shows throughout the States the group took a two–month break before beginning work on their next album.

The band would take it upon themselves to drastically update their sound and return with their best record in years. They had Vanda and Young back in tow for a full album, the first time since 1978. "With the three brothers working together, I think it's just the climax of many years of doing the right thing with music," Brian commented. "What I love to watch sometimes is Mal or Ang will look at George and just go 'ummm.' And George will go 'hmmm'. And they've just had a conversation. But it was through the mind, without words getting in the way. I think the boys believe in George more than anybody else in the world. They trust him, I do too." 'DC had enjoyed working with the veteran partners so much for *Who Made Who* that the choice of producers for the next full record was easily made.

"I don't think there is an ideal environment for writing songs. We've written songs under a hell of a lot of pressure, but then some songs just come when suddenly and spontaneously, like when you're not thinking and you're in the middle of a cab ride. We've even written songs on stage. But that's the key, I suppose, never knowing when to expect it." Angus Young

Together, the producers and musicians would record at the Miraval studios in the South of France. There was no air conditioning, but despite exceedingly warm temperatures a good time was had by all. There was ample time for AC/DC to enjoy their collective hobbies of bar–hopping and, less stereotypically, golf. Johnson admitted a fondness for 'French tarts' although in this instance, he meant the cakes. However one woman was particularly welcome.

"We had French women cooking us beautiful breakfasts. I couldn't stop eating. We had a ball!" Brian recalled.

"The studio where we record always plays a big part" he reckoned. "We need a place that's got a great live sound. We're not looking for technology, like effects and stuff. We rely mainly on getting the best sound out of whatever room we're in." Altogether, 19 tracks were composed and recorded but eventually only ten were chosen for the LP, called *Blow Up Your Video*. The title came from a line in the record's strongest tune, 'That's The Way I Wanna Rock N' Roll' and Brian Johnson thought MTV would appreciate it, being so relevant and descriptive.

The album would see a thoroughly rejuvenated AC/DC, capable of competing with the big boys of the eighties. They were still playing a modern form of rock n' roll but such was the sharpened presentation of their material, with Brian's rough voice and the striking riffs of the Young brothers that they could easily cut it alongside heavy metal acts of the day. Again the members distanced themselves from the style, though it was intriguing to note the band had longer hair than ever, especially Angus.

"It wouldn't be AC/DC if we did something different" said Angus. "And we're certainly not going to start putting dragons on the album covers." AC/DC kept it simple and in accordance with the title of their album they featured Angus exploding out of a television set – rather than the fantasy styled artwork preferred by many of the band's heavy metal rivals.

"Oh, we've had our share of hotels being smashed and all, but that was a long time ago. You get lousy room service... I mean, there is no use throwing a TV set out the window for the sake of throwing a TV set out the window. But if you get a lousy picture then you have an excuse." Angus Young

The songs had "to swing", according to Angus. "When we write songs the first thing is the feel. It's got to have that bottom edge to it and you take it from there. It's dumb to make a song fast just for the sake of it. The bottom line is we get out there and play rock n' roll music. I may wear that school suit but for me that just gives me that extra confidence. Then I can act like a real asshole."

Though Angus would demonstrate his guitar chops all over *Blow Up Your Video*, especially on 'Meanstreak' and 'That's The Way I Wanna Rock N' Roll' he wouldn't concede that he was in the same department as many of the '80s crop of super fast guitarists who loved to play high up the guitar neck and weren't exactly fond of standard songs. "I've never been impressed with someone who can zoom up and down the guitar neck, I can do that myself, but I call it practising," he would scoff.

"I don't like to play above or below people's heads. Basically, I just like to get up front of a crowd and rip it up." Angus Young

There was certainly a tinge of metal mania to Angus's style on the *Blow Up Your Video* LP but you sensed this was an almost ironic quip at the thousands of would be great guitarists releasing records in the saturated eighties rock music market. Angus was almost acknowledging the method but proving he could play it with greater style and ease, whilst still incorporating the blues scales he so loved. His opinion was reassuringly frank, "I've always liked Chuck Berry's music because it's simple and direct. You don't have to think about it. It makes you dance and tap your feet."

The metal rhetoric was quite removed from AC/DC even on stage in some ways. For one thing, they were only about showmanship in terms of performance. With the exception of Angus, who perpetually wore the obligatory school uniform, the group did not exactly dress to impress. There was no spandex, leather or huge, teased hair, just ordinary blokes with extraordinary talents. The lead guitarist was no prima donna, hogging the spotlight to satisfy his ego; it was just the way it happened. No one person in AC/DC begrudged another his time in the spotlight. Brian did not mind whether he received all the attention or not, he was just there to do a job of singing to the best of his ability, much like Bon had. And Malcolm, despite being the better guitarist according to Angus, did not care in the least that he was usually to be spotted in the distance, in fact he preferred it that way.

Angus also acknowledged regularly it was not by any means his band or even his guitar style, which defined AC/DC. He admitted to *Hit Parader,* "Malcolm is a big inspiration to me. He can always tell me if I'm playing good or bad. He's a very tough critic. I know if I can please Malcolm I can please the world. A lot of people say, 'AC/DC – that's the band with the little guy who runs around in shorts.' But I wouldn't be able to do it without Malcolm and the other guys pumping out the rhythm. They make me look good."

There was one thing the group rarely did on stage and that was to have Brian address the audience in typical metal mode. There were rarely any contrived sing–a–long moments from the crowd, no screaming for the crowd to be the best the band had ever played to. Sure, people in the audience sang along but it wasn't at the request of the performers – that was their job. As Brian would put it, "In fact, I never say anything onstage. The music's supposed to do the talking."

Also, despite AC/DC's rough and ready image, even swearing was a rarity. "Every other band has a front man who hogs the spotlight and swears," said Brian. "I think there's a school for it. One of the guys used to work for this band – I won't mention their name – and the singer said 'fuck' 165 times during one show. That was the record. Our guy used to count 'fucks' every night with a clicker. I've never said 'fuck' onstage. Well I said it once but and this woman said, 'I can't believe you swore onstage, I have my daughter here.' And I said, 'Jeez, I'm sorry.' And I've never said it since."

For *Blow Up Your Video* AC/DC would maintain their aversion to slower songs. "We're still as tough as ever and there's definitely no ballads," said Angus of the album. "I have a great aversion to slow songs. Apart from anything else the world is saturated with the damn things…I don't mind hearing a ballad every now and then, like once a year maybe, but even then I get pissed off after about two minutes. So whatever we try in the studio, it won't be a ballad!"

The mood in the studio was so light hearted and fun that the band enjoyed the recording of the album more than the last three they had put together. "We just went through the whole album with smiles on our faces," remembered Brian. "The album is smashing, and we just knew it was going to be good. George has this father –figure approach and he knows more about rock n' roll than any fucker! Then you've got Malcolm and Angus there, so happy to work with their own brother, and Harry too." The atmosphere in the studio came through on the album itself with the entire record having an upbeat vibe. Some of Johnson's favourite songs were 'That's The Way I Wanna Rock N' Roll' and 'Kissin' Dynamite' but the one he liked to sing most of all, chiefly because of what he described as having a "great sense of humour", was 'Meanstreak'. The lyrics were typically brazen AC/DC: "I ain't met no one who told me I got class, They say never feed the animal, the boy's got too much flash. I'm a guy they just can't teach, and I always kick the castle that's been built up on the beach."

Brian also acknowledged the last track on the album, 'This Means War' as being the fastest AC/DC song for some time and a "real cracker". Johnson reckoned it was as fast as a number the band had recorded a decade before, 'Riff Raff'. Though *Blow Up Your Video* would see AC/DC once again compared to heavy metal acts, it was still constructed from the usual components – AC/DC's trademark riffs, licks and melodies. The one difference from the likes of *Fly On The Wall* and *Flick Of The Switch* was the thicker sound buzzing throughout the album.

All this was even more impressive because unlike the distorted and literally buzzing sounds most metal outfits employed, Angus actually played with a clean guitar sound; it just sounded heavier when it was loud! "The amp is set very clean," he disclosed. "A lot of people who have picked up my guitar and tried it through my amp have been shocked at how clean it is. They think it's a very small sound when they play it and wonder how it sounds so much bigger when I'm playing. I just like enough gain so that it will still cut when you hit a lead lick without getting that sort of false Tonebender–type sound. I like to get a natural sustain from the guitar and amp."

The real secret with AC/DC was the way they interacted, not the ideal of playing as loud as possible just for the sake of it with maximum distortion. "It just depends on the nature of the room," Angus added. "If you've got a great sounding live room and everyone's in the same room, especially the drums and the guitars, then I think you'll really cook because there's more of a feeling of camaraderie. It makes for much more of a live feel. If you're in the control room or separated, sometimes you can be a little bit cut off. We've done it different ways, but a lot of it is still down to the room itself. If you've got a great sounding live room, you can get lucky." 'DC were most certainly lucky with *Blow Up Your Video*, though it was clearly more about talent than good fortune.

Fans were in agreement and sent the first single lifted from the album, 'Heatseeker' to number 12 in the UK charts. They loved the album just as much, seeing it in at number 2 on the British charts and number 12 in the United States. This was the best showing for an AC/DC album since the milestone *Back In Black*. After three days of rehearsals at the Entertainment Center in Perth, Australia, AC/DC would begin their world tour with a jaunt around Oz, beginning on February 1st 1989. This was the group's first live appearance in their spiritual homeland since 1981. Poignantly, Bon's parents Isa and Chick attended the show. Appropriately, AC/DC stuck to the early career material, plying the locals with mostly Scott–penned lyrics.

After their successful return to Australia, the band headed to the UK where they played in Birmingham and London, headed out to Europe, then returned for a second visit to Wembley Arena before the US leg of the tour.

But all was not well in the ranks. Before the North American jaunt, Malcolm Young dropped out, with the official excuse being 'exhaustion'. In fact, the temporary exit was an attempt to cure his alcoholism, which had been worsening for several years. Malcolm would later admit to his addiction and explain the long road back to sobriety.

"It went something along the lines of 'too much', 'a lot', 'not much', 'now nothing'. It's only a cup of tea for me these days," he explained. "I was drinking an awful lot before. I reckon you could have written a book about the things I got up to. But I had to give it up and get myself back together. I was bored of it, getting ripped all the time. It was always the same story and I couldn't leave it alone. I was a real Jekyll and Hyde character. I'd lost my self–control. I was still playing the songs OK, but I was always drunk. Things would get really bad after the gig, though. I was the first one to start drinking and the last to leave any club. I always had to be dragged out.

I've never been on tour without a drink inside me before and I never thought it would be a problem. So it's always difficult to stick with the tea when things get stressful." Angus would laugh, "He had to stop, it had just gone too far. From the age of 17, I don't think there was a day when he was sober. I suppose you could look at it as a record! I never knew how he could function like that. I don't drink, but everyone else was sure doing it for me!"

AC/DC had brought in another family member to take over from Malcolm in his hour of need. His nephew Stevie Young looked a lot like Malcolm and carried off his guitar parts with great aplomb. "He did a great job," Angus assured *Kerrang!* "most people thought it was Mal! They're very similar; he's got a strong personality. I was more nervous than he was." Stevie's first show with the band was at the Cumberland Civic Center in Portland, Maine, on May 3. "In both situations, I've always found that it works to put your best foot forward and don't be afraid," Angus said, about playing live and recording. "I suppose it's a bit like swimming. You can't just dip your little toe in the water. You've got to go all the way. I believe you've got nothing to fear, although a lot of people think that's strange. If you hit a bum note, that was fate. Some of those bum notes might be a great accident. I think that if you're too tight and restricted, then those sort of little spontaneous things just seem to give it that little bit of magic, they won't happen. Every now and again, we all hit a bum note. The ideal situation is just to hit less of them! I think that it just takes a bit of confidence when you're doing something. I've never been afraid. I guess I'm lucky for having grown up in a family of musicians. I think that gave me a lot of confidence about my playing and made it easier for me to be comfortable in any musical situation."

While Stevie Young was rocking packed arenas as Malcolm's double, the heart of AC/DC was enjoying time away from the rock n' roll circus, pursuing leisurely activities with his wife Linda and family in Sydney. For the first time in ages, he could relax away from the band. He even bought a racehorse, bringing something different to his otherwise music–dominated existence. However, music hadn't entirely disappeared from Malcolm's life, he was still cooking with ideas for the next AC/DC platter. The US tour had proved to be an enormous success for the group as they sold out most venues they visited throughout the world. By the end of the year *Blow Up Your Video* became the band's best selling album since *For Those About To Rock (We Salute You)*.

BRIAN JOHNSON EXPLAINS
what might have happened to AC/DC had they been easily per-suadable people

"In the middle eighties, we had a bit of a bad time, when all the music changed, long hairs... you know, Whitesnake and REO Speedwagon. The record company came to us to tell us change the clothes; they said, 'It would be best if you would change your image'. We were like 'Fuck you!' And all the bands that did change aren't here anymore. Because they let themselves be manipulated by the record companies, who quite frankly don't have a clue about music. They have only one thing; they know how to make money out of music. But that's it, that's where all ends. It's a funny world."

Chapter 15 – Days Of Thunder

"I am sick to death of people saying we have made 11 albums that sounds exactly the same. In fact, we've made 12 albums that sound exactly the same." Angus Young

At the end of 1989, AC/DC made headlines in a rather bizarre manner. American troops had invaded Panama, seeking to oust the country's leader, General Manuel Noriega. However, the general took refuge inside the Vatican diplomatic mission in Panama City. When all else failed, it was decided that only loud rock music would shake him out, and who better to annoy someone than AC/DC? 'Highway To Hell' was chosen, and a shaken Noriega surrendered on January 3, 1990. Angus explained: "They were trying to aggravate him so he couldn't get a restful sleep. It was pretty funny for us. I figure if our music is good enough for the U.S. army it's good enough for anybody."

With this unusual confirmation of the power and obnoxiousness of their music, AC/DC started work on their next album. It had by now become a running joke that the band made the same record over and over again. This was doubtless unfair: clearly *Blow Up Your Video* had been different from the material they recorded in the 1970s, but there was a specific AC/DC sound that the fans responded to, and provided the quality was maintained, the diehards weren't going to complain about a certain sonic consistency. However the material they were about to come up with would offer something different from the norm.

"We're a rock group. We're noisy, rowdy, sensational and weird."
Angus Young

Things were not easy during the preparation for the album. Simon Wright left to join Dio, the band fronted by the diminutive Ronnie James Dio, formerly of Elf, Rainbow and Black Sabbath.

Wright had previously guested on the group's *Lock Up The Wolves* album, but now decided to occupy the Dio drumstool on a permanent basis.

Brian Johnson was also going through a period of transition, as he was getting divorced from his wife Carol. He spent a lot of time in the USA dealing with legal matters, which meant it would be difficult for him to come up with lyrics for the LP. For the first time in the band's history, the singer would not compose the words for the new record. "Mal and I thought it would ease the pressure on him if we wrote the words" explained Angus. "We've always contributed in the past anyway. We'd sit down, all three of us, me, Mal and Bon, sometimes four of us with my brother George and we'd have this big shoot around. We always gave Bon a helping hand in the past; same with Brian, because if you have some lyrical idea while you're writing it can save you a lot of heartache and trouble at the end of the day."

"I just ran out of ideas," Brian would later say about this time. "I just can't think enough. I don't want to write same thing again. And Angus and Malcolm helped Bon with lot of the lyrics in the earlier days. Mal and Ang have this song writing in the blood, they are very good at it. They just let go. I just felt terrible when we were doing an album, I didn't have much idea wise. I thought I'd wait to see the boys and hear them playing the riffs. I was having a real tough time thinking of lyrics. That just happens sometimes, you just dry up. Well, the boys said 'We will give it a try'. And the boys gave it a thought, and it was great. It was from a different angle. And Angus has the craziest ideas. Angus is way out there, he comes back, get these things in his head and they are great. Angus and Malcolm are just that talented. But what I still do, and what I love very much is to meet Malcolm and Angus in London. They'll say, 'Come on Brian, we have few ideas'. And that's the best part of it, because I know I will be the first person in the world to hear them. And I help them to shape the songs. We just sit down there, and it's lovely. You are with your pals, drinking lots of coffee, I just love it."

The band was at least relieved to be able to write without a deadline looming over their heads. "We had plenty of time, which was good," said Angus. "In the past we've always been committed to something; sometimes we've even been committed to touring, with the dates set and we wouldn't even be finished with the record. This time, there was no pressure on us, which was great. We could write songs take some time and listen to them, say 'That's good' or 'That needs help.' Maybe change a piece here or there. We don't really like to go into the studio with nothing and try to do it there. We like to have it done and worked out, so that when you're recording you can concentrate on the performance and the sound."

AC/DC did, of course, need a replacement drummer, and the new man behind the kit was, in terms of style, a link with the band's past. Chris Slade had played with Manfred Mann's Earth Band, Uriah Heep, The Firm, Gary Numan, Gary Moore and many more. He also drummed on Tom Jones's 1965 chart topper 'It's Not Unusual'. Slade was originally approached to provide temporary percussive assistance. 'DC worked in a barn close to Brighton, and almost straight away it was clear they could consider Slade for a permanent position. As Angus explained, "His style is just perfect for the band, it is as solid and powerful as you can get. Chris is a bit similar to Phil Rudd; they both smash the drums as hard as they can. But Chris can be frightening to look at; you look at his bald head and it could scare you."

Slade's muscular, chrome–domed look made him stand out from his bandmates, who tended to be small and hairy, but his concrete backing was the ideal accompaniment to songs such as 'Fire Your Guns'. After rehearsals in Brighton, the band headed for Windmill Road Studios in Ireland to start work on the album proper. The choice of producer was a surprise to some observers. Canadian Bruce Fairbairn had worked his commercial magic for acts such as Bon Jovi and Aerosmith in the past and some were worried he would effect a change in the AC/DC style.

"You always make the best album you can for that period. We never have, never would, put something out unless we felt confident about it. This time, we kept pushing the deadline for completion further and further back so that the record was right." Angus Young

There was no chance of AC/DC losing their edge, however. All they were doing was to update the overall 'sound' of the album. The material they would create was to be as strong and defiantly unfashionable as ever. In fact the group showed a dark side on the title track, 'The Razor's Edge'. Angus's stroked a sinister riff and the vocals took on an epic edge. The song was unlike anything 'DC had created before and showed a distinct metal tinge, albeit unintentionally. "We had the main riff and there was something really ominous about it," remarked Angus. "And for that reason alone we decided to go ahead with it. In the past we'd stay away from things that sounded too musical."

Elsewhere it was business as usual with the likes of 'Got You By The Balls' and 'Goodbye & Good Riddance To Bad Luck'. But the real beauty of the album was in the opening track, 'Thunderstruck'. Beginning with a wonderful, one–fingered guitar hammer on/off trick the song built into a crescendo of hard–rocking perfection. "I was just fiddling around with my left hand when I came up with that riff," said Angus. "I played it more by accident than anything. I thought 'not bad' and put it on tape. That's how me and Malcolm generally work. We put our ideas on tape and play them for one another." The lyrical inspiration for the song was a suggestion by Angus. "I was in an airplane over East Germany and the plane got struck by lightning. I thought my number was up. The stewardess said we were struck by lightning and I said, 'No we were struck by thunder, because it boomed'."

'DC penned another memorable melody with 'Are You Ready' and a chorus which verged on the commercial in 'Moneytalks.' "There's a lot more melody on *The Razor's Edge* and we've always been wary of melody" Brian would explain. "A song like 'Moneytalks' or 'Thunderstruck', there are real melodies in those songs…I had to learn what to do again with that nonsense."

'Moneytalks', which would be released as a single, was another idea from Angus. "Money's the big divider," he would say. "Places other than America are not necessarily like that. In Europe they think you've got to be born with class. In the U.S. they think you buy it, like it comes with the tux. So it's just our little dig at the lifestyle of the rich and the faceless."

It seemed clear Bruce Fairbairn had a right to claim credit for the extra kick he had extracted from AC/DC. Rather than moulding them into his own sonic puppets, he simply honed their ever–present rock n' roll ideologies and made them slicker and stronger than ever before. For example, the prominence given to Cliff Williams' bass during 'Rock Your Heart Out' was a fine example of Fairnbairn's gift for finding previously hidden potential in something that had been present all along.

"Bruce told Malcolm that he didn't want to change AC/DC," Angus remembered. "And he didn't want us to do anything that we'd be uncomfortable with. These days it's hard to find people who are rock producers. A lot of people say they are, but as soon as you start working with them they'll push their ballads at you. The material was all ready to go when we got to Vancouver. Fairbairn just brought out the dynamics a bit. Bruce is a big fan of our older albums; he said he liked the excitement, rawness and lack of production on them. He wanted to capture that in your face sound again and did a good job doing it. There were very few overdubs. But sometimes somebody had picked their nose and hit the wrong chord so we patched up a couple of songs."

Brian felt it was a return to the no–pressure environment of his first year with AC/DC. "The studio experience reminded me of the old days when we would experiment with the arrangements and just try things out for the fun of it", he explained. "In the back of our minds we realised that there is a whole generation of fans that has sprung up in the three years since our last album was released. I want them to see what all this noise and fun is all about."

For *The Razor's Edge* AC/DC signed with the Atco label, and it was decided the first single to be released from the LP should be 'Thunderstruck'. which would go on to hit number 13 in the British charts. The album itself went top 5 in both Britain and America, taking the group's global album sales tally to over 60 million. In addition, they also charted in Britain with 'Moneytalks' and 'Are You Ready'. Touring the album began in the United States. Again 'DC travelled across Europe playing a series of 20 Monsters Of Rock festivals in 18 cities. When the band headlined the British show at Castle Donington for an unprecedented third time, they were supported by the likes of Metallica and Motley Crue. When Brian Johnson bumped into Crue's Nikki Sixx he told him that his tattoos looked as if someone had thrown up on his arms.

Comedy moments also prevailed at a show in Belfast in 1991, when Angus suffered the type of wardrobe malfunction that Janet Jackson would later make infamous. The moment was made more piquant by the fact that he was the last person to notice that 'little Angus's had made an unscheduled appearance. "I was wearing two pairs of shorts," remembered the guitarist. "And I didn't know the pair underneath had ripped at the front. So I pull these shorts down and Malcolm's looking at me funny, but I'm too busy in my own little world. I'm sort of thinking, 'What's he pointing at?' And the police are all sort of looking at me. And I turned around to the audience and they're all sort of stunned. And I sort of look down and there's all my wedding tackle hanging out for all the world to see."

But it wasn't all laughter. On January 18th 1991 tragedy was to befall AC/DC fans and the group itself. While the band were playing live at the Salt Palace in Salt Lake City, Utah, three youngsters – Curtis Child and Jimmie Boyd, both 14, and 19 year–old Elizabeth Glausi – were crushed as the crowd surged towards the front as the group began their set. A friend of Curtis Child, Scott Neil remarked, "It was chaotic it was hell. People were screaming. After they started another song, people started chanting, 'Stop the concert, stop the concert' until it echoed, but they wouldn't. When they started another song, I didn't think I was going to make it." According to another eyewitness, security had also attempted to alert the band to stop playing. One particular guard was "frantic, trying to get the lead singer's attention", said 39 year–old Gertrud Scheffler. "He was making motions across his neck, like to cut. You could see he was desperate."

A statement from AC/DC read: "The events of this calamity occurred in a very quick time frame. Once the gravity of the situation was communicated to the band, they immediately stopped performing, but stayed onstage in an effort to minimise the confusion. During this time singer Brian Johnson made several requests with the audience to clear the area. AC/DC's management co –operated with the Salt Lake City fire marshal and other health and safety officials to maintain calm and order. After 15 minutes, the decision to finish the performance was made with the fire marshal. This decision was motivated in order to maintain calm and order among thousands of fans who were unaware of what occurred."

Elizabeth Glausi died after her parents requested her life–support machine be turned off. Curtis Child's father filed an $8 million suit against AC/DC, as well as concert promoters and county officials. Later, Glausi's parents also sued the band. Less than a month later, on February 10th AC/DC were cleared of any involvement in the deaths of the teenagers although they continued to negotiate with the victims' relatives. The group did not know the teenagers were being crushed and were completely devastated at the news they received at the end of the show.

"Many a bootlegger has captured the whole feel of an AC/DC live gig. So we thought maybe it's our turn. And this was the best time, because we had done a lot of touring, nearly two years." Angus Young

AC/DC played a free show at the Tushino Airfield in Moscow on September 28 that attracted something between 500,000 and one million fans. The Moscow concert was presented as a "celebration of democracy and freedom" and as a gift to Russian youth for their resistance against the military coup that had recently failed. "It happened just thirty days after the coup attempt and it was the Moscow government's way of saying thank you to the kids for helping to stop the coup," explained Brian Johnson. "It was inspiring seeing these kids who'd put their lives on the line, rocking out to AC/DC like kids anywhere."

"The crowd was maybe crazier than any audience we ever played for. The government had insisted that the military be used to provide most of the security, but some of them started beating the kids with sticks. In the end, our security guys got them to pull back and just watch the show." Angus Young

The show was televised in Russia, filmed for a documentary by director Wayne Isham and recorded for a projected live album. The Russian concert was particularly significant in light of the fact that most Western rock music had been outlawed in the USSR until the advent of glasnost (the "openness" promoted by President Mikhail Gorbachev). Although AC/DC had long been popular among Soviet youths, the band's recordings were only obtainable on the black market. The concert almost didn't take place due to huge security concerns by the Russian Army, but as it turned out there were no greater problems than normally experienced in Russia at rock gigs. As other acts have found out, police brutality is commonplace and on the day AC/DC played there were many fans injured by the army security with 53 people requiring hospital attention. Authorities panicked when AC/DC wheeled out the cannon to accompany 'For Those About To Rock.' Angus said the military "really freaked! You saw their mouths drop. You almost heard them say, 'We've been tricked! It's a dirty imperialist trick!"

"We have been rioted upon by police; we've had all that," Angus continued. "But we are not telling people to do this; this is their own natural reaction. The biggest percentage of people who come to our show like to chant along to the songs they know really well. They like to throw their arms in the air and just release a bit of energy. There's nothing of 'This is aggressive.' I suppose if somebody were nodding his head or shaking his arms in the streets, people would say the guy's crazy. I could see that. But I can't see it when they are all together in a show and having fun; there's nothing at all aggressive in that."

The most aggressive head–shaker of all was, of course, Angus Young. He was asked if he ever got headaches from such intense head movement on stage. "No, when you first start, you are going to get sore bones," he admitted. "But I've never had any real headache from it. I've had headaches from travelling. Sitting around for 12 hours will give you a headache, because you're not doing anything." While on stage Angus would state that he didn't actually think about anything. "It's funny, but I don't. It's like two different people, sort of split. To me, the whole show is over and done within five minutes. It's like watching a movie."

1991 also saw the release of a video collection entitled *Clipped*, including material from both *Blow Up Your Video* and *The Razor's Edge*. It clocked in at 22 minutes. The lead track, 'Thunderstruck', became a classic in the AC/DC visual archives, encompassing everything from Chris Slade thumping the tom–tom drums, to Angus duck walking across a see through stage floor, and not least the inclusion of several hundred fans who were all housed in cages at the Brixton Academy. Unlike many acts that mime badly in videos, AC/DC looked as if they were giving their all, as if it was their last ever concert together. Brian Johnson is clearly singing properly, as he is at one stage caught spitting into the air, such is the intensity of his performance. And Angus's axe–wielding histrionics sometimes approach the level of air guitar.

'Moneytalks' was equally memorable. It begins with the burning of a specially designed dollar bill (bearing the image of a certain short–trousered guitarist rather than the customary George Washington). By the end of the video there are thousands of the dollars falling from the venue ceiling. Similar, but not identical dollars were later produced as inserts for the *Live* double album; any that were caught by fans in attendance at the Philadelphia video shoot are now collectors' items.

For the 'Are You Ready' video the band had a studio built to look like a prison. 10 volunteers had the AC/DC logo shaved into their heads especially for the video; one of the extreme haircuts was also used for the cover of the single. The audience was dressed in prison overalls, and to make the clip even more unusual, Angus was playing a black SG guitar rather than his usual red.

As ever, Angus was the visual focus. On 'Heatseeker' he exploded out of a television set, and returned (backwards) into the same set at the climax. On 'That's The Way I Wanna Rock N' Roll' he enters rooms where all manner of different characters reside, including a schoolgirl, a mechanic and several people at a hospital and an airport. As ever, he duck walks at the start of the song, boogieing along perfectly to the stuttering riff.

During 1992, AC/DC worked on the release of the *Live* album, which was mixed (and, according to the group, "re–touched") at Little Mountain Studios in Vancouver with producer Bruce Fairbairn. The tracks were recorded in various places during their world tour, notably at Castle Donington. It was made available in a single CD format, a double CD 'Special Collector's Edition', as well as a video, filmed in 35mm by David Mallet during the 'Monsters Of Rock' festival at Castle Donington. The album went straight into the US top 20 albums chart and went on to attain Double Platinum status in the States. "We wanted to capture it before the hair and the teeth drop out", laughed Angus. "We didn't want to be on life support systems. The album really is more for the AC/DC collector. When you're talking to them at shows, it's always the first thing they ask – 'When are you guys going to do another live album?' That's probably the most asked question of anyone in the band. But we wanted to wait until Brian had a lot of studio albums under his belt, so he'd get a fair shake."

The disc, the band's first official live album for 14 years, and Brian's first ever with the band, was a perfect representation of the group on a collective onstage high. The band had carved out an impressive array of songs with the Geordie vocalist and they were collectively itching to have the live renditions captured for posterity. Four of the 14 songs originated on *Back In Black*, including 'Shoot To Thrill', 'You Shook Me All Night Long', 'Hells Bells' and the iconic title track. Other Johnson–era tracks included the anthemic 'Thunderstruck' and 'Who Made Who', which was suitably pumped up and carried greater dynamism than the original. "We're constantly being bootlegged in Europe and Asia so we're bootlegging ourselves", said Brian of unofficial 'DC products. "Both the live double album and the video have odd songs that weren't singles or that we don't perform very often."

Unless they had access to these bootlegs, it was the first chance for some fans to hear Johnson–fronted versions of older AC/DC numbers such as 'The Jack', 'Whole Lotta Rosie' and 'Dirty Deeds Done Dirt Cheap'. Perhaps some were surprised at how capably Johnson attacked the Bon Scott songs, but he did so with remarkable ease – at least it seemed that way. Brian often suggested he had to try incredibly hard to carry off the older songs in an appropriate manner.

Unlike the often poor-quality bootleg material, *Live* was expertly produced and featured a clear mix that highlighted Johnson's shredding vocals. Often it was taken as read the Young guitar would be at the forefront of the sound but Fairbairn and mixing engineer Ken Lomas had been careful to assert Johnson's rightful place as front man. Credit also had to go to Chris Slade who seemed to be the strongest and most creative drummer the group had ever featured in its ranks. More likely to throw in a fill than previous sticks men, but equally as driven and solid with the beat, Slade was a sight to behold.

The downside to the album was the lack of atmosphere in between some songs, caused by the inclusion of tracks from several different live arenas. Rather than being the record of one continuous show, the songs jumped from venue to venue, which somewhat diluted the AC/DC live experience. "I'm not sure where all the songs on the record come from," said Brian candidly. "I've been so mixed up with all the tapes being sent back and forth. The songs come from Moscow, Donington, Scotland, Canada and America. They didn't want to put too much from one place because somebody would be insulted. They tried to be a bit diplomatic, but most of it is from America and Canada." He also said it was great being done this way, collecting tapes from shows "all over the world at different spots".

Nevertheless, the album was a timely gathering of the various strengths of an AC/DC gig. As Angus would testify, "I never hit a bum note, God forbid! I prefer to call it artistic license. If you were going to fix up that sort of thing, then it becomes a studio album. There's the inevitable feedback, the squeaks, the snare drum rattle, the technical things, you try to pull all that out..."

The album was to become the band's biggest seller since *For Those About To Rock...We Salute You*, which seemed to endorse Angus and Brian's assertion the material was strictly for the AC/DC connoisseur. An added bonus was the time it afforded the group to come up with new songs. "We're pretty lucky at this moment", said Angus. "We've got a little time to play with. The good thing about it is we can get to write a whole new record without somebody saying,

'Come on guys, you've got two weeks to finish it!' Hopefully we can do this next one exactly the way we want."

Brian added, "Sure, it gives us a little breathing space until the next studio album comes out. But we didn't want to put out a stopgap record. We wanted it to be a little special, to give the fans a wide choice… does putting out all this material mean we're cashing in and then packing it up? I'm being asked that and I'll tell you, definitely not."

THE PERILS OF ROCK N' ROLL

Apart from the disaster in Salt Lake City, the early nineties saw numerous negative incidents surround AC/DC. On November 11th 1990 21 year–old David Gregory was attacked outside the group's show at the Brendan Byrne Arena in New Jersey and died a day later in hospital. A state trooper was cleared of criminal wrongdoing in relation to the incident (though the Gregory family won a $250,000 settlement).

On November 13th 1991 while AC/DC were playing a show in Wellington, New Zealand two fans received stab wounds and several overdosed. After the show, unruly fans rampaged through the town damaging cars and shop windows. By the end of the day, 50 arrests had been made.

Chapter 16 – Vast Action Heroes

"We can't sit on our arses and say the world owes us a living because we've paid our dues. Me; I think if I fluff a note I'm robbing the kids. You're gonna pour it all on until you drop, so even if they hate you they can still say 'At least they tried.'" Angus Young

In 1993 AC/DC made a return to Hollywood, after the success of the *Who Made Who* soundtrack. There was less work for them this time; just one track, 'Big Gun' for the tie–in album for the Arnold Schwarzenegger motion picture *Last Action Hero*. AC/DC's song was the first track on the album, and one of the strongest – no mean feat on a compilation that included Def Leppard, Queensrÿche, Aerosmith, Tesla and Alice In Chains. The song was produced by Rick Rubin and once again kept AC/DC's name in the current musical spotlight, introducing them to new fans.

'Big Gun' was released as a single by Atlantic on June 28, backed with live versions of 'Back In Black' and 'For Those About To Rock...', both of which were recorded at the Moscow Monsters Of Rock show in 1991. The video for 'Big Gun' was filmed at Van Nuys Airport Hangar 104E in Los Angeles and featured Schwarzenegger, who was a fan of the band, wearing a schoolboy uniform while mimicking and 'playing' alongside Angus.

It was a wonderful combination of huge and tiny men, and the interplay between the pair worked well on screen. Angus recalled, "Well, I showed him a dance step for a video. I remember when I met him; he picked me up with his hand, lifted me to eye level and said, 'Hullo Ang–goose.' We had done a track for his movie, *Last Action Hero*, and the film studio wanted him to be part of the video. I said to him, 'It'd be cool if you were in the school suit like me' so they had a big school suit made for him. And the director said, 'Arnold, see that little run–around Angus does? It would be good if you could copy it.' So I showed him how to do it." The footage of the band was perfectly timed to coincide with the action in the movie and at the end it's left to Arnie to bid goodbye, with the Austrian saying, "that's what I call action".

The soundtrack album brought AC/DC into close proximity with metal bands such as Anthrax and Megadeth but 'DC just carried on doing their own thing, resisting easy categorisation.

"When you've hung together that long maybe people just get used to you. They might think, 'They've been around a lot. Maybe they *are* good,' laughed Angus when asked how the group had managed to carve out a 20–year career. "I think we have survived because we stayed the same. You try to be yourself. It's a bit late in the day for us to get out there and chase some trends. When we started playing, music was very mellow at the time, very middle of the road. If somebody had said, 'What's happening? What's the buzz out there for music?' It was the Village People, 'Macho Man'. There was Led Zeppelin and the Rolling Stones, of course, but these acts were rarely touring at the time. I thought of Zeppelin as a music trip, like a Yes or something. I never really saw them as a rock and roll band, even though they might have a stab at the rock and roll thing. The Stones were more rock and roll. We thought there was room for a good, tough approach with hard rock music."

Regardless of some connections with 'older' acts Angus still did not ever consider playing outside of AC/DC and either jamming with other major names, or making a solo album. "It's not a thing that's ever appealed to me," he explained. "I've never had the idea to go, even if anyone said to me, 'Come and play with me.' It doesn't give me a thing. Playing with the guys as AC/DC is what makes it for me. That's what makes the sounds. Outside of that, it's different. If I was standing there playing on my own, you'd find it dull. So, I need my brother, the two of us together. It's the combination."

After a break, AC/DC would begin to write for their second album of the 1990s. "We always seem to know when we've had enough of a break", said Angus. "Though it wasn't as long a break as some people think. We got together and jammed and the songs seemed to just fall into place."

At the dawn of 1995, rumours spread that Phil Rudd had returned to the band. At the end of the last 'DC tour, Malcolm and Angus had bumped into Rudd in New Zealand. Phil asked if there was any chance of playing with them again. So, when the group were rehearsing in England in early 1995, they asked him to sit down at the drums and see if the spark was still there.

"We've never tried to say we're better than our audience. There's a lot of people who come to see us and go, 'I can do what he does.' I've never said to an audience, 'You're going to have to applaud 'cause we're here, so stand up and go nuts.' AC/DC knows when we go onstage we go to work." Angus Young

In the 12 years since leaving the band Rudd had got his life back together. "I had plenty of ideas when I left the band that I hadn't had time to put into practice before," he says. "I raced cars, flew helicopters, learnt to shoot, became a farmer and planted some crops. I lived in New Zealand which was great; nice and quiet with nobody bothering me."

Rudd might not have been playing his preferred instrument much during the period away from AC/DC but he was still involved with music in other ways. Rudd: "I built my own 24-track studio and worked with a few bands, recording and mixing. But I didn't play drums at all for six years and even since then I've only played when I wanted to rather than when I had to. In the end I got together with a couple of close mates and started to play. We were a real 'Saturday night band' and we got a few tracks together that we could make a record with. We recorded them in my studio and gave them to a few people to listen to. They were impressed but if we had taken it further we would've had to go on tour and I wasn't ready for it at that point."

Rudd missed the camaraderie of the old days, not to mention the early material which AC/DC would always play live. "I loved *Powerage* and when we first started rehearsing in England we started with tunes like 'Gone Shootin' and 'What's Next To The Moon?' recalled Phil. "It was good. Even on tour we played older songs like 'Down Payment Blues' and 'Dog Eat Dog'. It only took five minutes to feel like I'd never been away."

According to his rhythm section partner Cliff Williams, **"Phil is really *the* groove. His play is simple, like mine, still being strong and fixable. Chris Slade was more a technician, kind of a 'studio shark'. Simon, he knew every song! His play was simple too, but he wasn't Phil Rudd. Phil's play is exactly what we need. Moreover, he's got this sixth sense, a natural feeling. Phil always had a natural feel for what the band was about. Chris is a fantastic drummer but Phil fits us like a hand in a glove. So it's nothing specific, more of a feeling. He was in the band even before I joined and when I came in the group already ran like a well–oiled machine. I had to fit in with it and that's what I did."

AC/DC had already begun to record their album in late 1994 at the Sony studios in New York but the sessions would be scrapped and the group then had to start all over again. They relocated to Ocean Way studios in Los Angeles and began work proper with co–producers Rick Rubin and Mike Fraser.

Malcolm Young, commenting on the move from New York to L.A., said, "we jammed a lot this time. And because of the delays in the studio, we jammed even more! I'd say we were together almost a year just playing, making this album. Things got really tight, the sort of thing you usually only get on tour. So that gave us a great vibe in the studio. We want our albums to sound like our best live gigs, and normally you have to shut your eyes and imagine you're back onstage again. But this time we were already in the stage mode."

Brian Johnson thought the five months AC/DC spent record-ing in L.A. were "Brilliant. We were having such a good time I didn't want to go home! When we all first got together it's always fun, because you haven't got a clue what is going to happen next. The boys just come in with some riffs – I don't know where they get them from, they're brilliant. And all I have to do is open my mouth and shout my tits off."

"Rick Rubin made us record every track about 50 times each to ob-tain the good dynamics and we kept those that had the best feelings. Sometimes, when we heard the whole tracks, our opinion changed totally. It was a bit disappointing and I thought we'd lose the sacred fire by playing all of those tracks again and again." Cliff Williams

The idea of recording an album with Rubin came from his work on the 'Big Gun' track. "From doing that he really wanted to try to do an album with us," said Angus. "Different folks, different strokes, I suppose. His approach is a little bit more bare bones. I don't know what Mutt Lange is up to now, but he was very into tuning in on what was current in the world." Rubin was certainly different; in no way did he follow any trends when working with musicians, especially a group who were as well established as AC/DC. As Angus would testify: "He's got a good approach because he doesn't sit there and say 'Let's make a hit single.' Some guys want you to do a filler because they say 'Let's make three hit singles'."

"One of the reasons we used Rick Rubin was to recreate the feel of the earlier albums," explained returning drummer Rudd. "We wanted to get that classic AC/DC sound back, the sound that suits us best. I'm really pleased with the results. I had the most fun I've ever had in a studio with this one." On Rubin, Cliff Williams would comment, "Yeah it's good to have young blood. He's loved the band for years – at least that's what he says – and wanted to work with us some more. He knew that the band has its own sound and knew what we wanted to hear. He doesn't try to get us to do things that don't suit us."

"Most of the kids in my high school were into bands like Led Zeppelin, Yes and Pink Floyd, and I spent a lot of time hating those bands. Two bands grabbed me, Aerosmith and AC/DC. 'DC were kicking with that great huge guitar. I remember being impressed by all the things they tell you are wrong – volume, power, the simple riffs. And Bon Scott was just brilliant." Rick Rubin, 1987

The album was to be called *Ballbreaker*, which summed up the band's sound, according to its members. "We just thought of the hardest and heaviest thing we could and it came from there," said Malcolm, "It just seemed to sum the whole album up." Equally descriptive was the first single from the record, 'Hard As A Rock'. This featured a glorious guitar lick that, like so much AC/DC material, combined simplicity with an irresistibly catchy quality. Released on September 22nd 1995, the album was a riotous update of the classic 'DC blueprint and would reach the number 4 spot on the US billboard charts.

There was no arguing about the direction of the material; it was more good time rock n' roll, honing decades of experience and dynamics into tight–knit riffs and melodies. "I'm really proud of this album," stated Angus. "I can honestly say I love very one of the songs – and that's saying something, coming from a band that started just after the Crucifixion." There were no surprises with *Ballbreaker*, just basic heads–down hard rock played with an audible sense of fun. 'Hail Caesar' was an update of 'For Those About To Rock…', a Roman tale of gladiatorial combat, with lyrics such as "Starring in the coliseum, tied upon the rack. Up comes the thumb of Caesar, to stab you in the back…All hail Caesar, hail, hail!"

"My first impressions of Rick Rubin was this big guy, twice my height, with sunglasses, lying on the floor doing yoga and telling us what a big AC/DC fan he was" Angus Young

Elsewhere, the group were in fine tongue in cheek lyrical form, penning lyrics such as the questionable paean to the female form, 'The Honey Roll': "Honey roll over, and lettuce on top. Strap you to the bed, and make you rock. Run it up the flag, send it on home, push you to the wall, and make you moan." AC/DC were not winning themselves any more devotees among the ranks of feminists, but then they had not exactly intended to. Likewise, they were not likely to be attracting too many new fans with their brand of wise old rock; though it did seem younger fans were coming to gigs all the time, eager to see masters at work. The likes of 'Caught With Your Pants Down' might not have been literary masterpieces but the music behind the lyrics was as raw and energetic as anything the group created in the late seventies. *Ballbreaker* received the overall thumbs up from dedicated fans and 'DC were always guaranteed to fill out concert halls. In some ways, writing a new album was simply an excuse to go on tour and rip it up.

As Brian Johnson put it, AC/DC was just "Five blokes who enjoy getting together and playing some music", making light of the band's place in rock folklore. But Angus was in agreement that the group was tightly knit, both as friends and musicians. "We play as a unit", he confirmed. "I think that's why we are what we are. We get out there and we don't try and go crazy. I mean, I'm standing out there jumping around a lot, but it's more nervous energy than anything. Same with Brian. We've always been pretty out front, and we always went onstage with that attitude. We always said, 'If you're gonna do something make sure you let 'em know you're doing it!"

"We have the best jobs in the world. Millions of people love us everywhere we go and we get to visit them whenever we want to tour. We'd have to be even dumber than we are to give that up. I know that some bands have internal problems that make life very difficult, but nothing could be less true where we're concerned; we love each other like brothers." Brian Johnson

For 'Hard As A Rock', the band worked with director David Mallet for the seventh time. Four hundred London–based AC/DC fans were invited to the shoot and driven by bus to a soundstage at Bray Studios in Windsor. Angus spent the majority of the day hanging in midair on a giant demolition ball, on which he eventually came crashing through a window amidst a hail of fake glass and (real) exploding fireworks. "It's scary," laughed Angus. "I'm not that brave, and they don't pay me any extra for it! My whole life was flashing before me up there! David Mallet is always coming up with these crazy schemes to try and kill me!"

"We have a gang of fans coming around," said Brian Johnson of the video. "From England, Switzerland, Germany, and we see them all the time, around the world. In Australia they turn up, and I'm like 'What the hell are you doing here?' 'Well, we knew you are down here playing so we came here for two weeks'. And in Japan, the same guys were there. I couldn't believe it. Well, my brother is a chef with the band – we just cook some great stuff, he's fantastic – and I see the lads, and ask have they eaten. 'No, we haven't, you know, it's a bit of an expensive place this, Japan'. And I say 'come on guys, have some beer and food'. It's the least you can do. On the last tour we gave them tour jackets that the band got. Sometimes I give them special shirts that I wear onstage. This is our way of saying thank you, it's the only way we can. But now I have noticed that I can spot some them in the audience during the show, like in Boston I was thinking 'Carl Allen? What the hell you are doing here?' It's absolutely stunning, I can't believe these guys. But it is a wonderful feeling, not many bands have that loyalty which kept us going through the good and the bad years."

AC/DC began its *Ballbreaker* world tour in America on January 12 in Greensboro, North Carolina, with The Poor as support act. Bon's mother, 78 year–old Isa Scott, showed up to give the boys support at the first date. Just two weeks into their American tour however, the band were forced to cancel four shows after the unexpected death of Brian Johnson's father. Brian left the tour in San Antonio on January 28 and immediately flew home to Britain to attend the funeral. He was back for the Oakland show on February 3rd. This not only proved his dedication to the band, but also the group's continuing allegiance to their legions of fans proved there was still a long way to go and more shows to play for AC/DC. Some people suggested the *Ballbreaker* tour would be the last for the band. Cliff Williams responded, "No way! As long as the public will want us and we're able to be good, there's no reason to stop. AC/DC is the best thing that ever happened to me, so I hope with of all my heart we'll continue. And our concerts are good, the kids have fun. We don't pretend to give something deep and intellectual, just good rock n' roll!"

"We want to go everywhere, even places no man or woman has boldly gone before," Angus said. "Now that the Wall has come down there's more and more places to play in the East. And Asia's opening up more, and it wants its slab of Western culture – and who better to do it than AC/DC!" Clearly the group were still doing something right, as many of the shows they played were sold out and during the year AC/DC received an award from Warner Music International to commemorate the sale of more than 80 million albums worldwide (this was with the exception of Australia and New Zealand, where the band had also sold millions of records). Also in the same year an 84–minute video, entitled *For Those About To Rock We Salute You* was released, taking in the footage of the

Moscow show AC/DC had played alongside Metallica, The Black Crowes and Pantera.

Malcolm shrugged off suggestions that *Ballbreaker* was AC/DC's last stand. "We've been going so long they always say that. No, we're gonna keep on rocking. We don't know any better!"

GOT YOU BY THE BALLS

The American part of the Ballbreaker tour ended in Dallas on April 4 1996. On April 20, the European tour began in Oslo with the British band The Wildhearts opening for AC/DC. In July, the band played three nights in the Plaza de Toros de Las Ventas in Madrid, Spain. The second show was filmed for a video project. The European part of the Ballbreaker tour ended on July 13 in Bordeaux, France, with a small festival with the French band Silmarils, The Wildhearts and Brazilian veteran metallers Sepultura.

In 2002 a DVD version of the Clipped video compilation was released, which also included the promos for 'Big Gun' and 'Hard As A Rock'. The latter was filmed in 130° heat but the fans, who had travelled from around the world to see the group in action did not seem to mind. One fan from Bavaria told the cameras he had "been following AC/DC for 17 years, the band is my life". The general performance was basic 'DC but there was an appearance from a wrecking ball in a demolition scene; whereby Angus was perched on top of the ball. This was some achievement as he doesn't like heights and was left 80 feet in the air!

Chapter 17 – Short Changed

"Take your 'save the trees' issue. I mean, my guitar is made of wood. A tree has been chopped down to make that guitar. I'd be a hypocrite 'cause I've got about 21 of those bits of wood. That's probably one tree in itself. Every rock n' roll musician's got a wooden guitar, including Sting. It's hypocritical." Angus Young

As the new millennium arrived, AC/DC prepared yet another studio album to placate their long time fans, originally known as *Smokin'* but eventually released as *Stiff Upper Lip*. Never mind reports of the band losing hair and being too old to rock n' roll, it seemed no one could prevent them from making music and travelling all over the planet to perform it live. However, tragedy was again to affect the group in 2000. During a concert in Ghent, Belgium, a fan climbed onto a chair during an encore before slipping and falling some 13 metres onto a concrete floor below. He later died in hospital.

The customary question of 'Is this the last AC/DC album?' was met with typical defiance from Angus Young. "It's the last one 'til the next one", he would say. Brian Johnson would concur, "Yeah it's a bit like a bus. There will be another one along in a minute."

There would always be an element of rebelliousness about AC/DC, even as its members passed their 50th birthdays. "As soon as they start liking you I think then you've got a problem", Angus told *Circus* magazine, referring to the media generally. "We've never been one to make yourself look nice or pretty or acceptable."

Angus recounted a story, which was typical of the kinds of remarks the media would often make to him or the other members of the band. "This DJ came into our dressing room and said, 'Hi, I'm so and so from so and so, I used to listen to your albums a few years ago and, to be honest with you, I didn't like them, but these kids kept ringing up and requesting them and gradually I've grown to like it.' And I just said to him, 'Pal, with us you either like it or hate it and if you didn't like it then I'll be buggered if you like it now.' I just told him what I thought and showed him the door."

"AC/DC has survived because we've never changed direction, never given in to trends. That's why there haven't been any solo projects from within the band. No one has ever wanted to. Our music doesn't go out of fashion because it isn't about fashion. I hear about all these different kinds of music: grunge, hardcore, death metal. And all it is is rock n' roll." Brian Johnson

Songs such as 'All Screwed Up' and 'Come And Get It' were once again the subject of prurient scrutiny. Interviewers asked whether AC/DC was still driven by their libidos. "It's what people on the street say, man," responded Brian. "Working lads, that's where their heads are at." "It's not just the fellas, either" added Angus. "Malcolm worked in a bra factory, and that was with, like, 1,000 women. You should have seen these women. They would go, 'Mal, my machine's down.' And he'd go in and say, 'There's nothing wrong with your machine.' And while he's on the floor, they're patting his head and rubbing his butt."

As for the explanation for still playing straightforward rock n' roll, the response was reassuringly basic. Brian Johnson: "Hell, I still like Chuck Berry playing rock and roll, and he doesn't turn around and come on like Martin Luther King and start giving me a lecture. I like Little Richard and he doesn't tell me what to do. These people lived it. I read this thing about Louis Armstrong and the hardships he went through in his life. And yet here's this guy coming on so happy just to be on a stage playing and performing. He's having a great time, and that's how I view it. We are in a great job. We get to do what we love most, make music. We get to travel. And we're happy."

"Our music comes from the heart. It's always been there. People put you down for playing rock n' roll you know. Well, fuck those people. You have got to do your own thing." Brian Johnson

The happiness was evident throughout the material on *Stiff Upper Lip*. Much like *Ballbreaker* it centred on composing familiar styled material, with a very slight modern twist in the production. The sound of the album was crisp, clear and upfront. At least in studio terms, AC/DC were brought crashing into the modern era. *Stiff Upper Lip* might have been on a par with material from the *Flick Of The Switch* album, which had received a mixed reception. At least, unlike that album, and certainly *Fly On The Wall*, the newest AC/DC record brimmed with a vibrant, punchy sound. Although there were a few complaints by some at the lack of ambition shown by the group, they were in the minority.

Furthermore, and more blatantly than previously, the band steered further into traditional blues on many of the album's tracks. It was still clearly AC/DC of course, as Angus confirmed. "It's good when you can hear something and straightaway go, 'That's them.' Somebody said to us once that you can instantly identify a Rolling Stones track. I said, 'Hey, with them you might hear it in a couple of chords, but we've got it in one!' You hear 'Back In Black' and it's just one chord. And that will crack it straight away. 'Highway To Hell' was another one."

The album was recorded in the Vancouver studio belonging to soft rocker Bryan Adams. "It was kind of strange", thought Johnson. "I didn't know it was his until we were recording, and one day, in walks Bryan Adams. Apparently, he's a non–smoking vegetarian, and here's our lead singer cooking all this meat and making bacon sandwiches. With this bacon smell floating around everywhere, he walks into the studio and it's full of cigarette smoke. So that was his introduction to us."

In a strange turn of events, Brian Johnson would have to go out and buy one of his own albums. As he was asked whether he collected AC/DC memorabilia, as had been a rumour for some time, he answered, "From us? No! Every time I get an AC/DC record, I just sign it and give it away to a fan. I don't have any of them left. But on this album, I had to go out and buy it. They forgot to send me one. And I got to the store and it was quite an embarrassment. They said 'What are you buying this for?' 'I haven't got a copy of it, that's why'. Sometimes they forget these silly things, like sending the record to the artist."

Brian was also peeved at the company's choice of single. "I'm still angry that they didn't release 'Can't Stand Still' as a single", he said later. "I couldn't believe that they chose 'Satellite Blues' instead of 'Can't Stand Still'. But that's just me personally. We don't have a choice; it's up to them. They just say, 'We want this, because we think it will sell more'. But I think on this they were terribly wrong. First single 'Stiff Upper Lip' was great. But I would have chosen 'Can't Stand Still' because it didn't have a high and low, just simple straight–ahead rock. It just rocks. And I'm amazed that it wasn't taken out as a single. We did that all the way through without any breaks. It is just beautiful rock n' roll."

Nothing, it appeared, could prevent AC/DC from knocking out material and entertaining their fans, which was what it was all about, according to Angus. "We are there as a rock n' roll band to give fun and entertainment," he said. "And we don't want to go out there and bullshit an audience. An audience can smell bullshit from a fucking mile away. It might wash once but when you come on twice, be prepared for the ripe tomato. When we started in the clubs our attitude was, we had one intention – rock n' roll! And we go for the same thing now…AC/DC never got sidetracked, to go this way or that way. We know what we do best, we play rock music."

Continuing his theories, Angus pondered, "I never take it seriously. Rock n' roll music was meant to be fun. I pick up a guitar and play it for enjoyment. If somebody says to me, do you think you're alienating an audience, are you being sexist, are you being this, are you being that? Are you doing harm to anyone out there? Hey, that's the last thing on my mind. The first thing is to get out there and have fun." In accordance with Angus's opinions, Brian remarked, "We're just pranksters more than anything. You're having fun. And that's all there is. It's not meant to harm anyone.

As for the long–term future of the band, Angus commented, "I don't think I could walk on that stage and do what I do or any of the lads do if we couldn't be honest. If it all went bad, we would feel it more than anyone. I couldn't get out there and rip people off in any way shape or form. If there's one thing I believe in, then it's that. "We've just kept plugging away at what we do. I know that sounds like a simple answer but I've never tried to write songs for any particular reason other than to do what I think is good. Yeah, there's a lot of people out there who write music they think other people will like, and then those people end up wondering why they're not successful at it. If we'd tried to write songs for those reasons, we'd probably be unemployed alongside those people. Luckily, we've been able to keep doing it, and hopefully it will continue for a while."

"There's not a day goes by when I don't pick up a guitar. And I'm getting there. I've got two fingers going now!" Angus Young

Brian was adamant that AC/DC always did things their way, even if that may have been different to other acts. "We've never pulled any punches", he stated. "We just play music that's fun and simple, the way our audience likes it. We're not gonna write some real serious political stuff that has no meaning to us – leave that for someone else to do. We're not here to save the world; we're here to play rock music. That's what we do, and that's why we're still around."

"A lot has happened since our days with Bon," Angus reflected. "But at the same time, I don't think music has really changed that much over the years. It's still all about making good music and the fans liking it. The business side of it hasn't really changed too much either, there's still the same kind of problems to deal with. You always hear about how all these revivals or new trends are taking place, but as far as I'm concerned we're just trying to do what we're good at."

2000 also saw the 20th anniversary of the death of Bon Scott, and there were many tributes. One in particular was a real reminder of the band's roots.

"Simon Croft, the guitarist with Thunderstruck – the world's no 1 AC/DC tribute band – rang me just after Christmas 2000 to let me know that his band was doing a special show on the 19th Feb which was the 20th anniversary of Bon Scott's death," explained Dave Evans, the man who preceded Bon as the band's singer. "I had worked with Simon in the 80's. As I had known Bon before he joined AC/DC, I asked Simon if he would like me to fly down to Melbourne from Sydney and do a couple of numbers with his band. He said it would be great and that I could do as many numbers as I wanted. I then realised that this was rock history in the making and that the AC/DC fans worldwide would be interested in this historic event so I arranged for the tribute to be recorded and videoed live."

As for the track listing, Evans commented, "I chose the first few songs from what I had recorded and sung with AC/DC to show my credentials. The other songs I felt told the story of Bon's rise, his pinnacle, his personal fears and his epitaph: 'It's A Long Way To The Top If You Want To Rock N' Roll', 'T.N.T.', 'Ride On' and 'Highway To Hell'. It was very electric, very emotional. The basic feel and excitement has never changed in over 30 years and so it continued to be a phenomenal success."

AC/DC's status as a sure–fire money–spinner was now set in stone. The merest hint of a gig by the legends could sell out venues in the most unlikely places, as the organisers of a jazz festival in Finland discovered in 2002. A man claiming to be George Young took a substantial advance from the organisers of the Pori Jazz Festival, claiming that AC/DC would perform as part of a three–concert tour, comprising the somewhat elongated itinerary of Melbourne, London and Pori, a town on the Gulf of Bothnia, in south–east Finland. Explaining the unlikely decision to book the no–frills rockers for a jazz event, the festival's managing director, Hannu Hakala, explained: "We were interested because the band is genuinely interested in the Aboriginals of their country, and some of them would have played at the Pori concert. Our part of the deal was to get Sámi (indigenous Lapp) musicians for the concert."

'George Young', unsurprisingly, vanished, having relieved the organisers of tens of thousands of euros.

BILLBOARD REPORT ON AC/DC SIGNING FOR EPIC RECORDS DECEMBER 2002

AC/DC Rides The Highway To Epic.

Australian rock icons AC/DC have signed a multi–album deal with Epic, the first fruit of which will be refurbished re-issues of seminal albums such as Back In Black, Highway to Hell, and Dirty Deeds Done Dirt Cheap, due early next year. Further reissues will follow, all of which will sport new liner notes and rare photos, and utilize Sony's proprietary Connected technology to unlock special online content created for each release.

It is understood that AC/DC's next studio album, due some-time next year, will complete the group's contractual obligation to Elektra. AC/DC has spent the past 26 years of its career recording under the Warner Music Group umbrella. The group's back catalogue is one of the most consistent sellers on Billboard's Top Pop Catalogue chart. According to Epic parent Sony, 1980's Back In Black has sold 41 million copies worldwide, making it the sixth highest–selling album in history. It has sold 318,000 copies this year alone, according to Nielsen Sound Scan.

The move to Epic reunites AC/DC with Epic chairman Dave Glew, who previously worked with the group at Atlantic, as well as Epic executive VP/GM Steve Barnett, formerly the group's manager. The new deal brings 16 of AC/DC's 18 U.S. releases to the label, which plans to also reissue some of the albums on vinyl and compile DVD releases.

"Today AC/DC is going stronger than ever, making it a true pleasure to welcome the band into the Sony Music family, and an honour to have the opportunity to bring both their classic repertoire and new releases to fans across the coun-

try and around the world," Sony Music chairman/CEO Thomas D. Mottola said in a statement.

AC/DC's last Elektra studio set, Stiff Upper Lip, debuted in March 2000 at No. 7 on The Billboard 200 and has sold 842,000 copies in the U.S., according to Nielsen Sound Scan. The title track from that album hit No. 1 on Billboard's Mainstream Rock Tracks chart.

Meanwhile, Image Entertainment has set a Feb. 18 release date for the DVD Rockmasters – AC/DC, capturing an Oct. 27, 1977, concert in London. The video finds the band, at the time fronted by the late Bon Scott, running through such favourites as 'Let There Be Rock,' 'T.N.T.,' and 'Bad Boy Boogie.'

Chapter 18 – For Those About To Rock Again

"I'm not going bald, my head's just getting higher" Angus Young

In 2003 AC/DC were inducted into the Rock & Roll Hall of Fame, a scenario that was accepted with the usual good grace and humour by the band. "Yeah, we got on and did a few songs and watched people wearing the tuxes and the evening gowns get up and go nuts," said Brian. "People were saying to us, thank fuck for AC/DC because it had been all speeches up until then. It's very nice that so many bands have respect for us, but it does make me feel very uncomfortable. I've always felt much of our appeal was based on the fact that anyone in the crowd could look up at us on stage and think, 'Hey, that could be me up there.' We are always making sure that we keep that good feeling between us and the fans, and I think if they look at us as 'legends' that would be difficult. I'd rather have everyone just think of us as a good rock and roll band."

That was unquestionable – but the fact remained that some of AC/DC's records had become imperishable rock classics. So, could the band members tell when they had a potential nugget on their hands? "Usually I can tell while we're making it," said Brian. "Obviously I think all our records are good, or we wouldn't release them. But there are certain songs that just get your foot tapping right away. I don't like to sell our music to people; I like to think that they buy it because they like it. But the fact that a lot of people seem to be buy our albums only makes me believe that we're doing what we're supposed to doing – and that's playing good ol' rock and roll."

Despite the band's back–to–basics, traditionalist approach, they have given in to many of the technological changes that have occurred in the music industry over the last 30–plus years, from videos and compact discs to, more recently, the Internet – do check out www.ac–dc.net for an idea of what a band site can achieve. Brian, however, had a particular gripe about the Internet. "I gotta tell you, one of the troubles in the Internet and some of the fanzine things, is rumours," he grumbled. "These mischief makers. Like, 'such and such is not going to make the gig this year', like Phil wasn't going to come on this tour. And we were looking at this and thought, why would anybody want to put that down? There is no reason for it. Or I won't be there. You know, like in America, in 21 years – in twenty –one years – I missed one gig. Because I was so sick that the doctor wouldn't let me, he said 'I can't let you on stage, Mr Johnson you're gonna mess the rest of the tour if you go tonight'. Blood level was that high, you know. We were just working too hard. So the doctor said 'I can't let you go, you're gonna kill yourself'. And I cancelled the gig. Within 24 hours I had left the band, I had been sacked; I was going to join other band, et cetera. I was like 'holy shit', one gig in 21 years. It wasn't that bad in the eighties, the rumours were just hearsay, you know it goes in to your left ear and out from your right. But now with the Internet, because it's the written word, people believe it. People believe anything that is written."

"For me, you just cannot whack rock n'roll, because it just does not tell any lies, you know?" Brian Johnson

Despite the obvious 'cyber waste', which could affect even an institution such as AC/DC, the band members still liked to keep an eye on fan–created websites, as Brian explained. "The band does that all the time. As we like to browse and see what's put on there that is true, what is not true. You know, you can't do anything about it, because if you write 'Hi, this is Brian... you lying piece of shit...' nobody would believe you. So they wouldn't believe it anyway. It's the problem of the Internet; people can put anything they like there, because nobody can identify them. Nobody knows who you are. You can get a nickname like Great Fish Blue – living in Kansas – and sitting in your room, mischief making. But thankfully there are lot of fans who are really good, they do try to get reliable information. Like the 'Dirty Deeds' boys – Michel Remy & friends from Belgium, they are good boys. In some cases they have been a little naughty too. We let them in the studio in Vancouver. They asked if they could come and visit, I said sure. And they came and we let them into the studio. They took photographs, but what they did was take a photo of a list of songs hanging on the wall..."

This supposed leak of details about a forthcoming album made it to the Internet. "You gotta be careful," Brian stated. "But that's their job, they want to get the info first. So I said 'Ten out of ten points to you'. To let them in and let them take photographs. But you see what happened straight after that, that was when the mischief started, people started make things up; the album was going to be called such and such, which it wasn't. Somebody's going to do this, which it never did..."

In this story the rumour was actually posted that Angus was going to sing on an AC/DC song, which of course was met with a mixture of surprise and elation for many fans. "It was me but they thought it was Angus", Brian recalled. "I was just starting *Stiff Upper Lip*, 'I was out on the drive'... and they thought it was Angus singing. Because Angus sings like that. And that kind of misinformation gets out there. Of course it's bad. But it's our part of the game – the music. And the good thing is that at least people are interested to know. Which makes us happy. When people like to know what we're going to do and what we're thinking. So it's got good and bad sides. The Internet is a curse and a wonderwall."

"I don't follow newsgroups that much myself. A lot of it is just not true so it's not worth watching. It's just like sitting in the pub. The weirdest rumours on the band can be heard in the pub, like somebody may have a sore throat, and at the end of the evening he is going to a throat operation" Brian Johnson

Although Brian was annoyed about the loose grasp of reality displayed on unofficial fan sites, he was even more damning about content providers who should have known better. "I think that the last time I went on the record company's website – which was Elektra's – I got on there but it's full of advertisements," he said. "You get the feeling 'What are you doing here?' So they use it as an advertisement platform, they can't win over the fan sites. They are our record company. I never forget about one situation... how dumb can they be? – fucking dumb!

Brian's scorn for 'the suits' extended beyond cyberspace, however. "We were in Argentina," he said, "and the head of our record company, the lady in charge, phoned up Sarasota (Florida) – where I live – and had a contact to my race shop, where we build racing cars. And she said 'Could I speak to Brian, I really need to talk to him immediately' and Tomas Ransen, a Swedish guy answered and asked 'Who is this?' 'Well, it's the record company, we want Brian to come and sing a song on this new band's album, to do a duet with the singer'. I have forgot the band's name by now. And Tomas said 'You are the record company? I'm afraid I don't believe you'.

"So the lady shouts 'How dare you, WE ARE THE RECORD COMPANY, this is our number, ring us back, and I'll prove it'. So Tomas rang back, and yes it was the record company. Tomas said 'You want Brian? So when do you want him?' The lady answered 'If he could try to get to Miami by tomorrow, that would be wonderful!' Tomas: 'You don't know he's in Buenos Aires?' Lady: 'Pardon?' 'He's in Buenos Aires, he's on tour. They have just been awarded a platinum album in Argentina from your company, and you don't know he is there?' So the lady was like 'Ooops, sorry...'

You know what I mean. It can be as dumb as that. She didn't even know that we were on tour, and she was the head of the record company. I won't give any names, to protect the innocents." AC/DC finally left the Atlantic label after almost 30 years but there was no love lost. As Angus put it, "We were one of their biggest selling artists, but I don't know what we meant to them. They put out some anniversary album to celebrate their acts and we weren't even on it."

"We always like to feed the kids who follow us everywhere. There's always a lot of food back stage; more then we can eat. So as soon as we are leaving the venue we say 'Okay guys!' And the kids come in with their haversacks and fill them up, so they can get to the next gig." Brian Johnson

In 2004 Angus Young discussed the outlook of the group in modern times. In typical fashion he observed, "The style of the music is still the same. We still play hard rock or rock and roll music.

That's what we started with and we still play it now. We just try to find new ways of presenting it, and for us, that is always a challenge – to come up with a new idea, turn it into AC/DC and still retain that style. We've recorded a lot of material over the years and, in a way, you have to be your own editor. We look at it all, but we don't let every one of the songs we write go out there. We try to pick the best of what we've got."

As for writing and presenting that music to the public, the outlook was reassuringly AC/DC. "I try to find new ways of playing things and I've always had a thing where I don't put a guitar lick into something just for the sake of putting a guitar lick into something," Angus said. "I like everything to have a groove and go with the track and besides that, you do like it to shine out, too, so it doesn't come across as just being in there as filler." As for Angus's guitar hero, Chuck Berry, it was nice to know the legendary player was still treading the boards on stage. "I saw him recently in Australia, and he was great" said Angus. "I saw Buddy Guy at the Roxy in L.A. while we were making the record, great show. To me these guys are timeless. Muddy Waters was the same. You look at them and they ooze youthfulness. Me and Malcolm both like the blues. It's between that and the early rock and roll, Little Richard and Chuck Berry. For us that is rock music. All the other things that you hear, like the current trends, Top 10s, and the latest, that's all that they are, trends. But I think all of those other things are timeless."

Angus was asked whether he enjoyed anything he might see or hear on the television or radio. "Not really", he responded. "I hear the odd tune or maybe I might hear a bit of classical on the TV. But I've never zeroed in and gone, 'What's that?' Whereas with blues music, even if I've seen an old documentary and there's somebody banging on a piece of wood in the back, I'll try and find out who it is. That's what I grew up with and liked best. Maybe it's the lack of rhythm in classical and other things. I like rhythm more than anything. But I know there's heaps of music out there, and I'm sure they're all good at whatever they're doing."

Still, there is not going to be any chance of an 'MTV Unplugged' album from AC/DC. When asked if the band would ever go unplugged, Angus's response was characteristically cheeky. "An 'undrugged' sort of thing? Haha. I don't know. When things are in fashion, you get one band to do something and they all do it. We tend to stray away from a lot of the trends. I suppose it's good for the people who can do it. Sometimes we've sat there, and Mal might pick up an acoustic…"

And there is the defining character of the group. They will never change, and for that their fans rightly love them. When AC/DC finally bow out of the world of rock, they will do so with their respect intact and an arsenal of classic records behind them, albums that will be successfully reissued for successive generations. The band has always appealed to the underdog, the naughty kid at school, the loner rocker and the heavy metaller as much as the biker and even the punk. You will be hard pushed to find a group with more widespread appeal than AC/DC, and for that they must be saluted.

October 2004 AC/DC now has a city laneway named after them. On October 1, 2004, Lord Mayor John So of Melbourne erected the sign for 'AC/DC Lane'. The unveiling was accompanied by cheers from fans present and a bagpipe player who belted out 'It's A Long Way To The Top (If You Wanna Rock N' Roll)'. The newly named AC/DC Lane is parallel with Swanston Street, which was the setting for the video to the song, filmed in 1976. The Mayor announced the sign with a quick speech, saying, "As the song says, this is a highway to hell. But I say this is a lane to heaven. Let us rock," as he pumped his fists in the air. The city made sure it produced plenty of copies of the sign, anticipating that the group's fans might take the original as a souvenir. Councillor Kimberley Kitching said, "We would expect it would be pretty hard to get it off though, you'd have to come with some pretty good equipment."

Many members of Australia's music scene were present to honour the band that made Melbourne their home in the 1970s. "I think the whole band would be blown away... I'm sure if Bon was still alive he would be very proud," said Aussie music business legend Ian 'Molly' Meldrum. The only downside, of which Bon would undoubtedly not approve, is the fact the Office of the Registrar of Geographic Names would not allow the lightning bolt between the 'AC' and the 'DC'.

Chapter 19 – The 'SG' Spot

"I'd always wanted an SG, I think the cutaway horns reminded me a bit of myself" Angus Young

Such is the importance attached to the guitar style of AC/DC, and indeed the guitar itself, you may have wondered where the guitar talk was for much of the book. Ladies and Gentlemen, here is the SG Spot, a dedication to Angus Young and his ubiquitous guitar and Malcolm and Angus's playing style, plus more. Though Angus will often tell interviewers his guitar style is simple, there is perhaps an element of modesty at play, characteristic of AC/DC's attitude to life in general. Angus and Malcolm stick to basic chords and also power chords, both of which are amongst the first things an aspiring rock guitarist will learn. However it's the quick combination of the varying chords, and a complicated spread of notes which sets AC/DC apart from modern rock n' rollers. For a small man Angus can sure spread his fingers across the guitar neck to get the best and most appropriate sounds. "I have a very small reach", says the guitarist. "When I sweat a lot, my fingers seem to go apart for miles. They'll stretch on their own once they get really loosened. I've only got a small hand so I use all my fingers to bend strings. I really push it with all my fingers backing it up."

Most of the speed for guitar work comes from his left hand, as Angus says there is a lot he can do without picking. In concert he often performs solos with just the left hand. "When I was smaller and wanted to learn to play, I thought maybe I'd toughen my left hand up," he explains. "But then I found it was always easier just to use the two as much as possible. Don't think of technique or anything, just play. Some guys play chords with their thumb, some guys with their pinkie. That's how I sort of learned for myself. I used to play with my thumb and make up my own sort of little chords, what I could do here and there. I just use them. I don't know any sort of positions or things like that."

"We fiddle about, usually," is Angus's perspective on creating riffs. "You go between different chords. We play a lot of open chords. Mal will fiddle around sometimes and try and come up with a couple of different things, even with chords and stuff. When we grew up, we never had chord books. We just played. It's like you see someone hit a chord and then you go, 'I've got six strings. I better use them all.' Now, we might use two or one. When we were recording things with my other brother, George, he used to say, 'Look, that string's rattling. Take it off.' We'd tape it up just for the sound. Sometimes people get all the bits and gadgets and everything and think, 'I'm going to use it all.' We listen and hear the song first. If something's not right we try some other way." Sometimes, playing live and jumping off monitors and generally up and down can create trouble in terms of the tuning of the guitars. "When you jump off things, yeah, you can have problems," confirms Angus. "But it's basically down at the guitar. Some guitars sit well the tunings stay in no matter what you do. I've got a few of them that won't for the love of anything stay in tune. You can just use them for a second and they go out."

"Are any of my solos particularly difficult? It depends. If somebody says, 'Roll around on the floor, and I want you to spin around at 100 miles an hour and whistle 'Dixie' or something,' it can be. The style of a solo might be difficult, but I don't think the actual thing itself is if you know what you're doing." Angus Young

Angus, like his brother, now has a wide range of guitars, including Fenders and acoustics as well as his trusty Gibsons. "I would say my favourite one is from about '67 or '68", he comments. "It used to have one of those engraved metal things on the back with the little arm the tremolo, but I replaced it with another tail piece. I've got a couple of them that have the vibrato arm." However, he rarely uses the tremolo arm. "There are songs where I can do it for the sake of convenience, for tuning or something. I've used it on some songs in the studio for growling, but mainly I would do that with a tuning key because you can go up a way or down a way. But

I've got one that's all set up and put there on the stage, and if I want to, I might use it just for a song."

When the boys were growing up, guitars were available in Australia but, as Angus has said, "It used to be very expensive there because they came from America. I bought one when they got cheap." The first electric guitar Angus ever purchased was the Gibson SG and he still uses it to this day. "I played other guitars too, though," he said. "I had an acoustic guitar first. My mum got it for 10 bucks when I was nine or so. She got both me and Malcolm one, so there would be no fighting over it. There was always a guitar around the house. Always some brother that had a guitar lying around somewhere. I always wanted an SG as a kid. I had a friend from San Francisco who went to school with me in Sydney. He had a Gibson guitar catalogue and when I looked through it and saw the SG, I said, 'That's my guitar!' I always liked the shape of it and when I got a hold of my first one, I was in love with it. I've always thought it was a great guitar. The shape of the SG has the little horns, it's red and it's a little devilish. It's also lightweight. Of course, I like the sound of it, too."

In the early years, Angus was tempted to shift his allegiance, but never seriously. "I tried a Les Paul once," he recalled, "but I'm a little guy and the SG just felt more balanced. Just as I came out of school, I saved up all my pesos and went to the guitar shop. As soon as I saw the SG, I knew it was that one I wanted. It was so easy for me to play. I always thought that it was just a run–of–the–mill Gibson, that they were all basically like that, and that you might get better ones. Over the years, I've never found one that was the same as it. And the other thing when I saw the Beach Boys with a Stratocaster, I think that also swayed me the other way. It didn't look right. And that surfing thing was popular at the time." So inextricably linked is Angus with the guitar, that there is now an Angus Young Signature model, made to his own specifications (and with a demonic Angus cartoon on the head).

Angus said that one of the things he loved was the "the double cutaway, for a start. If you think you're clever you'll get all the way up the neck, and you don't have to worry about being a contortionist and bending over. I know a lot of people that will go, 'Ah, yeah,

Les Paul, Les Paul,' but the SG's got the same neck. I don't think there's many more in the Gibson line with a similar neck. If you're a little guy like me, the balance makes it a lot easier to play. The only other guitar I could really get around on was a Tele, because of the size. But I've always liked the SG, plus with Gibsons you can get a certain tone. They're all different, whereas with a Fender type thing they've got a similarity that goes a lot of the way through. What I didn't like about Fenders, probably because I was never a fan of the surf type thing was they always make a clicky click click sound. With the SG you don't get that click. You get a mellower tone, a little bit more bottom end."

"Whatever you play, somewhere along the line guys will rip it off. People like Hendrix were always abused; everyone got into that sort of thing. I never did. I just sit on what I can do and feel" Angus Young

As far as the neck of the guitar is concerned Angus likes it as thin as possible. "The first one I had was a very small, thin neck. I showed it to a guy from Gibson, and he wanted to do some photos of it and look at the pick–ups. I said, 'Could you get me one the same as this?' And he went, 'I've never seen one like it.' It wasn't shaved either. It had come direct from their factory. It had all the original pieces. I've got another guitar that's a reject, and it's an incredible guitar. I said, 'If you can make a few more rejects, I'll like them, too!" "The pickups that they make are good," says Angus regarding the original Gibson pick–ups he likes to leave in the guitar. I've even got a couple of their newer ones that are really good. I've also got a few different pickups that a guy in England made for me once. He knows how I like guitars because he used to repair them all the time. They are basically the same as Gibsons. So, if I'm in England, I'll use him. If I'm in the U.S., I'll try and get a Gibson one.

"I'm more interested in bands than guitarists. I like the Yardbirds, some of the early Who, Stones. When it comes to solos and things, the guitar can be exciting. You like to see rock music be very hard

and tough, but a lot of that seems to be gone. People just seem to be worried about how many tricks they can do. Someone like Eddie Van Halen fiddles around a lot, and it tends to be like guitar exercises. People like Hendrix knew how to rip the hell out of it, but they still knew there had to be rhythm in there, too. That's what's missing a lot nowadays. It's a bit like Deep Purple, it's all technical, but there's none of the rhythm to back it up." Angus Young

EQUIPMENT

"Musicians with money usually buy expensive tuners when their sharps are a little flat. But who ever heard of a musician with money? If you're broke like the rest of us, here's an option: simply slap on AC/DC's 'It's a Long Way to the Top (If You Wanna Rock n' Roll).' The song has only one chord. If you can figure out which one it is, hold the chord with one hand and twist the pegs with the other until you sound just like Angus. If that fails, just follow the example of Sonic Youth and forego tuning altogether. Remember: one man's 'noise' is another man's 'art.' 'Turds of Wisdom', Guitar WORLD, April 1997

AC/DC Tour Equipment 1980 Back in Black UK Tour:

Angus

2 Gibson SG guitars
2 Radio Transmitters
3 Marshall 100 Watt Stacks

Malcolm

Gretsch Falcon
Gretsch Rock Jet
3 Marshall 100 Watt Stacks
1 Marshall 50 Watt Combo

Cliff

Fender Precision Bass
Fender Jazz Bass
3 Marshall 8 x 10s
3 Ampeg Suites

Phil

Sonor Custom Kit
Zildjan Cymbals

Brian

The Two–Ton Bronze Bell

THE RECORDING OF *BALLBREAKER*.

To record the Ballbreaker album Angus Young used 3 Gibson SG guitars. The primary guitar he used was a 1964 model and he played with Ernie Ball regular gauge strings .010 but with a .048 on the lower E. For solos he used a 1968 model strung with Ernie Ball super slinkys. For Power chords he played another 1968 model with Super slinkys. Malcolm Young used the same 1963 Gretsch Jet Firebird he has used since the start of AC/DC although the guitar has been altered through the years. For strings he used .012 – .056 Gibson strings with a wound G (.025).

When it comes to strings, Angus likes to change them fairly often, "Every show they have to be changed", he says. "Nobody plays them in. They just give them a tug and pull them in. And then I'll get a hold of them and pull them in just to make sure. There's nothing worse then going onstage and being out of tune." Angus rarely uses effects pedals, explaining, "I just have a Schaffer Vega wireless system. For me, it is probably the best. I've tried a few other ones, and they sort of cut out. The further you get away, the weaker the signal. The Schaffer seems to stay; it seems to keep going even if there are obstructions. I've been outside of buildings and played with that, and it still fires up really well." Equipment is important to Angus and AC/DC, but it is simply used as a means of getting a message across, there are no audio tricks being used to produce a specific sound. "I like it to work," is about as technical a view as Angus is likely to have but he does concede, "It is a big, important thing. On the stage, we know how to use those amps and everything. They are always repaired after the tours. They are a good, reliable amp, Marshall. I very seldom have ever had problems with them."
In 1995, Malcolm collaborated with guitar manufacturers Gretsch to come up with a new version of his guitar. The 'Malcolm Young Autograph' is based on his old Jet Firebird,

and comes in one and two–pickup models. It comes factory strung with .012's, which is the usual gauge that Malcolm uses. Malcolm played several of these, along with his old reliable one, during the Ballbreaker tour.

Malcolm has played a Gretsch 'Rock Jet' stripped of all controls except the volume for a number of years. He used to have a Gretsch White Falcon too, but says that after someone 'fixed' it, it lost the sound he liked it for and he got rid of it. In the 'Are You Ready' video, he is playing an orange Gibson; supposedly he was working with them on a new guitar, not for endorsement, but for himself since he only has one that he likes.
Phil Rudd plays a five–piece Sonor Designer Series kit in Stain Red. For sticks, Phil uses Easton Ahead, which are said to be unbreakable. He also uses the Swiss–made Paiste cymbals.

Cliff Williams uses a '76 Music Man strung with D'Addario flatwound strings.

"I always keep it simple. I think when you get onstage and you're playing rock and roll, the big lesson is this: If you've got too many toys up there, then there's too many things that can go wrong." Angus Young

THE ONSET OF THE SG

In the late 1950s the guitar of most connoisseurs up until then, the Les Paul had been declining in sales. However, its maker Gibson was enthusiastic about bringing in a new model as its successor. One advertisement for the new 'SG' with its distinctive shape boasted it was "An exciting new approach to the mahogany, solid body guitar... a solid success with players." The customary colour was, and has remained cherry red, though black is a popular second choice.

Though sales were initially slow, partly due to the popularity of folk music at the start of the 1960's, Gibson knew it was onto a winner, as an institution with a respectable name and diverse selection of instruments, and soon proved to be correct. By 1966 the company was the largest guitar maker in the world, with 250,000 square feet of manufacturing space.

Gibson's design for the SG weaved its way in slowly. At first they created the solid body Melody Maker guitar that was very similar to the Les Paul in appearance. By 1962 it had developed into an axe with the double cutaway and five years later developed the classic 'SG' shape, which also appeared as a 12-string model and a three-pickup version.

OTHER PROTAGONISTS OF THE DEVILISH AXE

Tony Iommi (Black Sabbath), Pete Townshend (The Who), Dave Grohl (Foo Fighters), Bernard Sumner (Joy Division, New Order), Damon Gough (Badly Drawn Boy), Eddie Vedder (Pearl Jam), Ian Mackaye (Fugazi), Mark Collins (The Charlatans), Matt Bellamy (Muse), Mike Campbell (Tom Petty And The Heartbreakers), Peter Holmstrom (Dandy Warhols), Ryan Peake (Nickelback), Todd Youth (Danzig), Bob Balch (Fu Manchu).

Chapter 20 – Fly On The Ball
– A Brian Johnson Profile

"Me, Phil and Cliff, we were watching Father Ted last night on telly. We have seen the episode about fifty times, but it didn't make any difference. We were crying and rolling on the floor; it was hysterical." Brian Johnson

(Some of the material in this chapter is from an interview by Jarmo published on the no nonsense webzine www.kolumbus.fi/nononsense/brian.htm)

He may have been in AC/DC for 25 years but Brian 'Jonna' Johnson is still something of an unknown entity to his legions of followers. He rarely speaks on stage and in most interviews he is asked repetitious, mind–numbing questions, leading to the same responses time after time. In many ways, Johnson keeps himself to himself, happy to take a back seat, even in the band he leads onstage hundreds of nights each year.

Perhaps this is a consequence of joining AC/DC at a time when modesty and a meek nature was required. It is to his eternal credit that Johnson did not seek to change AC/DC and adopt the typical lead singer mentality of 'me, me, me'. Instead he was astute enough to realise he was an addition to a perfectly run machine. He did not seek to overwhelm the 'DC chemistry with his personality, much less his voice. Instead he complimented the group with decent, honest and hard working dedication.

Brian's father, Alan Johnson, was a sergeant–major in the British army. During World War II, he was in the thick of campaigns in Italy and North Africa, but nothing could prepare him for his first experience of AC/DC in the raw. "I was at Monte Cassino when the Americans flattened the place," he said, "and I was at El Alamein when we knocked Rommel back with a big barrage of guns, but I've never heard anything as loud as this in my life."

"My father was a Protestant, Church of England, and my mother was a Catholic, an Italian," said Brian. "My father was in the Army. He took lessons to be a Catholic so he could marry my mother. So he was getting changed over to be a Catholic in the church and he was on his knees with his hands together. He was a sergeant–major. His captain walked in and said, 'Johnson, stand on your feet and walk out of this church.' My father said, 'What?' 'Get out of this church, now.' And my father said, 'Ah, captain, I don't think you understand. I'm being changed into a Catholic.' And the captain said, 'I'm your padre, Church of England.' The Catholic priest came in and said, 'Who do you think you are coming into my church,' and the two of them fought each other, the Catholic priest and the captain, the padre. My father has turned his back on religion ever since. Now he's a total atheist, total, because of two men of God, two men who have read the Bible back to front."

Brian was raised with affection and encouragement, although any child who was raised in an industrial town in the North–East of England during the fifties and sixties doubtless experienced a few hard knocks. It was no different for Brian, who though sensitive and almost shy, would later claim that he never showed his emotions. In cold, bleak towns like Newcastle to be seen as shy or thin–skinned meant you were a 'sissy' or a 'jessie'.

Acting in local television programmes as a young child encouraged Brian's confidence. He also performed Gang Shows with the Scouts, and joined the local church choir. He eventually went on to work in a factory. There he toiled alongside the Animals' Chas Chandler and both used a 'lucky' lathe. Brian explains, "There was a place where I served my apprenticeship in Newcastle. The foreman comes up to us and he said, 'Right son, you're going on that lathe there and I was like, 'That's a bit big for us' and he was telling me that it was the lucky lathe. He said Chas Chandler worked on that and he didn't know what strings I'd pulled, but I was on it."

Eventually, Brian would develop a strong Christian belief. As he put it: "I think even the hardest of men, the most cynical of men, people that are quite hard on the outside would have to say that at certain moments of depression, or when they're feeling really low and they're facing a big task, the hardest of men would have to ask for some help."

Actually admitting to a specific belief or suggesting others believe in the same things is never something Brian would do, however. "I keep it within myself", he says. "If I go to a church I'll go when the priests aren't in or the people aren't in. I don't like going with anybody else. But I'll tell you what I think about America's Sunday morning religious programs. When I see a man on television, telling me that he got a message from God; that we must fight the communists and saying, 'He told me, He came down and told me. So I'm starting a collection!' I've put my foot through many television screens before!"

For a rock singer, Brian admits it's seen as 'uncool' to be seen to say prayers every night, but for him it's a personal belief and something he does on a nightly basis. "I've been talking to Him since I was about five," he says, "and I've never stopped."

Brian has never been one for licentiousness but his concession to the stereotypical rock 'n' roll lifestyle is that he does like a drink. "I live in Sarasota, Florida, and there's a pub called Watson's Pub," he explained. "And they serve the beer like it is supposed to be served. These guys, when serving European beers, they serve them in glasses that they are supposed to be served in. Like German beer, real big Weiss beer, they are supposed to be served in these beautiful steins, glasses. The Belgian beers come in big balloon glasses. It gives something extra to the pleasure of enjoying beer."

Perhaps unsurprisingly, Brian's favourite brand of beer is the hometown speciality, Newcastle Brown Ale. "I used to drink Newcastle Brown... a lot! But unfortunately, the ale is just like taking drugs, you just can't stop drinking. It's a beautiful drink, and I had to get off that. You know, it's too easy to drink that stuff. God, I love it. But now I have to watch it, as I'm getting old, and I gotta watch my stomach. I better keep fit. I go to the gym, life a few weights and I do a lot of breathing exercises. I've cut down on the ciggies too. I used to smoke three packs a day; now it's a lot less, a packet at most. They were knackering me. I hope I'll give them up completely one day. I feel a whole lot better."

HOMELY PURSUITS

"Because we keep a low profile we can walk around relatively unrecognised", Brian says of AC/DC's popularity. "And it's where we are living also. Phil lives in a small place in New Zealand, Malcolm lives in a small village, Angus is living in a small village. And Cliff lives in North Carolina, and I'm in Florida, but they are both small places. Everybody knows you, the kids just say 'Hey Brian' when I go to get French bread. So people know who you are, but it's an enjoyable situation. It must be hard to be a superstar; I never could handle that kind of shit."

Brian can still become star struck himself. "I got to see George Thorogood and the Destroyers in Helsinki," he said, "and as far as I'm concerned, it's been a fabulous rock band for years and years. And I went to say 'Hi' to them before they went onstage. They were like 'Oh man, it's a real honour'. And I was 'Fuck, it's an honour for me'. So I still get thrills when I see someone who I think is famous in my eyes. It's wonderful. The people you meet in your life, some of them are just rude arrogant bastards. But you get that in every form of life, in a factory, in the music business, in the business world. If I meet an arrogant one, untouchable, you know, I tell them what they are. I don't like the arrogant ones, they are not good."

In the singer's house there is "Nothing to do with music, certainly no home studio! When I go home, that's the end of music. I have a bar though, English bar, which is an exact replica of a pub in Newcastle I used to go – Queen's Head – I took photographs of it, and told them to build it exactly to be the same. My house is all cars, just cars. Cars, cars, and more cars."

Brian races cars in his spare time, as part of a lifelong obsession with vehicles. He spoke of his participation in the Indy 500 "I was at the championships of '97 to '98. In '99 I had to stop it, to do the album. I really can't wait to get back on the track. It's all over America, it's not round and round. It's real racing, road racing – as we call it in America. I can't wait, just the thrill of it, all the competition, crashing..."

Talking of crashing, Brian has had more than his fair share of scrapes over the years. "The worst time was in Atlanta when I had to get cut out of my car", he recalls. "I hit the bridge. I had slick tyres, and I was in the lead. It was my first race, I couldn't believe I was in the lead; I was just going faster than anybody else. The car was a Lotus Cortina Mark I, this was my first race, all the Porsches were behind me. And I came up the hill towards the bridge at the speed of 120 miles per hour. And the bridge was behind the hill; it was a blind spot. You see the bridge and you see the sky. You just got to take your chances because the road turns rapidly after the hill. And I turned my steering wheel, but nothing happened, I just went straight ahead. I got a film of it – there are these cameras in the car. 'This is gonna hurt!' And bang! And the car went upside down; it was nasty. So from first, I was last. But I didn't finish the race, obviously. They took me away by ambulance. But it was funny, just seeing your life flashing. I was very calm, I just sat there, 'This is it', you know."

"I didn't get injured," he says, "apart from feeling pretty stupid – because there was nothing I could do. Because once I hit the grass, which is like ice and water, and that was the end of me. I didn't have a chance; I was just a missile. It didn't stop me; I was in the next race. We were in the first class area with all these businessmen, and in Japan when you're not working, you have to sleep. We had lots of fun, the crew was there, everybody was on. It's a nice country. I hadn't been there since 1982. And we'd forgotten how it is to be there. We know that the Japanese like these 'pretty boy' bands more. So we went out and did three shows there.

The promoters said 'You've gotta understand that they won't go crazy, they just sit down and give applause between the songs'. Which was totally wrong. They went nuts, they were like wild monkeys. It was brilliant. I couldn't speak to them; I don't have a clue about the Japanese language. Too difficult to handle."

Japan continues to provide an element of culture shock to the band. "It's a funny culture, you know," says Brian. "These young kids walking around with their long hair, they look like women. And these bands... some of them are not even bands. They'll get together, like four good –looking young guys getting together. And they just call themselves 'The Boys', they don't play instruments, they don't sing, they don't do nothing. But they book into a hotel and put an advert in the newspapers 'The Boys will be signing autographs'. And the chicks just go nuts. And the boys won't do anything. But then they will be picked up to do an advertisement for Nike shoes or something, and then they do an album. And all of sudden they are famous... for nothing. It's just amazing. Because I was asking the record company what they do. 'They don't do anything, they just get together and call themselves 'The Gang'!' All they do is that they walk around like The Beatles. But the food is good, and the people are lovely."

Brian has been confronted with the mindbending commitment of some devoted fans. "This guy had his whole back tattooed, the Fly On The Wall album cover... in colours. I kept thinking 'Boy, that must hurt'. I haven't got a tattoo; I'm too chicken, I guess. I've never seen one that I liked enough. I nearly had one when I was in the in the parachute forces. And we all went in, 12 of us, and we were drunk. The only reason I didn't get one was because I was last in the line. And by the time there were two in front of me, it was, like, four in the morning, and the tattoo guy just had it. 'That's enough, I can't take anymore'."

TOO CLOSE TO HOME

Brian had been married to Carol Johnson, but it was their divorce which was causing him problems at the time of the Blow Up Your Video album. In an amazing coincidence, Carol went on to marry Malcolm 'Supermac' MacDonald, the famous Newcastle United centre forward, who played for the club 187 times between 1971 and 1976. Newcastle have been Brian's football heroes since childhood and he remains a dedicated fan today.

Carol and Malcolm married at a secret ceremony in Tyneside after redhead Carol had moved in with Macdonald (in a flat in Jesmond, Newcastle) to help him dry out after he admitted his battle with alcoholism several years ago. Carol's experiences with AC/DC, with whom she toured as a teenager, led to a long battle of her own with whiskey and cocaine, and she drew upon this part of her life to aid MacDonald into a rehabilitation programme.

He said: "Carol is the one who has given me a kick up the backside, and she has been there for me. I couldn't have done it without her." The twice divorced former striker is now enjoying a life of punditry, has seven children and two former wives.

BRIAN'S DESERT ISLAND DISCS

'Delta Lady' (Joe Cocker)

'Here, There And Everywhere' (The Beatles)

'Boom Boom' (John Lee Hooker)

'Blue Bayou' (Roy Orbison)

'Jailhouse Rock' (Elvis Presley)

'Bad Bad Boy' (Nazareth)

'Seven Seas Of Rhye' (Queen)

'Bad To The Bone' (George Thorogood)

'Brown Sugar' (Rolling Stones)

'Get Back' (The Beatles)

...any Louis Armstrong record

Chapter 21 – They Salute You

"AC/DC is one of my favourite bands and our first album, Iron Balls, *was made, in a way, like the Young brothers with the same arrangements and song structure. At the present time our style is far from AC/DC, but we covered 'Back In Black' to show our roots."*
Lead Weight, Kazakhstan metal band

There are more AC/DC tribute bands throughout the world than there are actual AC/DC songs; such is the level of worship at the altar of the Gods of rock n' roll. From banjo–playing hillbillies to down–tuned death metal grunters every type of musical act has tipped a hat to Angus Young and co. There are groups who have made whole careers out of covering AC/DC, and then there are those who merely record one or two tracks to show their allegiance more discreetly. In this chapter, the art of the tribute is examined.

In recent times one outfit in particular has made waves with fans of all types of music, from hardcore 'DC fans to lovers of traditional country. Hayseed Dixie's career kicked off with the album *A Hillbilly Tribute To AC/DC*, reworking the songs of the rock titans using the traditional bluegrass line–up of mandolin, fiddle and banjo, not to mention some terrific straw–in–the–mouth singing and grumbling. Singer and violin player Barley Scotch explains: "It became revealed to me – that Lost Highway of Brother Hank Williams and that Highway to Hell them boys was singing about, well, I knew: they're the same damn road! So, we just set about playing some of them songs, in with our regular ones, you know, at church socials and such, and the next thing we knew, this fellow from Nashville had us down there making a record. Before I knew it, I was talking on the radio every day and the record was in every Wal–Mart in the country".

The boys of AC/DC have never been the type to take themselves too seriously, and they are, in turn, fans of the Hayseeds. Cliff Williams invited the group to play at a tour–wrap party, and even joined them onstage to play bass on 'Have a Drink On Me.'

"Yeah, so we didn't know what to expect, you know" recalls Barley, "But Cliff was about the coolest fellow we ever met. He said the whole band really liked our record, and I figured, after him saying that, well, I didn't give a damn what any of them critics had to say about it, you know. So we got out there touring around, spreading the message, you know . . . about that Lost Highway and that Highway to Hell being the same road and such".

People seemed to enjoy the different take on a familiar style. The band often appeared on radio throughout the United States and sold over 100,000 copies of the album worldwide. "Nobody expected that record to do like it did", laughs Barley. "I guess the message just hit home with a lot of folks. I mean, verily, verily I say to ya'll, there's four key elements in any good mountain song – drinking, cheating, killing and going to hell. That's what we've been singing about our whole lives. And that's just what them AC/DC songs was about too. So you know, there's a lot of stuff the same between rock and mountain music. You listen to some old Stanley Brothers stuff and you'll hear what I'm talking about."

"I think AC/DC is the only band that can rewrite a song over and over and over and have it still be classic and good. I think that a lot of records suffer from one good song and nine pale imitations of the one good song" Jizzy Pearl, Love/Hate, L.A. Guns

Unsurprisingly, the hard rock and metal community provides the most fervent admirers of the band. American traditional metallers Iced Earth recorded versions of both 'Highway To Hell' and 'It's A Long Way To The Top (If You Wanna Rock N' Roll)'. Matt Barlow sang with the band when they recorded these 'DC classics, and although he's a natural baritone, he managed to follow Bon's screechy tone easily enough. He certainly believes AC/DC was a major influence on himself and Iced Earth. "Yeah, that was the stuff that I cut my teeth on, listening to hard rock, that was the shit back when I was a kid," he acknowledges. "Before that I was basically spinning my dad's country and Elvis 45s. So that was like the first influence down the road to hell basically. *Highway To Hell* was the first AC/DC record that my brother brought into the house and I just listened to it over and over. Then, of course, 'It's A Long Way To The Top (If You Wanna Rock N' Roll)' is something that Jon (Schaeffer, guitar) picked because it makes perfect sense. If there's a message in a song on the record, that's the one."

Another group appealing to listeners in both metal and rock camps is the Florida–based Six Feet Under, a death metal outfit that has now recorded two albums entirely consisting of covers. One, *Graveyard Classics* was a mixed selection of rock, punk and metal standards that included AC/DC's 'T.N.T.'. True to their usual style, the track was heavily down–tuned, and highlighted vocalist Chris Barnes's death–metal growl. The album was generally well received but when, in 2004 Six Feet Under decided to record *Back In Black* the whole way through, in a death metal style, the punters weren't so happy.

Many wondered why the band did it at all, and those AC/DC purists out there were hard pushed to find a positive note regarding a group completely deadening the impact of the originals. A review on www.SMNnews.com had this to say about the record: 'Without a doubt, words cannot fathom the disgust and contempt I feel about this release from Six Feet Under. Shockingly titled *Graveyard Classics 2*, there is nothing classic about it. It's a disgrace to AC/DC, a disgrace to metal, and a disgrace to Metal Blade Records who actually paid for such a thing to be made. For those of you unaware of what this monster is – it is a feeble attempt at covering the entire AC/DC album *Back in Black* all the way from 'Hells Bells', right through 'Rock and Roll Ain't Noise Pollution'.'

Many purists listening to Barnes's vocals thought he was having a joke, but the group was actually seriously paying tribute to a band they grew up with, and one they respect. Barnes does say though, "I'm not the AC/DC aficionado of a mass of useless knowledge on the subject. I've seen them a lot of times when I was growing up and that was about it. I didn't need to find out too much about them apart from being dragged to Bon's grave site in Perth when we were on tour." As for the furore surrounding the *Back In Black* reworking, Barnes makes light of it, but is somewhat hurt by the vilification that has been stirred up.

"Oh my God, man…it's haunting me worse than the first one," Barnes says of the album. "What can I say, I get a vision and I have to follow through on it, it's a tunnel for me, I have to get through to the other side. I love it, man. Those guys did such an awesome job laying the music down. I couldn't believe the leads Steve (Swanson, guitar) laid down. If you want to you can set that thing up on two different CD players and play the original and ours together on top of each other and it doesn't change except for the end of 'Back In Black', because I couldn't chop that lead, it was just too good."

Unlike many cover artists, SFU were scrupulous in their fidelity to the original. "It's exactly the same tempo and the CD is exactly the same length, exactly the same time between songs which no one really picked up on," Barnes points out. "I thought it was great, man. I know people rip me to shreds because of my vocals, but I don't get it. I don't know what they expect – I'm not going to start singing like Rob Halford. How I felt about it is, if you can't sing and scream like Brian Johnson it's not worth trying. I just had to do it my own way. My favourite song is 'Let Me Put My Love Into You'. It just reminds me of night time, I don't know why. If that's the most I get out of it I'm happy with it and I'm glad I did it." Contrary to popular belief, the album has actually reached quite a few fans, eager to hear a new take on a well–known set of songs. "The sales have been pretty good," confirms Barnes. "Over here on the college radio charts it was surprisingly doing well."

SOMETHING FOR EVERYONE

"We gotta do something like that." Joe Perry & Steven Tyler *of Aerosmith after seeing an AC/DC concert.*

Other expressions of love for the band range from the all–female tribute act Hell's Belle's, formed in 2000 by guitarist Amy Stolzenbach (aka Angus), to the German football team FC St Pauli, noted for their hardcore support among the anarchists and punks of Hamburg and the fact that they begin every game with a rousing rendition of 'Hell's Bells'. As Four Four Two magazine mused, "it's hard not to fall in love with FC St. Pauli. The politics, the passion, the counter–culture, AC/DC..."

But perhaps the greatest tribute ever paid to AC/DC was for the remembrance service for Bon Scott. For the 25th anniversary of his death, in 2005, a pipe band marched to his gravestone, while tribute bands from Spain to Sydney paid their respects through several commemorative concerts.

"I like AC/DC." Keith Richards, Rolling Stones

As for original AC/DC members, most are creating music and touring. Original singer Dave Evans reports: "I have been gigging in Europe during the last two years and have recorded a new CD called Sinner in Newcastle, New South Wales (and mixed in Germany) for my record company CM records, out of Hamburg. I am looking forward to heading back there again this year." Dave also recorded two songs live for the Bon Scott memorial gig on the A Hell Of A Night album. He also adds that he wrote and performed two songs with AC/DC, called 'Sunset Strip' and 'Fell In Love', which stayed in the band's repertoire under new titles. "My lyrics were rewritten with Bon and released under the titles 'Show Business' and 'Jean'". Dave Evans and Hot Cockerel did record and release some music but this might be hard to

*track down, as Dave explains, "It was only for a film, which
I starred in, called Coming Of Age, which only received
a video release. I played a rock star called Rexx Rated,
frontman of The Banned. The guys from Hot Cockerel
played as The Banned. Including the title track, there
were four or five of our tracks in the movie. Hot Cockerel
was much heavier than Rabbit and blacker in genre." As
mentioned previously, Dave has also performed with AC/DC
tribute group Thunderstruck.*

*MARK EVANS HAS ALSO BEEN BUSY, AS HE SAYS;
"I've been doing lots of things since leaving the band. I've
been primarily back in Australia, based in Sydney. The last
year I've been actually dealing with vintage guitars. And
there's a guy outside my office playing 'Jailbreak', ha ha.
But I'm also doing lots of playing now. I'm in a band called
Headhunters. And also I have done bits and pieces of work
with Rose Tattoo, I've been doing some bass work with them.
I also toured America with a band called Heaven, which
was managed by Michael Browning. I'm still pretty active in
playing, but the main thing at the moment is my passion for
guitars. And my family, of course."*

*According to Angus, his older brother George has been
"writing songs. He is always writing songs. And he is
opening up a new studio somewhere in England. I never talk
to him. I'm his little brother."*

*Bon still lives on in reissues of his original recordings
with AC/DC but there are still little–heard tracks featuring
Scott's voice. 1996 saw the release of the last recordings he
made as a solo performer. As the press release put it: "Bon's
back! Two new songs, three tracks. One CD single released
October 20 is the closest thing you're ever likely to hear
to the solo album he talked about but never got the chance
to complete. Now re–produced for the Nineties. 'Round
And Round And Round' and 'Carey Gully' are the last two
songs Bon Scott committed to tape a month before joining*

AC/DC and the only released from a three–year period in his career between Fraternity's Flaming Galah in April 1972 and AC/DC's 'Baby Please Don't Go' in March 1975. In their original form, the tracks are genuine Australian long lost 'Basement Tapes', recorded a few months after Bon's motorbike accident. Recently re–discovered, both 'Round And Round And Round' and 'Carey Gully' have been extensively reworked to create musical pieces, which the project's collaborators believe Bon would have been proud of."

The tracks were recorded in July 1974 and were written by Mount Lofty Rangers' musical director Peter Head. He teamed up with a friend of Bon's, Ted Yanni to isolate Bon's vocal track and re–record the backing track from scratch. The original version is also included on the CD, featuring former members of Headband and Fraternity. The press release boasts, "'Carey Gully', a lilting country–flavoured ballad has been tastefully augmented with strings – the Classically Blue String Quartet. The song celebrates the Mount Lofty Rangers' stomping ground at the time, then home to one of South Australia's leading artists. Vytas Serelis, whose stunning photo portraits grace the CD cover. The whole project has been achieved by many people – musicians and technicians donating time, talent and studios in order to pay tribute to an old friend. The result is one of the best recordings available by Bon Scott displaying a side to his vocal ability that wasn't as evident in subsequent releases." Although the original release was very limited, there are plans to issue a full–length album.

THE ULTIMATE ACCOLADE

AC/DC songs recorded or performed by other artists, and where to find them.

16 volt (Eric Powell's one–man industrial group, straight out of the bedroom) – Dirty Deeds Done Dirt Cheap (from the album *Wisdom,* Cargo Records 1993)

Aerobitch (Spanish punk band) – High Voltage (from the album *An Urge to Play Loud,* People Like You Records 2000)

Alivaltiosihteeri (Finnish rockers) – Highway To Hell (from the album *Yeah Baby Yeah,* Hiljaiset Levyt 1992)

A.N.I.M.A.L. (Argentinian metal band) – Highway To Hell (from the album *USA Toda Tu Fuerza,* Warner 1999)

Anthrax (Veteran New York thrash metallers) **& Dee Snider** (Twisted Sister vocalist) – Walk All Over You, (from the album *Back In Black – A Tribute To AC/DC,* Zebra 2000)

Baron Rojo (Spanish veteran heavy metal act) – Girls Got Rhythm (from the album *Desafio,* Avispa 1992)

Beck (American experimental artist) – Highway To Hell (from the 12" single *Mixed Bizness,* White Label 2000)

Pat Boone (Smooth singer most popular in the 50s and 60s) – It's A Long Way To The Top...If You Wanna Rock N' Roll (from the album *In A Metal Mood: No More Mr Nice Guy* Hip –O Records 1997)

Birmingham6 (Obscure industrialists) – Thunderstruck (from the album *Covered In Black – An Industrial Tribute To The Kings Of High Voltage AC/DC,* Cleopatra 1997)

Black Obelisk (One of the first Russian thrash metal bands) – Touch Too Much (from the album *Stena,* JetNoise 1994)

Bob Rivers (American radio presenter and novelty musician) – Jingle Hells Bells (from the album *I Am Santa Claus,* Atlantic 1993)

Casanovas (Australian band very much influenced by AC/DC) – Riff Raff (from the single *Shake It,* Rubber/Shock 2003)

Cowlicks (Self confessed rip–roaring and shin –kicking country rockers) – You Shook Me All Night Long (from the album *The Cowlicks Live & Unplugged*, Tres Payasos 2005

Bruce Dickinson (Iron Maiden lead singer) – Sin City (from the single *Dive Dive Dive*, EMI 1990)

D4 (New Zealand indie rockers) – High Voltage (from the album *Garage Days V/A* Soundtrack, Mercury 2002)

Dandy Warhols (alternative/psychedelic unpredictables) – Hell's Bells (from the single *Bohemian Like You*, EMI 2000)

De Heideroosjes (German punk rockers) – Bad Boy Boogie (Played live only)

Diamond Dogs (The Swedish Rolling Stones) – You Shook Me All Night Long, (from the album *A Salute To AC/DC*, Tribute 1996)

Die Krupps (Industrial Metallers) – It's A Long Way To The Top…If You Wanna Rock N' Roll (from the album *Covered In Black*, Zebra 2002)

Céline Dion (French–Canadian diva) & **Anastacia** (American songstress) – You Shook Me All Night Long (Played live only)

Downstroke (German modern thrash metal act) – Overdose (from the album *A Salute To AC/DC*, Tribute 1996)

Everclear (American alt –rock trio) – Sin City, (from the single *Heartspark Dollar Sign,* Capitol 1996)

Exodus (San Franciscan thrash metal veterans) – Overdose (from the album *Fabulous Disaster,* Music For Nations 1988), Dirty Deeds Done Dirt Cheap (from the album *Good Friendly Violent Fun*, Combat 1991)

John Farnham (Australian rock legend) – It's A Long Way To The Top… If You Wanna Rock N' Roll (from the album *Age Of Reason,* BMG 1989)

Femme Fatale (Lorraine Lewis –fronted glam rockers) – It's A Long Way To The Top…If You Wanna Rock N' Roll (from the single *Falling In And Out Of Love*, MCA 1988

Fuckemos (Texan punk rockers) – Thunderstruck (from the album *Hell Ain't A Bad Place To Be ... A Tribute To AC/DC,* Reptilian Records 1999)

Genitorturers (Dominatrix fronted industrial act) – Squealer (from the album *Covered In Black*, Cleopatra 1996)

Girlschool (All –female quartet, popular in the 80s) – Livewire (Played live only in 1980)

Godflesh (British industrial metal icons) – For Those About To Rock...We Salute You (from the album *The World's Greatest AC/DC Tribute*, Big Eye Music 2004)

Lesley Gore (Popular 60s female singer helped by Quincy Jones) – Dirty Deeds Done Dirt Cheap – (from the album *When Pigs Fly – Songs You Never Thought You'd Hear,* Xemu Records 2002)

Great White (Glam rockers most popular in the 80s L.A. scene) – Sin City, (from the album *Thunderbolt A Tribute to AC/DC,* Triage 1996)

Guns N' Roses (legendary L.A. rock quintet) – Whole Lotta Rosie (from the German 12 –inch Single *Sweet Child O' Mine*, Geffen 1989)

Hard Corps (Early rap metal group) – Back In Black (from the album *Def Before Dishonour*, Interscope 1991)

Hayseed Dixie (See main text) – Covered Several AC/DC Tracks On Their Tribute Album *A Hillbilly Tribute To AC/DC,* Dualtone 2003)

Honeygun (obscure rock outfit) – High Voltage (from the album *Honeygun*, 1996)

Honeymoon Killers (Legendary Sub Pop blues noise group) – Get It Hot (from the single *Get It Hot*, Sub Pop 1989)

Hotwire (German hair band) – You Shook Me All Night Long (from the album *Middle Of Nowhere*, 2001)

Hullabaloo (Hardcore/rock/ska crossover act) – Back In Black (from the album *United Colors Of Hullabaloo,* Musical Tragedies 1992)

Hundred Reasons (UK emo rockers) – Back In Black (from the single *How Soon Is Now*, Sore Poiint, 2004)

Iced Earth (See main text) – It's A Long Way To The Top...
If You Wanna Rock N' Roll (from the album *Tribute To The Gods*, Century Media 2002)

Jackyl (Chainsaw–wielding friends of Brian Johnson) – Live
Wire (from the album *Stayin' Alive*, Shimmering Tone 1998)

Joan Jett (Female rock icon) – Dirty Deeds Done Dirt Cheap
(from the album *Hit List*, Epic 1989)

Kanuuna (Finnish act who record in their native language)
– Touch Too Much (from the album *Kanuuna,* A & M 1992)

Sam Kinison (American comedian rock fan, now deceased)
– Highway To Hell (from the album *Leader Of The Banned*,
Warner Bros 1990)

Knorkator (German punk rockers) – Highway To Hell, (from
the album *Hasenchartbreaker*, Mercury 1999)

Mark Kozelek (Red House Painters frontman) – 10 cover versions of AC/DC tracks (from the album *What's Next To The
Moon*, Badman 2001)

Ed Kuepper (Australian singer–songwriter) – Highway To
Hell (from the album *A King In The Kindness Room*, Hot
2002)

Alan Lancaster (former bassist of Status Quo) – High Voltage (from the album *Life After Quo*, Eagle 1998)

Lead Weight (Kazakhstan metal band) – Back In Black (from
the album *For Thine Is The Kingdome*, Maximum 1999)

Living Colour (crossover funk–metallers) – Back In Black
(from the album *Collideoscope*, Sanctuary 2003)

Local H (American two–piece in Nirvana style) – It's A Long
Way To The Top...If You Wanna Rock N' Roll (Played live
only)

Marilyn Manson (The self –styled God Of Fuck) – Highway
To Hell (from the album *Detroit Rock City*), Mercury 1999

Metallica (Multi–million selling metallers) – Back In Black,
Highway To Hell, High Voltage Live Versions (Played live
only)

Motley Crue (Glam metal legends of the Sunset Strip) – Bad Boy Boogie, (from the album *Girls, Girls, Girls*, Hip –O 1987)

Motörhead (Lemmy–fronted Brit rock n' rollers) – It's A Long Way To The Top…If You Wanna Rock N' Roll, (from the album *The World's Greatest AC/DC Tribute*, Big Eye 2004)

Nashville Pussy (Dirty punk metal rockers) – Kicked In The Teeth, Shot Down In Flames, Highway To Hell (Played live and available as bonus tracks)

Nitronic (Featuring ex–Ratt vocalist Stephen Pearcy) – Whole Lotta Rosie, (Played live only)

Omen (American traditional heavy metal group) – Whole Lotta Rosie (from the EP *Nightmares*, Metal Blade 1987)

Onslaught (UK thrash metal titans) – Let There Be Rock (from the album *In Search Of Sanity*, London 1989)

Pearl Jam (Seattle grunge legends) – Sin City (Played live only)

Phish – (Alt rock quartet) Highway To Hell (Played live only)

Psychopomps (Danish industrial outfit) – Badlands, (from the album *Covered In Black*, Zebra 2002)

Quiet Riot (Veteran Canadian hard rock act) – Highway To Hell (from the album *Alive And Well*, Axe Killer 1999)

Red Star Belgrade (Alternative country experimentalists) – Highway To Hell (from the album *Telescope*, Checkered Past 2000)

Refused (Swedish modern punk innovators) – Back In Black (Played live only)

Reo Speedealer (Metal/punk band now known as Speedealer) – Rocker (Played live only)

Henry Rollins (former Black Flag/current Rollins Band vocalist and spoken word performer) and **The Hard Ons** (Aussie punk rock veterans) – Let There Be Rock (single, Vinyl Solution 1991)

Screaming Jets (Aussie hard rockers, popular in early nineties) – High Voltage, Ain't No Fun Waiting Round To Be

A Millionaire (from the single 'Living In England', Rooart 1993)

Shakira (Tiny Colombian pop singer) – Back In Black (from the album *Live And Off The Record*, Sony 2004)

Six Feet Under (See main text) – T.N.T. (from the album *Graveyard Classics*, Metal Blade 2000) Complete re–recorded version Of *Back In Black*: *Graveyard Classics 2,* Metal Blade 2004)

Skid Row (American hard rockers fronted by Sebastian Bach) – T.N.T., Little Lover (Played live only)

Slash's Blues Ball (Guns N' Roses/ Velvet Revolver guitarist's side project) – Night Prowler, Highway To Hell (Played live only)

Spahn Ranch (Industrial/electronic rock outfit) – Shot Down In Flames (from the album *Covered In Black*, Zebra 2002)

Sprung Monkey (Hardcore funsters) – Thunderstruck (from the album *Varsity Blues*, Hollywood 1999)

Straitjackets (Surf rockers from Nashville) – Hell Ain't A Bad Place To Be (from the album *A Salute To AC/DC*, Tribute 1996)

Andrew Strong (Irish star of *The Commitments* movie) – Girl's Got Rhythm (from the album *Strong*, MCA 2003)

Supersuckers (Punk rockers with a country side) – Rock N' Roll Singer (Played live only)

Surf Rats (Professional surfers who also make music) – Rocker (from the album *Straight Between The Eyes*, Lost Moment 1989)

Andy Taylor (Ex–Duran Duran) – Live Wire (from the album *Dangerous,* A&M 1990)

Lydia Taylor Band (Female–fronted Canadians) – Highway To Hell, (from the album *Lydia Taylor Band*, Passport 1981)

Terminal Sect (Industrial two –piece) – Who Made Who (from the album *Covered In Black*, Zebra 2002)

The Donnas (All Female alternative punk quartet) – Shot Down In Flames (Played live only Coney Island High, New York, 11/5/98)

The Dwarves (Punk legends famous for naked guitarist) – Big Balls (from the album *Hell Ain't A Bad Place To Be ... A Tribute To AC/DC,* Reptilian Records 1999)

The Fargone Beauties (Australian rock act) – Highway To Hell (from the album *It's Hard When You're Ugly*, Mercury 1992)

The Hives (Swedish garage quintet) – Back In Black (Played live only)

The Offspring (Million selling modern punk rockers from Orange County) – Sin City (Played live only)

Tiny Tim (aka Herbert Khaury, eccentric 60s entertainer) – Highway To Hell (from the single 'I Love Rock N' Roll', Regular 1992)

Tornado Babies (Swedish 80s hard rock band) – Jailbreak (from the album *A Salute To AC/DC*, Tribute 1996)

Transport League (Swedish metal crossover group) – Let There Be Rock (from the album *A Salute To AC/DC*, Tribute 1996)

Travis (Scottish alternative act) – Back In Black (Played live, Leeds, England 28th May 2001)

Trust (French hard rock group from the 70s/80s) – Love At First Feel (from the album *Paris By Night,* Melodia 1978)

Turbo Acs (American punk group) – Riff Raff (Played live in Vienna, June 2001)

Twisted Sister (Recently re –formed outrageous 80s glamsters) Sin City (from the album *Twisted Forever,* Koch 2001)

Ugly Kid Joe (Defunct early 90s funk metal crew) – Sin City (from the single *Everything About You,* Mercury 1992)

Vulcain (Hard rock band, known as the French Motorhead) – Hell Ain't A Bad Place To Be (from the album *Live Force*, Musicdisc 1987)

Warrant (Lipstick –wearing rockers, famous for the 80s hit 'Cherry Pie') – Down Payment Blues (from the album *Under The Influence*, Downboy 2001)

W.A.S.P. (Los Angeles' shock rockers from the 80s) – It's A Long Way To The Top...If You Wanna Rock N' Roll, Whole Lotta Rosie (Played live only)

Wax Tadpole (Obscure Aussie punk rockers) – Let There Be Rock, (from the album *Hometown Tribute*, GOH International 2000)

Wolfsbane (British rock/metal band who once supported Iron Maiden) – If You Want Blood...You've Got It (Played live 1987)

Zakk Wylde (Ex Ozzy Osbourne guitarist) – Hell Ain't A Bad Place To Be (from the album *Thunderbolt: A Tribute To AC/DC*, De Rock 1998)

NOTE: Aussie band The Stetsons released an album called The Stetsons 97, *featuring a cover of the Bon Scott song 'Up In The Hills Too Long' which he wrote while working with the Mount Lofty Rangers.*

Chapter 22 – Did You Know?

When Norman and Marilyn White sued the band for £120,000 because their phone number was mentioned in 'Dirty Deeds Done Dirt Cheap', Angus remarked: "The numbers don't refer to any particular phone number. They are simply my dream girl's vital statistics 36–24–36. I thought any red–blooded male would realise that".

AC/DC is an enduring band with a fervent set of highly knowledgeable fans, but there may be nuggets contained in this section that even the best–informed admirer may not have known.

MEMBERS OF AC/DC – PAST & PRESENT

Guitar
Malcolm Young,1974 – present
Angus Young, 1974 – present
Stevie Young, 1988 (on tour)

Vocals
Dave Evans, 1974
Bon Scott, 1974 – 1980
Brian Johnson, 1980 – present

Bass
Larry Van Kriedt, 1974
Rob Baily, 1974
Bruce Howe, 1974
George Young, 1974
Malcolm Young, 1974 – 1975
Mark Evans, 1975 – 1977
Cliff Williams, 1977 – present

Drums
Colin Burgess, 1974
Rob Carpenter, 1974
Peter Clack, 1974
Bon Scott, 1974
Tony Kerrante, 1974 – 1975
Phil Rudd, 1975 – 1983
Simon Wright, 1983 – 1989
Chris Slade, 1989 – 1994
Phil Rudd, 1995 – present

50 AMAZING FACTS

1. AC/DC was offered a chance to star in the movie *Dracula Rocks* but they declined.
2. Some Christian Church groups believe the lightning bolt between the AC and DC to be a Satanic 'S'.
3. Cliff Williams has been known to bleach his hair.
4. Bon had six tattoos including an eagle, a snake, and a cartoon lion. He also pierced both ears out of boredom.
5. Geordie, Brian Johnson's former band, spent a total of 35 weeks on the UK singles chart during 1973. Their biggest hit was 'All Because Of You' which reached Number 6 in March of that year.
6. Bon's parents still refer to him as Ron.
7. One of AC/DC's first supporters in England was the magazine *New Music Express* (*NME*), a publication not known for its love of hard rock.
8. Angus lives in Groningen in the Netherlands, Malcolm lives in England, Cliff lives in Fort Myers, Florida and North Carolina. Brian also resides in Florida, while Phil lives in New Zealand.
9. AC/DC's first strongholds in America were Jacksonville, Florida and Columbus, Ohio.

10. Angus first mooned the audience during the last Australian show the band played before leaving for England.
11. Malcolm had originally intended to be the sole guitarist in AC/DC. Instead of another guitar, he wanted to have a piano player.
12. Bon was born in the Scottish county of Angus.
13. AC/DC came close to being dropped by Atlantic's U.S. division, but retained its spot thanks to the support of U.K. division manager Phil Carson.
14. Angus's hobby is to paint landscapes.
15. The band prefers to use buses rather than planes when they are on tour.
16. When AC DC appeared as musical guests on *Saturday Night Live*, wrestling star The Rock was the presenter.
17. Readers of music magazine *Sounds* picked AC/DC as the leader of the 'New Order' in 1976.
18. On August 18th 1979, AC/DC opened for The Who at Wembley, at the headliners' request.
19. In common with most other performers, AC/DC's lyrics are sometimes prone to creative misunderstanding. In 'Money Talks', people thought that Brian was singing 'Mommy Dogs'. In 'You Shook Me All Night Long' the lyric 'She had sightless eyes' was heard as 'She had me circumcised'. And in 'Back In Black the 'Forget the hearse cause I'll never die' line was misinterpreted as 'I've got a hairstyle that'll never die'. These mistakes are known as mondegreens.
20. Angus and Malcolm originally wanted to call the band Third World War.
21. In 2004, an Australian movie called *Thunderstruck* was released. It's a comedy about five friends who go to an AC/DC show in 1991, and agree that when the first one of their number dies, he will be buried next to Bon Scott.
22. In Australia, the song 'Thunderstruck' was used in commercials for the Holden Commodore SS Ute (utility vehicle). The adverts were about an Australian –built Ute creating a storm in the outback.

23. For AC/DC's last show as Cheap Trick's opening act, Angus, Malcolm and Bon bounded onstage for the headliners' encore, which included renditions of 'Sin City' and 'School Days'. The encore also found a roadie hoisting Cheap Trick guitarist Rick Nielsen on his shoulders, a pose that Angus tends to enjoy.

24. McFarlane Toys released an Angus Young doll in October 2001.

25. Former Buffalo member Chris Turner has a unique place in the history of AC/DC. His are the fingers on the guitar fret board on the cover of the Australian *Let There Be Rock* album. Recently Chris has released a few solo albums that are reported to feature Mark Evans.

26. If you look closely at the cover of Green Day's *Dookie* album, you will see a picture of AC/DC's Angus Young. (Look at the guitarist standing on the roof of the building on the bottom right hand corner).

27. On the 15th September 2000, AC/DC were inducted into the famous Hollywood Rock Walk. Further details of their induction, including pictures and video clips can be found at www.rock-walk.com.

28. In October 1983 a Fort Lewis soldier caused $20,000 in damage to the Tacoma Dome by firing a military flare into it during an AC/DC concert.

29. The title 'Crabsody in Blue' is a parody of George Gershwin's 'Rhapsody in Blue'. The song appeared on the Australian and UK vinyl releases of the *Let There Be Rock* album. The track was later replaced by 'Problem Child' on the North American release.

30. Bob Defrin designed the classic AC/DC logo.

31. Ozzy Osbourne is quoted as saying that he wrote the track 'Suicide Solution' to honour the memory of the late Bon Scott.

32. Bon met Rosie (the inspiration for 'Whole Lotta Rosie') at Freeway Gardens Hotel in Melbourne.

33. Part of Angus's solo in 'Let There Be Rock' is lifted from the song 'B.O.G.I.E.' by Bill Haley and the Comets.

34. The MTV Cartoon Beavis & Butthead features the Butthead character wearing an AC/DC T–shirt.

35. The *Maximum Overdrive* movie opened in the U.S.A on 18th July 1986.

36. The first Australian AC/DC single to have a picture sleeve was the 12 –inch of 'Rock n' Roll Ain't Noise Pollution'.

37. The press launch for the *Razor's Edge* album was at the School Dinners restaurant in London.

38. The band filmed a performance of 'Dog Eat Dog' for the 5th anniversary show of *Countdown* on Australian television.

39. 'My Favourite Things', from the Rodgers and Hammerstein musical 'The Sound of Music' is reinterpreted as 'Jingle Hells Bells', and AC/DC parody by 'Bob Rivers and Twisted Radio', a band from Seattle that performs unusual versions of classic rock songs. At the start of the song they chant "Ho! Ho! Ho!", spoofing the "Oye! Oye! Oye!" chant of 'T.N.T.'. It is available on a Christmas music compilation.

40. Bon used to walk the streets with his pet boa constrictor hanging round his neck.

41. Bon's brother Graeme has been seen in various parts of the world singing in numerous rock and blues bands.

42. The *Let There Be Rock* concert was filmed on December 9th 1979. However, the guitar solo at the beginning of the film is taken from Angus's sound check at Metz (France) on December 6th.

43. Lee Richardson, one time midfielder with Aberdeen FC was quoted in *The Sun* as saying he would rather play drums with AC/DC than play for Inter Milan. Sadly, he did neither. After leaving Aberdeen he joined Oldham Athletic.

44. During December 1993 it was reported on Radio 1 that AC/DC were under surveillance by the K.G.B. from the late 70's until the breakup of the Soviet Union.

45. Malcolm joined the Australian band Velvet Underground in 1971. The only recordings by Velvet Underground were from the time before Malcolm joined the band.

46. In 1985 Brian contributed to a charity single called 'Try Giving Everything' along with other musicians from the North–East of England, under the group name Geordie Aid.

47. AC/DC met Mark Evans at the Station Hotel, a live venue in the Trahan district of Melbourne.
48. Malcolm plays lead guitar on 'Soul Stripper', 'Show Business', 'You Ain't Got A Hold On Me', and 'Can I Sit Next To You Girl'.
49. At the beginning of the movie Mad Max, the 'Night Rider' character steals a police car, and during the chase he is ranting over the police radio. One of his rants is, 'I'm a rocker, I'm a roller, I'm a right out of controller!' This from the 'DC song 'Rocker'.
50. AC/DC are among only 12 Australian rock n' roll artists honoured with a postage stamp. The 'Australian Rock n' Roll' stamp set was issued May 26, 1998 by Australia Post. The AC/DC stamp features a picture of Angus, with 'It's A Long Way To The Top' written across his school satchel. The other artists were Johnny O'Keefe, Col Joye, Little Pattie, Normie Rowe, The Easybeats, Russell Morris, Masters Apprentices, Daddy Cool, Billy Thorpe, The Aztecs and Sherbert.

AC/DC'S LIVE REPERTOIRE

Here is a complete list of the songs AC/DC has performed since the beginning of their stage career on stage, noting the first year in which a song made an appearance, or the first time it was sung by a specific frontman.

DAVE EVANS ON VOCALS

1973
Baby, Please Don't Go
Heartbreak Hotel
Jailhouse Rock
Jumping Jack Flash
No Particular Place To Go
Shake, Rattle & Roll

That's Alright Mama
The Old Bay Road
Sunset Strip
Can I Sit Next To You Girl
Rockin' In The Parlour
Fell In Love
Midnight Rock
Rock N' Roll Singer
Soul Stripper

BON SCOTT ON VOCALS
(* originally sung by Evans)

1974
*Can I Sit Next To You Girl
Little Lover
School Days
She's Got Balls
Show Business
*Soul Stripper
Stick Around
The Jack
You Ain't Got A Hold On Me
*Shake, Rattle And Roll
*Honky Tonk Women
*Jumpin' Jack Flash

1975
High Voltage
It's A Long Way To The Top
Live Wire
Rock N' Roll Singer
Rocker
T.N.T.
*Jailhouse Rock
*That's Alright Mama
*Heartbreak Hotel

*Roll Over Beethoven

1976
Dirty Deeds Done Dirt Cheap
Jailbreak
Problem Child
Tutti Frutti (only 5.12.76)

1977
Bad Boy Boogie
Dog Eat Dog
Hell Ain't A Bad Place To Be
Kicked In The Teeth (only 3.9.77 – half a year before the release date)
Let There Be Rock
Up To My Neck In You (only 3.9.77 – half a year before the release date)
Whole Lotta Rosie

1978
Beating Around The Bush (only 27.5.78)
Down Payment Blues
Fling Thing (played only on Glasgow and some London gigs up to date)
Gimme A Bullet (only 29.5.78)
Gone Shootin'
Riff Raff
Rock'N'Roll Damnation
Sin City

1979
Girls Got Rhythm
Highway To Hell
If You Want Blood (You've Got It)
Shot Down In Flames
Walk All Over You

BRIAN JOHNSON ON VOCALS
(** originally sung by Scott)

1980
Back In Black
**Bad Boy Boogie
Given The Dog A Bone
**Hell Ain't A Bad Place To Be
Hell's Bells
**High Voltage
**Highway To Hell
**Let There Be Rock
**Problem Child
**Rocker
Shoot To Thrill
**Shot Down In Flames
**Sin City
**The Jack
**T.N.T.
What Do You Do For Money Honey
** Whole Lotta Rosie

1981
**Dirty Deeds Done Dirt Cheap
For Those About To Rock (We Salute You)
Inject The Venom (only on few dates)
Let's Get It Up
Lucille (only 25.1.81)
Put The Finger On You
Rock And Roll Ain't Noise Pollution

1982
C.O.D. (only 3., 4. and 5.10.82)
**Live Wire (only 9.10.82 and 30.9.82)
Have A Drink On Me

1983
Badlands (only 9., 11. and 13.11.83)
Bedlam In Belgium (only on a few dates)
**Dog Eat Dog (only on a few dates)
Guns For Hire
Landslide (only 3.11.83)
Nervous Shakedown
Rising Power
This House Is On Fire

1985
Fly On The Wall
**Jailbreak
Shake Your Foundations
Sink The Pink (this song was performed on the first part of the European tour)
Playing With Girls (only at 4.9.85)
First Blood (only at 4.9.85)

1986
**She's Got Balls (on the whole US tour.)
Who Made Who

1988
Go Zone (only on a few dates)
Heatseeker
Nick Of Time
That's The Way I Wanna Rock N Roll

1990
Fire Your Guns
Moneytalks
The Razor's Edge
Thunderstruck

1991
Are You Ready

1996
Ballbreaker
Boogie Man
Cover You In Oil
**Dog Eat Dog (only for one date before 1996)
**Down Payment Blues
**Girls Got Rhythm
Go Down (only 5.7.96)
**Riff Raff (only 5.7.96)
**Gone Shootin' (only 5.7.96)
Hail Caesar
Hard As A Rock

Songs that were also rehearsed:
The Furor – Rock'N'Roll Damnation – Rocker – Dog Eat Dog –
High Voltage – Live Wire – Fire Your Guns – What's Next To The
Moon – Burning Alive – Big Gun – D.T. – Chase The Ace – Rock
And Roll Ain't Noise Pollution – Jailbreak – Problem Child

2000
Get It Hot
Stiff Upper Lip
Meltdown
Safe In New York City
Satellite Blues

Soundcheck in Pittsburgh: Riff Raff (According to Mark Erb, ear
witness)

2001
**Ride On
**Up To My Neck In You

Also rehearsed:
Night Prowler

OTHER FACTS RELATING TO AC/DC

The following is a list of other bands of which the main members of AC/DC have been members as well as a checklist of non –'DC albums that they have appeared on.

MALCOLM YOUNG
Velvet Underground 1971 – 1972
Marcus Hook Roll Band 1973
Stevie Wright 1973 (guest on album)

ANGUS YOUNG
Kentuckee 1971 – 1973
Tantrum 1973
Marcus Hook Roll Band 1973
Stevie Wright 1974 (guest on album)
Ray Arnott 1979 (guest on album)

BON SCOTT
The Spektors 1965 – 1966
Valentines 1967 – 1970
Fraternity 1970 – 1973
Blackfeather 1971 (guest on album)
Vince Lovegrove 1972 (guest on single)
Mount Lofty Rangers 1974

MARK EVANS
Finch 1977 – 1978
Contraband 1978 – 1979
The Beast 1982
Heaven 1983 – 1984
Headhunters 1988
Bob Armstrong 1990 (guest on album)
Chris Turner 1990 (guest on album)

PHIL RUDD
Buster Brown 1974

CLIFF WILLIAMS
Home 1970 – 1974
Al Stewart 1974 (touring band)
Bandit 1975 – 1977
Alexis Korner 1977 (touring band)
Adam Bomb 1986 (guest on album)

BRIAN JOHNSON
Geordie 1972 – 1980
Jackyl 1997 (guest on album)
Neurotica 1998 (producer and guest on album)

STEVIE YOUNG
Starfighters 1980 – 1984
Little Big Horn 1989

SIMON WRIGHT
Tora Tora 1980 – 1981
AIIZ 1981 – 1982
Tytan 1982 – 1983
Dio 1989 – 1991
Rhino Bucket 1993 – 1995
UFO 1995, 1997 – 1999

CHRIS SLADE
Tom Jones 1963 – 1969
Session Drummer 1969 – 1971
Manfred Mann's Earth Band 1972 – 1979
Session drummer 1979 (Frankie Miller & Kai Olsson)
Uriah Heep 1980 (*Conquest* album)
Session Drummer 1980 – 1983 (Gary Numan, Mick Ralphs Band)
David Gilmour 1984 (touring band)
The Firm 1984
Gary Moore 1989 (touring band)

MORE TRIVIA

The Valentines' first single 'Everyday I Have To Cry B/W Can't Dance With You' was released in May 1967 and reached the top five in the Western Australian charts.

The Valentines recorded a Coca Cola commercial.

MONSTERS OF ROCK AND DONINGTON FACTS

1984 Monsters of Rock line –up:

AC/DC topped the bill plus Van Halen , Ozzy Osbourne , Gary Moore , Y & T, Accept, Motley Crue. Compere was Tommy Vance. 65,000 people attended.

1991 Monsters of Rock line –up:

AC/DC topped the bill, plus Metallica, Motley Crue, Queensrÿche, The Black Crowes.

The width of the Donington stage in 1991 was 72.45 metres. It included 250 tonnes of steel, plus a further 250 tonnes of production equipment, which required 34 articulated lorries to ferry everything around. 116 production workers were contracted to AC/DC alone. AC/DC hit the Donington stage at 8.20 pm playing 'Thunderstruck'. 72,500 people attended.

1991 Monsters of Rock tour

20 concerts in 18 European cities finishing with a special free concert at the Tushino airfield on the outskirts of Moscow on September 28th. 500,000 people attended this show. The tour also included Donington, Basel & Dortmund.

Old Fossils?

Fossils discovered in Australia have been named after brothers Angus and Malcolm Young. *(As published in the records of the Australian Museum, Volume 50, Number 3, November 1998).*

The fossils are of two species of an animal named Maldybulakia, believed to be related to millipedes or horseshoe crabs.

One species was named for Malcolm (*Maldybulakia malcolmi*) and one named for Angus (*Maldybulakia angusi*). *Malcolmi* was deposited in a lake in volcanic terrain in southern New South Wales 383 million years ago. *Angusi* was deposited in floodplain sand in a river system not far from Canberra about 414 million years ago. The only closely related species to these two Australian Maldybulakias comes from Kazakhstan (two Russian palaeontologists named it for the farm, Maldybulak, where they found their fossils). A complete animal would have reached about 15 cm or so in length.

Senior research scientist Greg Edgecombe from the Australian Museum named the two species after the Young brothers.

Chapter 23 – Discography

In 2004 a report in the Australian Financial Review suggested that AC/DC's *Back In Black* album has been certified by the Recording Industry Association of America (R.I.A.A.) as the second biggest selling album of all time.

Although the album has indeed sold tens of millions of copies, the report was possibly slightly overenthusiastic. It sits at sixth in the R.I.A.A. list (which refers to sales in North America) but, as John Henkel of the Association points out there is no official world statistic for album sales. Each country keeps their own figures and in most cases those figures are never made public. "We only certify titles based on domestic sales which is basically the United States and its territories," says Henkel.

Therefore it is difficult to find out exactly how many AC/DC records have been sold, or how their sales stand in comparison with other artists. The only information made available worldwide is when a particular album hits a sales level, resulting in a Gold, Silver or Platinum disc. In 1976 the definitions were different from today. For instance, in order to qualify for a Silver award, an artist's album had to clear £100,000 profit. This is based on the revenue received by manufacturers after export sales and tax have been deducted. By 1977 the Silver mark rose to £150,000, with Gold increasing to £300,000 (from £250,000 in '76). However, for both years the figure for a Platinum award remained at a cool £1,000,000.

Everything changed in 1979. Firstly, the basis for qualification became units sold rather than cash. From the beginning of that year, the qualifications were: Silver 60,000 units; Gold 100,000 units; Platinum 300,000 units.

This has remained in place ever since, but for AC/DC specifically the changes mattered little. This is because every single long form release of theirs has turned Silver and then Gold virtually instantaneously. It took just a month for *Back In Black* to hit 60,000 units, but by the end of 1980 it had risen to 100,000 and Gold status. Today it stands at multi, multi platinum level. *Blow Up Your Video* had been available for just 11 days when it attained Gold status, proving the late 80s was a fruitful period for the band.

Of course, it takes time for Platinum status to accrue; yet much like their recorded output, AC/DC has remained consistent in this respect also. Each release, from *Dirty Deeds Done Dirt Cheap* to *Ballbreaker* and even the box set *Bonfire*, now sits comfortably in Platinum territory. Even the video releases from the group occupy a place in the high sales list. The *No Bull*, *Stiff Upper Lip* and *Who Made Who* releases all made Gold status, while *Live At Donington* rose to Platinum level.

The likeable act remain a guaranteed seller, yet true to their roots they stringently control the quality of their releases. A case in point is the 2005 DVD release, *Family Jewels*. It contains early television appearances, as well as the previous long–form video re-leases, *Let There Be Rock*, *Fly On The Wall* and *Clipped*. A perfect entry into the age of the digital versatile disc, the action–crammed product is a perfect accompaniment to AC/DC for fans young and old.

What follows in the discography section is the definitive list of all available AC/DC products, which includes everything from general albums to bootlegs, and interview discs. Of course, with such a long standing band, and one who appeal heavily to collectors it would take far more space than available at the end of a biogra-phy, to do full justice to the overall amount of 'DC paraphernalia available. Thus, this does not claim to be the ultimate collectors' guide (this would necessitate a separate tome), yet it certainly does stand as the most authoritative directory ever produced on an endur-ing and prolific group.

The current "Top 10" sellers of all time as certified by R.I.A.A. are:

1. The Eagles – Their Greatest Hits (28 million)
2. Michael Jackson – Thriller (26 million)
3. Pink Floyd – The Wall (23 million)
4. Led Zeppelin – Led Zeppelin IV (22 million)
5. Billy Joel – Greatest Hits Vol 1 and II (21 million)

6. AC/DC – Back In Black (19 million)
6. Shania Twain – Come On Over (19 million)
6. Fleetwood Mac – Rumours (19 million)
6. The Beatles – The White Album (19 million)
10 Soundtrack – The Bodyguard (18 million)
10. Boston – Boston (18 million)

ALBUMS

HIGH VOLTAGE: *Baby Please Don't Go / She's Got Balls / Little Lover / Stick Around / Soul Stripper / You Ain't Got A Hold On Me / Love Song / Show Business*
LP, Cassette – Albert 1975 Australia Only

T.N.T.: *It's A Long Way To The Top (If You Wanna Rock 'n Roll) / Rock 'n Roll Singer / The Jack / Live Wire / T.N.T. / Rocker / Can I Sit Next To You Girl / High Voltage / School Days*
LP, Cassette – Albert 1975 Australia Only

HIGH VOLTAGE: *It's A Long Way To The Top (If You Wanna Rock 'n Roll) / Rock 'n Roll Singer / The Jack / Live Wire T.N.T. / Can I Sit Next To You Girl / Little Lover / She's Got Balls / High Voltage*
CD, LP, Cassette – Atco 1976

DIRTY DEEDS DONE DIRT CHEAP: *Dirty Deeds Done Dirt Cheap / Ain't No Fun Waiting Around To Be A Millionaire / There's Gonna Be Some Rockin' / Problem Child / Squealer / Big Balls / R.I.P. (Rock In Peace) / Ride On / Jailbreak*
LP, Cassette – Albert 1976 Australia Only

DIRTY DEEDS DONE DIRT CHEAP: *Dirty Deeds Done Dirt Cheap / Ain't No Fun Waiting Around To Be A Millionaire / There's Gonna Be Some Rockin' / Love At First Feel / Big Balls / Problem Child / Rocker / Ride on / Squealer*
CD, LP, Cassette – Atlantic 1976

LET THERE BE ROCK: *Go Down / Dog Eat Dog / Let There Be Rock / Bad Boy Boogie / Crabsody In Blue / Overdose / Hell Ain't A Bad Place To Be / Whole Lotta Rosie*
LP, Cassette – Albert 1977 Australia Only

LET THERE BE ROCK: *Go Down / Dog Eat Dog / Let There Be Rock / Bad Boy Boogie / Problem Child / Overdose / Hell Ain't A Bad Place To Be / Whole Lotta Rosie*
CD, LP, Cassette – Atco 1977

POWERAGE: *Rock 'n' Roll Damnation / Down Payment Blues / Gimme A Bullet / Riff Raff / Sin City / What's Next To The Moon / Gone Shootin' / Cold Hearted Man / Up To My Neck In You / Kicked In The Teeth*
CD, LP, Cassette – Atlantic 1978

IF YOU WANT BLOOD…YOU'VE GOT IT: *Riff Raff / Hell Ain't A Bad Place To Be / Bad Boy Boogie / The Jack / Problem Child / Whole Lotta Rosie / Rock 'n' Roll Damnation / High Voltage / Let There Be Rock / Rocker*
CD, LP, Cassette – Atlantic 1978

HIGHWAY TO HELL: *Highway To Hell / Girls Got Rhythm / Walk All Over You / Touch Too Much / Beating Around The Bush / Shot Down In Flames / Get It Hot / If You Want Blood (You've Got It) / Love Hungry Man / Night Prowler*
CD, LP, Cassette – Atlantic 1979

BACK IN BLACK: *Hells Bells / Shoot To Thrill / What Do You Do For Money Honey / Given The Dog A Bone / Let Me Put My Love Into You / Back In Black / You Shook Me All Night Long / Have A Drink On Me / Shake A Leg / Rock and Roll Ain't Noise Pollution*
CD, LP, Cassette – Atlantic 1980

FOR THOSE ABOUT TO ROCK (WE SALUTE YOU): *For Those About To Rock (We Salute You) / Put The Finger On You / Let's Get It Up / Inject The Venom / Snowballed / Evil Walks / C.O.D. / Breaking The Rules / Night Of The Long Knives / Spellbound*
CD, LP, Cassette – Atlantic 1981

FLICK OF THE SWITCH: *Rising Power / This House Is On Fire / Flick Of The Switch / Nervous Shakedown / Landslide / Guns For Hire / Deep In The Hole / Bedlam In Belgium / Badlands / Brain Shake*
CD, LP, Cassette – Atlantic 1983

'74 JAILBREAK: *Jailbreak / You Ain't Got A Hold On Me / Show Business / Soul Stripper / Baby Please Don't Go*
CD, LP, Cassette – Atlantic 1984

FLY ON THE WALL: *Fly On The Wall / Shake Your Foundations / First Blood / Danger / Sink The Pink / Playing With Girls / Stand Up / Hell Or High Water / Back In Business / Send For The Man*
CD, LP, Cassette – Atlantic 1985

WHO MADE WHO: *Who Made Who / You Shook Me All Night Long / D.T. / Sink The Pink / Ride On / Hells Bells / Shake Your Foundations / Chase The Ace / For Those About To Rock (We Salute You)*
CD, LP, Cassette – Atlantic 1986

BLOW UP YOUR VIDEO: *Heatseeker / That's The Way I Wanna Rock 'n' Roll / Meanstreak / Go Zone / Kissin' Dynamite / Nick Of Time / Some Sin For Nuthin' / Ruff Stuff / Two's Up / This Means War*
CD, LP, Cassette – Atlantic 1988

THE RAZOR'S EDGE: *Thunderstruck / Fire Your Guns / Money Talks / The Razor's Edge / Mistress For Christmas / Rock Your Heart Out / Are You Ready / Got You By The Balls / Shot Of Love / Lets Make It / Goodbye & Good Riddance To Bad Luck / If You Dare*
CD, LP, Cassette – Atco 1990

LIVE: *Thunderstruck / Shoot To Thrill / Back In Black / Who Made Who / Heatseeker / The Jack / Dirty Deeds Done Dirt Cheap / Money Talks / Hells Bells / You Shook Me All Night Long / Whole Lotta Rosie / Highway To Hell / T.N.T. / For Those About To Rock (We Salute You)*
CD, LP, Cassette – Atco 1992

BALLBREAKER: *Hard As A Rock / Cover You In Oil / The Furor / Boogie Man / The Honey Roll / Burnin' Alive / Hail Caesar / Love Bomb / Caught With Your Pants Down / Whiskey On The Rocks / Ballbreaker*
CD, LP, Cassette – Elektra 1995

STIFF UPPER LIP: *Stiff Upper Lip / Meltdown / House Of Jazz / Hold Me Back / Safe In New York City / Can't Stand Still / Can't Stop Rock 'N' Roll / Satellite Blues / Damned / Come And Get It / All Screwed Up / Give It Up*
CD, LP, Cassette – Elektra 2000

SINGLES

CAN I SIT NEXT TO YOU GIRL
Can I Sit Next To You Girl / Rockin' In The Parlour
7" – Albert (Australia only) 1974

DOG EAT DOG
Dog Eat Dog / Carry Me Home
7" – Albert (Australia only) 1975

IT'S A LONG WAY TO THE TOP (IF YOU WANNA ROCK 'N' ROLL)
It's A Long Way To The Top (If You Wanna Rock 'n' Roll) / Can I Sit
Next To You Girl
7" – Atlantic 1976

JAILBREAK
Jailbreak / Fling Thing
7" – Atlantic 1976

HIGH VOLTAGE
High Voltage / It's A Long Way To The Top (If You Wanna Rock 'n'
Roll)
7" – Atlantic 1976

DIRTY DEEDS DONE DIRT CHEAP
Dirty Deeds Done Dirt Cheap / Big Balls / The Jack
7" – Atlantic 1977

LET THERE BE ROCK
Let There Be Rock / Problem Child
7" – Atlantic 1977

ROCK 'N' ROLL DAMNATION
Rock 'n' Roll Damnation / Sin City
7" – Atlantic 1978

WHOLE LOTTA ROSIE (LIVE)
Whole Lotta Rosie (Live) / Hell Ain't A Bad Place To Be
7", 12" – Atlantic 1978

HIGHWAY TO HELL
Highway To Hell / If You Want Blood (You've Got It)
7", 12" – Atlantic 1978

GIRLS GOT RHYTHM
Girls Got Rhythm / Get It Hot / If You Want Blood (You've Got It) /
Hell Ain't A Bad Place To Be / Rock 'n' Roll Damnation
7" – Atlantic 1979

TOUCH TOO MUCH
Touch Too Much (Live) / Live Wire (Live) / Shot Down In Flames (Live)
7" – Atlantic 1980

YOU SHOOK ME ALL NIGHT LONG
You Shook Me All Night Long / Have A Drink On Me
7" – Atlantic 1980

ROCK 'N' ROLL AIN'T NOISE POLLUTION
Rock 'n' Roll Ain't Noise Pollution / Hell's Bells
7", 12" – Atlantic 1980

BACK IN BLACK
Back In Black / What Do You Do For Money Honey
7", 12" – Atlantic 1981

LETS GET IT UP
Lets Get It Up / Back In Black (Live) / T.N.T (Live)
7", 12" – Atlantic 1982

FOR THOSE ABOUT TO ROCK (WE SALUTE YOU)
For Those About To Rock (We Salute You) / Let There Be Rock (Live)
7", 12" – Atlantic 1982

GUNS FOR HIRE
Guns For Hire / Landslide
7", 12" – Atlantic 1983

FLICK OF THE SWITCH
Flick Of The Switch / Badlands
7" – Atlantic 1983

NERVOUS SHAKEDOWN
Nervous Shakedown / Rock 'n' Roll Ain't Noise Pollution (Live) / Sin City (Live) / This House Is On Fire (Live)
7", 12", Cassette – Atlantic 1984

DANGER
Danger / Back In Business
7", 7" Picture Disc, 12" – Atlantic 1985

SHAKE YOUR FOUNDATIONS
Shake Your Foundations / Send For The Man / Stand Up / Jailbreak
7", 7" Picture Disc, 12" – Atlantic 1986

WHO MADE WHO
Who Made Who / Guns For Hire / Who Made Who (Collector's Mix)
7", 7" Picture Disc, 12" – Atlantic 1986

YOU SHOOK ME ALL NIGHT LONG
You Shook Me All Night Long / She's Got Balls (Live) / She's Got Balls (Extended)
7", 7" Picture Disc, 12" – Atlantic 1986

HEATSEEKER
Heatseeker / Go Zone / Snake High
7", 12" Picture Disc, 12" – Atlantic 1988

THAT'S THE WAY I WANNA ROCK 'N' ROLL
That's The Way I Wanna Rock 'n' Roll / Kissin' Dynamite / Borrowed Time
/ Shoot To Thrill (Live) / Whole Lotta Rosie (Live)
7", 12" Picture Disc, 12", Cassette, CD – Atlantic 1988

THUNDERSTRUCK
Thunderstruck / Fire Your Guns / DT / Chase The Ace
Year Of Release – 1990
7", 10" Picture Disc, 12", Cassette, CD – Atlantic 1990

MONEYTALKS
Moneytalks / Mistress For Christmas / Borrowed Time

7", 12" Picture Disc, 12", Cassette, CD – Atlantic 1990

ARE YOU READY
Are You Ready / Got You By The Balls / Razor's Edge
7", 12", Cassette, CD – Atlantic 1991

HIGHWAY TO HELL
Highway To Hell (Live) / Hell's Bells (Live) / High Voltage (Live) /
Hell Ain't A Bad Place To Be (Live) / The Jack (Live)
7", 12", Cassette, CD – Atlantic 1991

DIRTY DEEDS DONE DIRT CHEAP
Dirty Deeds Done Dirt Cheap (Live) / Shoot To Thrill (Live) / Dirty
Deeds Done Dirt Cheap
12", CD – Atlantic 1993

BIG GUN
Big Gun / Back In Black (Live) / For Those About To Rock (We Salute
You)
7", 12", Cassette, CD – Atlantic 1993

HARD AS A ROCK
Hard As A Rock / Caught With Your Pants Down
7", CD – Atlantic 1995

HAIL CAESAR
Hail Caesar / Whiskey On The Rocks / Whole Lotta Rosie (Live)
Cassette, CD – Atlantic 1996

COVER YOU IN OIL
Cover You In Oil / Love Bomb / Ballbreaker
CD – Atlantic 1996

STIFF UPPER LIP
Stiff Upper Lip / Hard As A Rock (Live) / Ballbreaker (Live)
CD – Atlantic 2000

SOUNDTRACKS

WHO MADE WHO: *Who Made Who / You Shook Me All Night Long / D.T. / Sink The Pink / Ride On / Hells Bells / Shake Your Foundations / Chase The Ace / For Those About To Rock (We Salute You)*
CD, LP, Cassette – Atlantic 1986

LAST ACTION HERO: Big Gun
CD, Cassette – Sony 1993

BEAVIS AND BUTTHEAD DO AMERICA: Gone Shootin'
CD, Cassette – Geffen 1997

PRIVATE PARTS: You Shook Me All Night Long (Live)
CD, Cassette – Warner Bros 1997

SIXTEEN CANDLES: Snowballed
CD, Cassette – MCA 1998

DETROIT ROCK CITY: Thunderstruck (performed by Sprung Monkey)
CD, Cassette – Universal 1999

BOOTLEGS

During the course of AC/DC's live career there have been literally hundreds of unofficial products on vinyl and CD. In fact, although the band is generally not seen as visually appealing, they could easily have a full book written simply about the rarities and collectibles, which have amassed over the years. Therefore it would take far too much space to list every bootleg recording of the band in these pages, but here is a selection of the best.

1976 (LP):
Side 1: Angus Int. (78) / Can I Sit Next To You Girl / Live Wire (BBC Sessions 3 Jun 76) / Bon Int. (79) / Jailbreak (London (Wimbledon Theatre) 'Rollin Bolan' TV Show 13 July 76) / Angus Int. (78) / Rock & Roll Singer / School Days (Reading 29 Aug. 76)
Side 2: It's A Long Way To The Top / Soul Stripper / Baby Please Don't Go (London (Marquee) Jul. 76) / Bon Int. (78) / Little Lover (BBC Sessions 3 Jun 76)
Various live 76 and interviews 78 –79

A GIANT DOSE OF ROCK & ROLL! (CD/LP):
Side 1: Jailbreak / The Jack / She's Got Balls
Side 2: Can I Sit Next To You Girl / T.N.T. / Rocker
Live Sydney (Hurtsville Civic Centre) 5 Feb. 77
YD 004 (Matrix) (1998, Germany)

...AND I CURDLED HER CREAM – THE LITTLE CUNTS REVISITED (2 LPs):
Side 1: Love Song (intro) /Dirty Deeds Done Dirt Cheap / She's Got Balls / Problem Child
Side 2: Live Wire / The Jack
Side 3: Jailbreak / T.N.T. / Can I Sit Next To You Girl / High Voltage
Side 4: Baby Please Don't Go / Rocker
Live in Hobart, Aust (City Hall) 7 Jan. 1977
RRR 1040 (Oct. 2002, USA)

BBC TRANSCRIPTION SERVICES (LP):
Side 1: Live Wire / It's A Long Way To The Top (If You Wanna Rock & Roll) / Soul Stripper/High Voltage
Side 2: Def Leppard Live Reading 1980.

283

Live London (Marquee Club) Jul. 76.
London Wavelength 2647S (1990, UK)

CAN I SIT ON YOUR FACE GIRL... YOU CAN SIT ON MINE (LP):
Side 1: Jailbreak / The Jack / Can I Sit Next To You Girl
Side 2: High Voltage / Rocker / It's A Long Way To The Top (If You Wanna
Rock 'n' Roll)
Live Sydney (Haymarket) 30 Jan. 77.
AC 201 (Matrix) (Nov. 02, Sweden)

DIRTY DEEDS DOWN UNDER (LP):
Side 1: Love song (intro only) / Dirty Deeds Done Dirt Cheap / She's Got
Balls / Problem Child/Jailbreak (cut)
Side 2: The Jack / T.N.T. / Baby Please Don't Go (cut)
Live Brisbane (Festival Hall) 18 Dec. 76.
AC1 (1986, Germany)
THE DEVIL ROCKS (CD):
Dirty Deeds Done Dirt Cheap / She's Got Balls / Problem Child / Live
Wire / Jailbreak / The Jack / Can I Sit Next To You Girl / T.N.T. / Rocker
/ Interview
DC –DR –01 (Matrix) (Dec. 2002, Germany)

THE LITTLE CUNTS HAVE DONE IT (CD):
Intro / Dirty Deeds Done Dirt Cheap/ Problem Child / Live Wire / The
Jack / Jailbreak / T.N.T. / Can I Sit Next To You Girl / High Voltage / Baby
Please Don't Go / Rocker
Rosie's Revenge Records RRR 1040 (June 2001, USA)

LIVE IN ENGLAND FEATURING BON SCOTT (7" Single):
It's A Long Way To The Top (If You Wanna Rock n' Roll) / Jailbreak
Azimuth AM 301 62 (1989, UK)

NO AFRAID... ...IT'S ONLY ROCK 'N ROLL (LP/CD –R):
Live Wire / Rock N' Roll Singer / Jailbreak / She's Got Balls / Rocker /
High Voltage / Baby Please Don't Go
No Afraid Records 2 –39 –56 (1997, Germany)

SCOTTISH BASTARDS (LP):
Live Wire / She's Got Balls / It's A Long Way To The Top (If You Wanna

Rock n' Roll) / Can I Sit Next To You Girl / The Jack / High Voltage /
T.N.T. / Baby Please Don't Go
Wolf Records WOLF 003 (Jan 2002, Sweden)
SIN SYDNEY 76 (LP):
Dirty Deeds Done Dirt Cheap / She's Got Balls / Problem Child / Live Wire
/ Jailbreak / The Jack / Can I Sit Next To You Girl / Stone Cold Crazy
Home Grown MEFW –01/02 (1991, Germany)

110/220 (LP/CD):
Live Wire / Problem Child / High Voltage / Hell Ain't A Bad Place To Be /
Dog Eat Dog / The Jack / Whole Lotta Rosie / Rocker
Impossible Recordworks IMPI.31 (1979, USA)

AC/DC (Live At The Atlantic Studios) (LP):
Live Wire / Problem Child / High Voltage / Hell Ain't A Bad Place To Be /
Dog Eat Dog / The Jack / Whole Lotta Rosie / Rocker
Bobop A –7925 (Jan. 83, Germany)

THE NUCLEAR BOMB OF ROCK N' ROLL (LIVE WITH BON SCOTT)
Live At The Mayfair, Newcastle (UK) 01.01.1980 (LP):
Live Wire / Problem Child / Gone Shootin' / Bad Boy Boogie / Rock 'n'
Roll Damnation / Highway To Hell / Soul Stripper / Baby, Please Don't
Go
For The First Session For 'Highway To Hell ' 1979:
If You Want Blood / Back Seat Confidential / Touch Too Much

WE CAN'T STOP ROCK N' ROLL (D –CD):
Recorded Live In Paris, November 2000
Disc 1: You Shook Me All Night Long / Stiff Upper Lip / Shot Down In
Flames / Thunderstruck / Hell Ain't A Bad Place To Be / Hard As A Rock
/
Shoot To Thrill / Angus Young Guitar Solo / Rock 'n' Roll In Noise
Pollution / I Feel Safe In New York City / Bad Boy Boogie
Disc 2: Hell's Bells / The Jack / Dirty Deeds Done Dirt Cheap / Back In
Black / Highway To Hell / Whole Lotta Rosie / Let There Be Rock / T.N.T
/ For Those About To Rock (We Salute You)
EUROBOOTS: EB 67/2 (2001, Luxembourg)

SHE'S GOT BALLS REMASTERED (CD):
Live In Towson, Maryland, USA 16.10.1979
Live Wire / Shot Down In Flames / Hell Ain't A Bad Place To Be / Sin City / Problem Child / Bad Boy Boogie / The Jack / Highway To Hell / High Voltage / Whole Lotta Rosie / Rocker/Guitar Solo / If You Want Blood (You Got It) / Get It Hot (early version, different lyrics and vocals) / Dirty Eyes
(Early version of 'Whole Lotta Rosie', completely different)
Bontow: BT CD 7879 –2 (2002, Germany)

THE BBC TAPES (LP):
London 1980
Live Wire / Shot Down In Flames / Hell Ain't A Bad Place To Be / Sin City / Walk All Over You / The Jack / Highway To Hell / Girls Got Rhythm / High Voltage / If You Want Blood (You've Got It) / Let There Be Rock
London 1976
Live Wire / It's A Long Way To The Top (If You Wanna Rock 'n' Roll) / Soul Stripper / High Voltage

THE BBC TAPES VOL. 2 (LP):
'Rock Goes To College' TV Show ABC University, Colchester, Essex 28.10.1978
Live Wire / Intro / Problem Child / Sin City / Bad Boy Boogie / Whole Lotta Rosie / Rocker / Let There Be Rock
Radio 1 Broadcast, Maida Vale Studios, London 03.06.1976
High Voltage / Live Wire / Can I Sit Next To You Girl? / Little Lover
Bonus Tracks: High Voltage (Video Version) / Jailbreak (Video Version)

IN THE STUDIO (LP):
Live radio broadcast, Atlantic Studios, N.Y 07.12.1977
Live Wire / Problem Child / High Voltage / Hell Ain't A Bad Place To Be / Dog Eat Dog / The Jack / Whole Lotta Rosie / Rocker / Dirty Eyes / Crabsody In Blue / Cold Hearted Man / Get It Hot / If You Want Blood / Back Seat Confidential / Touch Too Much

IN ROCK WE TRUST – THE RARITIES (CD):
Can I Sit Next To You / Rockin' In The Parlor / Love Song / She's Got Balls / Little Lover / Stick Around / High Voltage / School Days / Rock

In Peace / Crapsody In Blue / Carry Me Home / Down On The Borderline / Fling Thing / Cold Hearted Man / Hell Ain't A Bad Place To Be / The Jack / Whole Lotta Rosie (All tracks are single B –sides, Australian only album tracks or otherwise unobtainable material)

MILESTONES OF DYNAMITE – THE RARITIES VOLUME 2 (CD):
Dirty Deeds Done Cheap (only released on aussi vinyl) / Dog Eat Dog (released by mistake only as a German 7" B –side) / Highway To Hell (Live
on "Rock Pop" German TV 28.08.1978 / Johnny B Goode (Rare Live Version,
Sioux Falls, USA 07.07.1979) / Ride On (Last recording of Bon Scott, Scorpio Studios, London 13.02.1980) / Guns For Hire (tour rehearsals, Los
Angeles 05.10.1983) / Flick Of The Switch (tour rehearsals, Los Angeles 05.10.1983) / Nervous Shakedown (tour rehearsals, Los Angeles 05.10.1983) / Rising Power (tour rehearsals, Los Angeles 05.10.1983) / That's
The Way I Wanna Rock 'n' Roll (studio outtake from 1987) / Heatseeker (Studio outtake from 1987) / For Those About To Rock (We Salute You) / Live, Moscow, 28.09.1981 from a rare Maxi CD) / Highway To Hell (mega rare
live version only ever released on a French 5 –track –maxi) / Back In Black (Previously unreleased VH1 session track, London 05.07.1996) / Stiff
Upper Lip (The tracks live world premier, MTV 2Total Request Live" 10.03.2000) / Back In Black (The tracks live world premier, MTV 2 'Total Request Live' 10.03.2000) / Stiff Upper Lip (Live on NBC's 'Saturday Night
Live' TV Show, March 2000) / You Shook Me All Night Long

HAIL GEEZER – SPANISH FLY (CD):
The Bullring, Madrid, Spain July 3, 4, 5 1996
Back In Black / Shot Down In Flames / Thundershock / Girls Got Rhythm /
Hard As A Rock / Shoot To Kill / Boogieman/Heatseeker / The Jack / T.N.T
/ Highway To Hell / For Those About To Rock (We Salute You)
Buddy Knox Music (1996, USA)

MADRID 1996 (D –CD –R):
Live in Madrid at Plaza De Toros De Las Ventas, Spain, 10.07.1996
Disc 1: 1ˢᵗ Intro 'Beavis & Butthead' / 2ⁿᵈ Intro 'Stage Destruction' /
Back In Black / Shot Down In Flames / Thunderstruck / Girl's Got
Rhythm
/ Hard As A Rock / Shoot To Thrill / Boogie Man / Hail Caesar / Hell's
Bells / Dog Eat Dog / The Jack / Ball Breaker / Rock 'n' Roll Ain't
Noise Pollution / Dirty Deeds Done Dirt Cheap
Disc 2: You Shook Me All Night Long / Whole Lotta Rosie / T.N.T / Let
There Be Rock / Highway To Hell / For Those About To Rock (We Salute
You)
(1997, France)

BACK IN RHYTHM (D –CD):
Westfallenhalle, Dortmund, 08.05.1996.
Disc 1: Intro / Back In Black / Shot Down In Flames / Thunderstruck /
Girl's Got Rhythm / Cover You In Oil / Shoot To Thrill / Boogie Man /
Hard As A Rock / Hell's Bells / Dog Eat Dog / Down Payment Blues /
The
Jack
Disc 2: Ballbreaker / Rock 'n' Roll Ain't Noise Pollution / Dirty Deeds
Done Cheap / You Shook Me All Night Long / Whole Lotta Rosie / T.N.T /
Let There Be Rock / Highway To Hell / For Those About To Rock (We
Salute You)
(1996, USA)

LIVE AT THE APOLLO STADIUM (LP):
Apollo Stadium, Adelaide, Australia 12.04.1976.
Jailbreak / She Got The Jack / Can I Sit Next To You / High Voltage /
I'm A Rocker – I'm A Roller / Long Way To The Top / Baby, Please Don't
Go / Problem Child

LIVE AT LEITH THEATRE (LP):
Leith Theatre, Edinburgh, Scotland 12.06.1976.
Live Wire / She's Got Balls / It's A Long Way To The Top (If You Wanna
Rock 'n' Roll) / Can I Sit Next To You Girl / The Jack / High Voltage /
T.N.T. / Baby Please Don't Go

ROUTE 666 – VOL 1 (CD/LP):
Warners Theatre, Fresno, California, USA 09.08.1979

288

Highway To Hell (German TV) / Live Wire / Shot Down In Flames / Sin City / Problem Child / Walk All Over You / Bad Boy Boogie
Haizea Prod. HP010301 (2003, USA)

ROUTE 666 – VOL 2 (CD/LP):
Warners Theatre, Fresno, California, USA 09.08.1979
The Jack / Highway To Hell / Whole Lotta Rosie / Rocker / Let There Be Rock / Unknown Jam (Unreleased)
Haizea Prod. HP010301 (2003, USA)

LIVE AT THE MYER MUSIC BOWL (D –CD):
Myer Music Bowl Melbourne, Australia 27.02.1981
Disc 1: Hell's Bells / Shot Down In Flames / Sin City / Back In Black / Bad Boy Boogie / The Jack / What Do You Do For Money Honey / Highway To
Hell / High Voltage
Disc 2: Whole Lotta Rosie / Rocker /You Shook Me All Night Long / Rock 'n' Roll Ain't Noise Pollution / T.N.T / Let There Be Rock

FLY ON TOUR (D –CD):
Frank Erwin Centre, Austin, Texas, USA 11.10.1985
Disc 1: Fly On The Wall / Back In Black / Shake Your Foundations / Dirty Deeds Done Dirt Cheap / You Shook Me All Night Long / Sin City / Jailbreak / The Jack / Shoot To Thrill
Disc 2: Hell's Bells / The Jack / Dirty Deeds Done Dirt Cheap / Highway To Hell / Whole Lotta Rosie / Let There Be Rock / T.N.T / For Those About To Rock

LIVE AT THE PEPSI CENTRE (CD):
Pepsi Centre Denver, Colorado, USA 11.04.2001
You Shook Me All Night Long / Stiff Upper Lip / Shot Down In Flames / Thunderstruck / Hell Ain't A Bad Place To Be / Hard As A Rock / Shoot To
Thrill / Rock 'n' Roll Ain't Noise Pollution / Safe In New York City / Bad Boy Boogie / Hell's Bells / Get It Hot / The Jack / Back In Black / Dirty Deeds Done Dirt Cheap / Highway To Hell / Whole Lotta Rosie / Let
There Be Rock (We Salute You)

RIDE ON PARIS (D –CD):
Stade De France Paris, France 22.06.2001
Disc 1: Stiff Upper Lip / You Shook Me All Night Long / Problem Child /
Thunderstruck / Hell Ain't A Bad Place To Be / Hard As A Rock / Shoot
To Thrill / Rock 'n' Roll Ain't Noise Pollution / What Do You Do For
Money Honey / Bad Boy Boogie / Hell's Bells
Disc 2:Up To My Neck In You / The Jack / Dirty Deeds Done Dirt Cheap
/
Back In Black / Highway To Hell / Whole Lotta Rosie / Let There Be
Rock

SELECTED PROMOS

As with many collectible bands, the prices for promotional items can be fairly high, and for some of the following items it might well be astronomical. Many of the following were issued in very small numbers. Collectors will often state the value of something is merely based upon how much a person is willing to pay, but the promo only items listed below rate as the crème de la crème of the AC/DC collecting world and you should expect to pay rather a lot to complete your collection!

10 Of The Finest Items Of Promotional Memorabilia

Here are some of the most unusual and sought after AC/DC items which were usually scarcely produced as items for serious fans. All memorabilia is promotional only and will have been produced from the record company of the time.

SET OF 5 CREDIT CARDS – This incredible set was made to promote the 'Money Talks' single. There is one credit card for each member of the band. There are only 6 complete sets in existence.

SATCHEL
For the 1976 Lock Up Your Daughters tour a satchel was produced which came with a red sticker, badge and lyric sheets. It was given to the winner of radio contest. This was a supremely rare gem as it was a complete one –off.

STOPWATCH
The 'Are You Ready' single was promoted with a rare stopwatch. The watch is white with red logo.

PROMOTIONAL TIE
For the release of the *If You Want Blood…You've Got It* album in the United Kingdom, certain record stores were giving these mock Angus ties to the first paying customers.

DECK OF PLAYING CARDS

For the release of 'The Jack' (live version) 7" single there was a set of playing cards produced. However this item was never distributed due to 'The Jack' never being released; it was therefore locked away in the Atlantic vaults. Only 25 sample decks were made.

SET OF EARPLUGS

This item was produced for the *Blow Up Your Video* American tour. The earplugs came with a black case with gold logo. The edition was strictly limited to 200 sets.

MATCHBOX SEMI –TRUCK

For AC/DC's Australian tour in 1991 the band held a press conference in Sydney beforehand. A matchbox truck was placed on each table. There are less than 50 in existence. There is a picture of one of the trucks on *Live* double album insert.

CARDBOARD GIBSON SG

200 cardboard replicas of Angus's SG were made for 'That's The Way I Wanna Rock N Roll' video shoot which was filmed in Sydney. Afterwards Angus signed as many as he could.

SPRAY CAN AND PLASTIC FLY

These items were made to promote the *Fly On The Wall* album. The insect can is blue and it has a red AC/DC logo on it. The plastic fly, known as Looy is around 2 inches in size.

WATCH

For the song 'Nick Of Time' a watch with a gold rim, white face and red AC/DC logo with black strap was produced.

THE JAPANESE EFFECT

All the AC/DC albums before *Powerage* were issued in the 80's specifically for Japanese fans as they caught onto the band. As Japanese fans often find, the albums packaged in their country are generally far nicer than in terms of general production and with AC/DC it was no different.

The front sleeves were similar all over the world but the back sleeves were lavishly illustrated. The albums were contained OBI strips (a customary Japanese inclusion) as well as lyric sheets.

The *Blow Up Your Video* and *The Razor's Edge* albums were promoted with CD singles. Both are in generous and colourful packaging.

ALBUMS

(with inserts, OBIs and lyric sheets)

Powerage (LP P10533A, CD, 1978)

If You Want Blood (LP P10618T, CD, 1978)

Highway To Hell (LP P10719, CD, 1979)

Back In Black (LP P10906, CD, 1980)

High Voltage (LP P10926T, CD, 1980)

Dirty Deeds Done Dirt Cheap (LP P10994, CD, 1980)

Let There Be Rock (LP, CD, 1980)

For Those About To Rock (LP P11068, CD, 1981)

Flick Of The Switch (LP P11399, CD, 1983)

'74 Jailbreak (LP P6196, CD, 1984)

Fly On The Wall (LP P13152, CD, w/flexi disc, 1985)

Who Made Who (LP 13269, CD, 1986)

Blow Up Your Video (LP 13634, CD, 1988)

The Razor's Edge (LP, CD AMCY –138, 1990)

Live (2LP) (LP, CD AMCY –656, with extra track, 1992)

Ballbreaker (CD AMCY –888, 1995)

Bonfire (CD 251541, w/ booklet in Japanese, 1997)

PROMOTIONAL ALBUMS

Japan Tour '81 (LP PS180, picture disc, 1980)
AC/DC vs. Foreigner (LP PS205, 6 tracks each, 1982)
The Heavy Metal (LP PS171, special DJ copy, v.a., 2 AC/DC tracks, 1981)

The Heavy Metal '81 (LP PS187, v.a., 1981)

Heavy Metal 1964 –1984 (2LP PS239/40, v.a., 2 AC/DC tracks, 1984)

Hard Rock 1985 (LP PS269, v.a., 2 AC/DC tracks, 1985)

WEA Top Hits September '85 (LP PS271, vol 26, v.a., w/Danger, 1985)

The Atlantic Times (CD ASCD –10, v.a., 3 AC/DC tracks)

CD SINGLES

Heatseeker / Go Zone (105W –9, 3" CD, w/PS, 1988)

That's The Way I Wanna Rock N' Roll / Kissin' Dynamite (105W –49, 3" CD, w/PS, 1988)

Thunderstruck / Fire Your Guns (3"CD, w/Long PS, 1990)

Moneytalks / Borrowed Time (AMDY 5040, 3" CD, w/Long PS, 1991)

7" SINGLES

The 7" singles from Japan are also of appeal to AC/DC collectors. These are generally very nicely packaged and tend to be quite different in appearance from the regular releases. Also in the mid eighties two Japanese flexi–singles were pressed, 'Guns For Hire' and 'Danger'. Both are incredibly hard to find.

Back In Black / What Do You Do For Money Honey

Danger / Back In Business (7/85)

For Those About To Rock / T.N.T. (live) (5/82) (P1649)

Guns For Hire / Landslide (10/83) (P1809)

Heatseeker / Go Zone (3/88) (P2377)

Highway To Hell / If You Want Blood (9/79) (P464)

Let's Get It Up / Back In Black (live) (2/82) (P1615)

Rock N' Roll Damnation / Sin City (7/78) (P311A)

Shake Your Foundations / Send For The Man (11/85) (P2038)

Touch Too Much / Walk All Over You (3/80) (P544A)

Who Made Who / Guns For Hire (live) (6/86) (P2134)

Whole Lotta Rosie (live) / Hell Ain't A Bad Place To Be (live) (1/79) (P372A)

You Shook Me All Night Long / Back In Black (10/80) (P631A)

5" FLEXI SINGLES

Danger (Came with the *Fly On The Wall* album)

Guns For Hire (Came with the *Flick Of The Switch* album)

BOXED SETS

AC/DC (Volume 1) (Australia only) LP
High Voltage / T.N.T. / Dirty Deeds Done Dirt Cheap / Let There Be Rock / Powerage / Highway To Hell
Also includes: 12" Maxi Single with 'Cold Hearted Man'
Iron –on transfer
Originally released in November 1981. Available in Australia & New Zealand only.
Reissued in 1987 without transfer, and in 1989 without 12". CD reissues without transfer & 12".

AC/DC (Volume 2) (Australia only) CD
Back In Black / For Those About To Rock…We Salute You / *Flick Of The Switch* / *Fly On The Wall* / *Who Made Who*
Also includes: Poster
Originally released in November 1987. Available in Australia & New Zealand only. Reissued in 1989 without poster. CD reissues without poster

BOOM BOX / AC/DC (Australia only) CD
High Voltage / T.N.T. / Dirty Deeds Done Dirt Cheap / Let There Be Rock / Powerage / If You Want Blood…*You've Got It / Highway To Hell / Back In Black / For Those About To Rock / Flick Of The Switch / Fly On The Wall / Who Made Who / Blow Up Your Video / The Razor's Edge / Live (Special Collectors Edition) / Ballbreaker (On 2002 reissue only) / Stiff Upper Lip (On 2002 reissue only)*
Originally released in 1991 (without *Live*), reissued in October 1995 (All remastered CD's until *Live*), and in December 2002 as *AC/DC*. Available in Australia & New Zealand only. CD's are in jewel cases & booklet with lyrics, same as standard remastered Australian CDs. Original release in different package.

Live: *Thunderstruck / Shoot To Thrill / Back In Black / Sin City * / Who Made Who / Heatseeker / Fire Your Guns * / Jailbreak * / The Jack / The Razor's Edge * / Dirty Deeds Done Dirt Cheap / Money Talks / Hells Bells / Are You Ready * / That's The Way I Wanna Rock 'n' Roll * / High Voltage * / You Shook Me All Night Long / Whole Lotta Rosie / Let There*

Be Rock * / Bonny * / Highway To Hell / T.N.T. / For Those About To Rock (We Salute You)
* Box Set Only Tracks; Special Longbox Collectors edition (which contains fold –out Booklet and AC/DC dollar)
1992

BONFIRE (CD)
DISC 1: Live From The Atlantic Studios: Live Wire / Problem Child / High Voltage / Hell Ain't A Bad Place To Be / Dog Eat Dog / The Jack / Whole Lotta Rosie / Rocker
DISC 2: Let There Be Rock – The Movie – Live In Paris: Live Wire / Shot Down In Flames / Hell Ain't A Bad Place To Be / Sin City / Walk All Over You / Bad Boy Boogie / The Jack / Highway To Hell / Girls Got Rhythm / High Voltage / Whole Lotta Rosie / Rocker / T.N.T. / Let There Be Rock
DISC 3: Volts: Dirty Eyes / Touch Too Much / If You Want Blood You Got It / Back Seat Confidential / Get It Hot / Sin City / She's Got Balls / School Days / It's A Long Way To The Top (If You Wanna Rock 'n' Roll) / Ride On
DISC 4: Back In Black: Hells Bells / Shoot To Thrill / What Do You Do For Money Honey / Given The Dog A Bone / Let Me Put My Love Into You / Back In Black / You Shook Me All Night Long / Have A Drink On Me / Shake A Leg / Rock and Roll Ain't Noise Pollution
1998 Elektra

AC/DC (Europe only)
High Voltage / T.N.T. / Dirty Deeds Done Dirt Cheap / Let There Be Rock / Powerage / If You Want Blood…You've Got It / Highway To Hell / Back In Black / For Those About To Rock / Flick Of The Switch / Fly On The Wall / Who Made Who / Blow Up Your Video / The Razor's Edge / Live (Special Collectors Edition) / Ballbreaker / Live From The Atlantic Studios
All CD's included are the vinyl –replica reissues in card sleeves.

2000 (Available in Australia & Europe only): Stiff Upper Lip – Tour Edition
Stiff Upper Lip: Stiff Upper Lip / Meltdown / House Of Jazz / Hold Me Back / Safe In New York City / Can't Stand Still / Can't Stop Rock 'N' Roll / Satellite Blues / Damned / Come And Get It / All Screwed Up / Give It Up

Bonus Disc enhanced CD: *Cyberspace* (Non –album track) / *Back In Black* (Live Madrid July 96) / *Hard As A Rock* (Live Madrid July 96) / *Ballbreaker* (Live Madrid July 96) / *Whole Lotta Rosie* (Live Madrid July 96) / *Let There Be Rock* (Live Madrid July 96) / *Stiff Upper Lip* (Video Clip) / *Safe In New York City* (Video Clip) / *Satellite Blues* *(Video Clip)*
2001.

BOOKS

HIGHWAY TO HELL: THE LIFE AND TIMES OF AC/DC LEGEND BON SCOTT, Clinton Walker, Verse Chorus Press, U.S. 2001

ROCK N ROLL FANTASY – MY LIFE AND TIMES WITH AC/DC, VAN HALEN, KISS..., Susan Masino, Badger Books Inc 2003

AC/DC: SHOCK TO THE SYSTEM, Mark Putterford, Omnibus Press 1992

AC/DC – AN ILLUSTRATED RECORD COLLECTORS GUIDE VOLUME 1 & 2, Chris Tesch, C.M. Tesch 1992

SINGING IN THE DARK – A ROCK 'N' ROLL ROADIE STEPS INTO THE LIGHT, Barry Taylor, Kingsway Communications, 1990

HELL AIN'T NO BAD PLACE TO BE, Richard Bunton, Omnibus Press 1982

AC/DC THE WORLD'S HEAVIEST ROCK, Martin Huxley, Saint Martin's Press 1996

GET YOUR JUMBO JET OUT OF MY AIRPORT (RANDOM NOTES FOR AC/DC OBSESSIVES), Howard Johnson, Helter Skelter Publishing 1999

AC/DC HARD ROCK LIVE PHOTOS 1976 – 1980, Von Wolfgang Heilemann, Schwarzkopf and Schwarzkopf 2004

AC/DC, Malcolm Dome, Jewish Pubn. Soc. of America 1982

AC/DC STORY, Paul Ezra, Babylon Books 1982

AC/DC: THE DEFINITIVE HISTORY, The Kerrang! Files (Various), Virgin Books 2001

MAXIMUM AC/DC, THE UNAUTHORISED BIOGRAPHY OF AC/DC (Audio Book), Chrome Dreams 2000

INTERVIEWS

CDs

The Conversation Disc Series, ABCD, 1989

The Interview, Baktabak, 1992

Dirty Words, Holoview Ltd, 1994

Monsters Of Rock, Kokopelli Records, 1996

Monsters Of Rock, Rockview, 1996

AC/DC X –Posed, The Interview, Chrome Dreams 2005

7"s

An Interview With Angus Young and Brian Johnson Parts 1 and 2, 10/01/82, 1984

12"s

Limited Edition Interview Picture Disc, Tell Tales 1986

AC/DC Interview Picture Disc, Baktabak, 1987

AC/DC Interview Disc, RDPD, 1987

Rock Sagas – The Chris Tetley Interviews, Fotodisk, 1988

AC/DC, Tell Tales, 1988

Mini Disc

The Razor's Edge, Atco, 1992

(This is a Japanese released interview and the only official AC/DC mini disc ever produced).

DVD

No Bull Live
Warner 1996

Stiff Upper Lip Live
Elektra 2001

Live At Donington
Sony 2003

No Bull Live/Stiff Upper Lip Live
Warner 2003

Guitar Method In The Style Of AC/DC
MVP 2003

And Then There Was Rock: AC/DC Unauthorised Documentary
Chrome Dreams 2005

Family Jewels
Sony 2005

VIDEOS

PROMOTIONAL VIDEOS

Can I Sit Next To You Girl (1974, w/ Dave Evans vocals)
High Voltage (1975)
It's a Long Way To The Top (1975) (version 1 studio)
Dirty Deeds Done Cheap (1976)
Jailbreak (1976) (version 1 studio)
Jailbreak (1976) (version 2 outdoors)
Jailbreak (1976) (version 2 edit)
Jailbreak (1977) (version 3 studio / stage)
It's a Long Way To The Top (1977) (parade float)
Let There Be Rock (1977) (both edit and unedited versions)
Dog Eat Dog (1977)
Rock n' Roll Damnation (1978)
Riff Raff (live, 1978)
Bad Boy Boogie (Live, 1978)
Highway To Hell (1979)
Walk All Over You (1979)
Touch Too Much (1979)
Shot Down In Flames (1979)
If You Want Blood (1979)
Walk All Over You (live, 1979 LTBR movie)
Hells Bells (1980)
Back in Black (1980)
What Do You Do For Money Honey (1980)
You Shook Me All Night Long (1980)
Rock n' Roll Ain't Noise Pollution (1980)
Let Me Put My Love Into You (1980)
Back In Black (live 1981) (B&W and Colour)
For Those About To Rock (live 1981)
Put The Finger On You (live 1981)
Let's Get It Up (live 1981)
Guns For Hire (1983)
Flick Of The Switch (1983)
Nervous Shakedown (1983) (version 1)
Nervous Shakedown (1983) (version 2)

Fly On The Wall (1985)
Danger (1985)
Sink The Pink (1985)
Stand Up (1985)
Shake Your Foundations (1985)
Who Made Who (1986)
You Shook Me All Night Long (1986)
Heatseeker (1988)
That's The Way I Wanna Rock n' Roll (1988)
Thunderstruck (1990)
Money Talks (1990)
Are You Ready (1990)
Highway To Hell (live, 1992)
Dirty Deeds Done Dirt Cheap (live, 1992)
Back in Black (live, Moscow, 1992)
Big Gun (1993)
Hard As A Rock (1995)
Hail Caesar (1995)
Cover You In Oil (1995)

OFFICIAL RELEASES

Let There Be Rock
1980

Fly On The Wall
1985

Who Made Who
1986

Clipped
1990

Live At Donington
1992

AC/DC Uncut
1996

No Bull Live
1996

WEBSITES

www.ac –dc.cc

www.highwaytohell.net

www.crabsodyinblue.com

www.acdccentral.com

www.acdcfrance.com

www.acdcrocks.com

www.acdcband.com

www.gotmacdc.de

www.acdc1.com

www.squealer.net

www.kolumbus.fi/nononsense/

www.thereddevil.com

www.ac –dc.net/

www.accadacca.net

www.bigguns.galea.com

ADDITIONAL MATERIAL

What follows is a brief synopsis of the various Bon Scott and Brian Johnson recordings outside of AC/DC. This does not claim to be complete as there are undoubtedly other bootlegs etc which are available, but here is the significant material each singer recorded before joining AC/DC.

BON SCOTT

THE SPEKTORS
Bon Scott With The Spektors: CD E.P. released in 1992 by See For Miles Records (SEACD 6). This CD contains The Spektors only known recordings, all from a television broadcast. The track listing is as follows: *Gloria (lead vocal: Bon Scott)*
On My Mind (drums: Bon Scott) / Yesterday (Bon Scott does not play drums or sing lead vocals on this, but it's suggested he sang backing vocals) / Interview with Vincent Lovegrove (by Alan Mannings) the interview lasts 23 minutes and contains sound clips of several Valentines songs / Gloria* / On My Mind* / Yesterday*
*The last 3 songs are the same as the first 3 except that they include the announcer's introduction and crowd applause
FRATERNITY

ALBUMS

Livestock: *The Race Part 1 / Seasons Of Change / Livestock / Summerville /*
Raglan's Folly / Cool Spot / Grand Canyon Suites / Jupiter's Landscape / You
Have A God / It / The Race Part 2
LP, Sweet Peach / Astor 1971

Flaming Galah: *Shape I'm In / If You Got It (Single Version) / Welfare Boogie /*

Annabelle / Seasons Of Change / You Have A God / Hemming's Farm / Raglan's
Folly / Getting Off / Summerville
LP, RCA 1971

Fraternity – The Complete Sessions 1971 –72 (2 –CD): *Seasons Of Change / Livestock / Sommerville / Raglan's Folly / Cool Spot / Grand Canyon Spot / Jupiter's Landscape / You Have A God It / The Race (Pts 1 & 2) / Why Did It Have To Be Me / Question / Shape I'm In, The / If You Got It (Single Version) / Welfare Boogie / Annabelle / Seasons Of Change (II) / You Have A God (II) / Hemming's Farm / Raglan's Folly (II) / Getting Off / Sommerville R.I.P. / Canyon Suite / If You Got It (II) / 'Battle Of The Sounds' Sequence / Bon Scott Talks With David Day of 5KA, Adelaide 1977 / Bon Scott Talks With Sheila Renay of KSJO, San Jose, 1978*

SINGLES

Seasons Of Change
Seasons Of Change / Summerville
7" – Sweet Peach / Astor 1971

The Race Part 1
The Race Part 1 / The Race Part 2
7" – Sweet Peach / Astor 1971

Welfare Boogie
Welfare Boogie / Getting Off
7" – RCA/Victor 1971

If You Got It
If You Got It / Raglan's Folly / You Have A God
7" – Raven/Festival 1971

THE VALENTINES

ALBUMS

The Legendary Bon Scott with the Spektors and the Valentines SEECD 704: The Spektors: *Gloria / It Ain't Necessarily So / On My Mind / Yesterday / Interview by Allan Mannings featuring Vince Lovegrove / Gloria (As original TV Broadcast) / It Ain't Necessarily So / (As original TV Broadcast) / On My Mind (As original TV Broadcast) / Yesterday (As original TV Broadcast)*
Bon Scott With The Valentines: *To Know You Is To Love You / She Said / Every Day I Have To Cry / I Can't Dance With You / Peculiar Hole In The Sky / Love Makes Sweet Music / I Can Hear Raindrops / Why Me / Sooky Sooky*

SINGLES

I Can't Dance With You
I Can't Dance With You / Everyday I Have To Cry
7" Clarion / Festival 1967

She Said
She Said / To Know You Is To Love You
7" Clarion / Festival 1967

Why Me?
Why Me? / I Can Hear The Raindrops
7" Clarion / Festival 1968

Peculiar Hole In The Sky
Peculiar Hole In The Sky / Love Makes Sweet Music
7" Clarion / Festival 1968

Ebeneezer
Ebeneezer / My Old Man's A Groovy Old Man
7" Philips 1969

Nick Nack Paddy Whack
Nick Nack Paddy Whack / Getting Better
7" Philips 1969

My Old Man's A Groovy Old Man
My Old Man's A Groovy Old Man / Nick Nack Paddy Whack / Ebeneezer
/
Getting Better
7" EP Philips 1969, 1970

Juliette
Juliette / Hoochie Coochie Billy
7" Philips 1970

VARIOUS

Blackfeather – At The Mountains Of Madness: *At the mountain of Madness / On this Day that I die / Seasons of change (pt1) / Mangos Theme part 2 / Long Legged Lovely / The Rat suite – Main title (The Rat) – The trap – Spanish Blues – Blazwaorden (Land of dreams) – Finale (The Rat)*

Round And Round And Round, CD single: *Round And Round And Round/Carey Gully* Released: 24/01/1999 Cat: MB619622
Bon Scott Seasons Of Change 1967 –1972: *To Know You Is To Love You / She Said /*
Everyday I Have To Cry / I Can't Dance With You / Peculiar Hole In The Sky / Love Makes Sweet Music / I Can Hear The Raindrops / Why Me? / Sooky Sooky / Getting Better / Ebeneezer / Hoochie Coochie / Billy / My Old Man's A Groovy Man / Nick Nack Paddy Wack / Julliette / Annabelle / Welfare Boogie / Hemming's Farm / Sommerville / R.I.P. / Getting Off If You Got It / Seasons Of Change / Interview with David Day of 5Ka in Adelaide

BRIAN JOHNSON
GEORDIE

ALBUMS

Hope You Like It (EMI EMC 3001): *Keep on Rockin' / Give You Till Monday / Hope You Like It / Don't Do That / Because of You / Old Time Rocker / Oh Lord / Natural Born Loser / Strange Man / Ain't It Just Like a Woman / Geordie's Lost His Liggie* CD, LP EMI 1973 Reissued on CD (Repertoire REP 4033 –WZ, 1991)

Masters Of Rock: *Geordie Stomp / Can You Do It / Give You 'Till Monday / Red Eyed Lady / Don't Do That / Black Cat Woman / Keep On Rockin' / Electric Lady / Natural Born Loser / Ain't It Just Like A Woman / All Because Of You* CD, LP EMI 1974

Don't Be Fooled By The Name (EMI EMA 764): *Goin' Down / House Of The Rising Sun / So What / Mercenary Man / Ten Feet Tall / Got To Know / Little Boy / Look At Me* CD, LP EMI 1974 Reissued on CD (Repertoire 4124 –WZ, 1991)

Save The World (EMI EMC 3134): *Mama's Going To Take You Home / She's A Teaser / Goodbye Love / I Cried Today / You Did This To Me / Save The World / Rocking Horse / Fire Queen / She's A Lady / Light In My Window / Ride On Baby / We're All Right Now* CD, LP, EMI 1976 Reissued on CD as part of 'A Band From Geordieland' (Repertoire REP4515 –WY, 1996)

No Sweat (Neat 1008): *No Sweat / This Time / Move Away / Time To Run / So You Lose Again / Rock & Roll / Oh No! / Hungry / We Make It Rock* CD, LP, Neat 1983

Geordie Featuring Brian Johnson (Redbus RBMP 5001, vinyl compilation): *All Because Of You / Keep On Rockin' /Natural Born Loser / Rocking With The Boys / Going Down / Black Cat Woman / Electric Lady / Can You Do It / Don't Do That / Ain't It Just Like A Woman / Hope You Like It / Fire Queen / Mercenary Man / Treat Her Like A Lady* (Anchor/DCC – U.S. CD compilation, ANZ 700, 1989)

SINGLES

Don't Do That
Don't Do That / Keep On Rockin'
7", Regal Zonophone 1972

All Because Of You
All Because Of You / Ain't It Just Like A Woman
7", EMI 1973

Can You Do It
Can You Do It / Red Eyed Lady
7", EMI 1973

Electric Lady
Electric Lady / Geordie Stomp
7", EMI 1973

Rock n' Roller
Rock n' Roller / Geordie's Lost His Liggy
7", EMI 1973

She's A Teaser
She's A Teaser / We're All Right Now
7", EMI 1974

Ride On Baby
Ride On Baby / Got To Know
7", EMI 1974

Goodbye Love
Goodbye Love / She's A Lady
7", EMI 1975

Also Available from Chrome Dreams

Maximum AC/DC
The Unauthorised Biography of AC/DC
Cat: ABCD054

A 60-minute spoken word biography of AC/DC featuring
interview clips throughout and covering all eras of their
extraordinary career.
Comes in deluxe packaging with outer slipcase, 8-page
illustrated booklet and free fold out poster.

**Available from all good record stores,
online at Amazon and other good sites and from**
www.chromedreams.co.uk

Also Available from Chrome Dreams

AC/DC X-Posed
Upublished and Rare Interviews Set
Cat: CTCD7038

AC/DC X-Posed provides further insight into this remarkable group with a series of interviews covering two distinct eras of the band's history. The first, with the late but sorely missed original frontman Bon Scott, is a very rare recording never previously heard. This is followed by another rare interview with Bon's replacement in AC/DC, Brian Johnson. A unique opportunity to hear both of this legendary band's singers revealing all.
Comes in deluxe packaging with outer slipcase, 4-page illustrated booklet and free fold out poster.

**Available from all good record stores,
online at Amazon and other good sites and from**
www.chromedreams.co.uk

Also Available from Chrome Dreams

AC/DC - And Then There Was Rock
DVD Documentary
Cat: CVIS379

AC/DC: And Then There Was Rock charts the band's early years, up to the tragic death of their enigmatic front man, Bon Scott. This DVD documentary takes the cameras where they have never previously preyed, interviewing AC/DC's original singer Dave Evans, original drummer Colin Burgess, school friends of Bon, Angus and Malcolm, Bon's lifelong friend Vincent Lovegrove, and AC/DC biographers Malcolm Dome and Clinton Walker among others. This DVD is a fitting tribute to the memory of Bon Scott, containing rare footage and music of him in his earlier bands, previously unseen photographs and much, much more!

**Available from all good record stores,
online at Amazon and other good sites and from**
www.chromedreams.co.uk